D1383949

#IDLENOMORE

#IDLENOMORE

AND THE REMAKING OF CANADA

KEN COATES

 University of Regina Press

Printed and bound in Canada at Marquis.

COVER AND TEXT DESIGN: Duncan Campbell
COVER IMAGE: Alan Clarke

Library and Archives Canada Cataloguing in Publication
Cataloguing in Publication (CIP) data available at the Library and Archives Canada web site: www.collectionscanada.gc.ca and at www.uofrpress.ca/publications/#idlenomore

10   9   8   7   6   5   4   3   2   1

University of Regina Press, University of Regina
Regina, Saskatchewan, Canada, S4S 0A2
tel: (306) 585-4758 fax: (306) 585-4699
web: www.uofrpress.ca

U OF R PRESS

The University of Regina Press acknowledges the support of the Creative Industry Growth and Sustainability program, made possible through funding provided to the Saskatchewan Arts Board by the Government of Saskatchewan through the Ministry of Parks, Culture and Sport. We also acknowledge the financial support of the Government of Canada through the Canada Book Fund and the Canada Council for the Arts for our publishing program. This publication was made possible through Culture on the Go funding provided to Creative Saskatchewan by the Ministry of Parks, Culture and Sport.

*This book is dedicated to Aboriginal children across Canada.
May they be inspired by Idle No More and understand
the potential for a better future.*

CONTENTS

Idle No More event: Elsipogtog Solidarity
rally in Vancouver on October 18, 2013.
Photo: Lukasz Szczepanski

QUIET NO MORE

P rairie winds often start gently. At first, the long prairie grasses and stands of wheat and canola begin to sway, almost im-
perceptibly. The softness in the onset of these winds is like
a caress that, even on a cool fall day, carries more promise
than risk. The movement of air is hardly noticeable, but it is
there, possessing power and substance. Perhaps it is that, the absence
of danger but the presence of real power, which makes prairie winds
so invigorating.

Prairie winds rarely stay calm. At times, they die down completely,
bringing near silence to the land and leaving the impression that the
power has dissipated, that the threat has disappeared, and that all will
stay as it is. More often, the breeze picks up slowly, the soft swaying of
foliage replaced by a noisier rustling, a persistent background sound
that heightens unease and speaks to an untapped power. You can feel
the wind at these times; it is strong without being severe, bold but not
ominous. You can see this iteration of the wind, or so it seems. It is
that which pushes the prairie grasses and sways the roadside trees.

When it further intensifies, the wind can be staggeringly strong. In
winter, it whips the dry, western snow into a frenzy, pushing a white
wall across the landscape that obliterates the vast skies and reminds

humanity of its smallness and vulnerability. In summer, it picks dirt up off the farmers' fields, and thus the wind gains a body with taste and grit, driving dust into eyelids and through tightly clenched teeth. In this form, the wind can usher in a storm, complete with rainclouds and torrential downpours. Midday skies turn black. Rain or hail beats down ferociously. The wind can terrify us as it threatens to uproot safe and comfortable lives.

The temptation to hunker down, to avoid the threatening storm, is overwhelming.

Is it surprising that the prairie wind, with its many faces and great strength, also carries a transformative power that can allow us to see the world in a different light? The storm clouds pushed along by this wind provide relief for the lightning, sharp and powerful, that illuminates the sky with a subtlety that defies description. So soft and pervasive is the reach of this light that colours change hue and landscapes are seen anew. And the same wind that brought in vast banks of clouds also creates small openings: light peaks through in strange and beautiful ways. Fear is replaced by wonder as the storm clouds that moments ago seemed full of danger become things of beauty. Black and imposing on the top, they are radiant and sunlit on the bottom. It is here, in a landscape transformed, that one of the most fundamental lessons of prairie life is learned: consider the wind; do not turn away from it. Do not hunker down, and do not assume the worst. Turn toward it and wait for the light. In that moment of luminescence, those precious seconds during which the clouds part, you will see light, power, and beauty rise from below.

The world recently experienced a personification of the prairie winds: Idle No More, a movement as surprising and as transformative as a sudden prairie storm. Frightening for some, difficult for most to understand—including those at the hundreds of events that sprang up across Canada in 2012 and 2013—Idle No More arose as does a perfect prairie storm. Unleashed on a surprised nation, propelled by forces that, like the gentle winds, turn in a matter of seconds into a formidable blizzard, Idle No More swept across Canada with stunning speed and strength.

As a political movement, it had almost everything: a powerful message, legions of supporters, and a hungry media eager to forage off the turmoil. Everyone in Canada knew Aboriginal people were angry. Aboriginal political leaders have described the poverty and despair that engulf many of their communities. Academics have described the hardships, cultural dislocation, and historical injustices that shape First Nations, Métis, and Inuit realities. Journalists have chronicled the glue-sniffing, health crises, domestic violence, over-stuffed penitentiaries, and political unrest that percolates across the country. In an Aboriginal political world defined in the public's eye by conflicts at places like Burnt Church (New Brunswick), Gustafsen Lake (British Columbia), Caledonia (Ontario), the Oldman River (Alberta), and Oka (Quebec), anger seemed both just and inevitable. That hundreds would take to the streets in protest was far from surprising.

But as political protests go, key elements were missing. Idle No More had founders but no leaders. There was no manifesto at first, no real organization, and an almost complete absence of an effort to manipulate, aggregate, or intimidate. At first glance, the arrival of hundreds of Aboriginal people in shopping malls and on street corners seemed deliberately threatening. Yet the people were singing instead of yelling. They didn't demonstrate but danced. They had a purpose, but to many people it seemed deeply buried or, at least, confused. This was a protest, if it was that at all, of mothers and children more than warriors and activists. All events associated with Idle No More were astonishingly calm. Culture mattered more than politics.

Idle No More started in Saskatchewan. Like a prairie breeze, it picked up strength, as fast as a gathering storm. The country hunkered down, preparing for and assuming the worst. This, it seemed, was the long-promised storm of the century, the much-anticipated Aboriginal uprising that had lain, for decades, in the grass, building into a dangerous and potentially violent crescendo that would shake the very foundations of the Canadian system.

But the violence never materialized. Instead, decades of anger manifested as celebration and determination, not denunciation and vitriol. Rocks did not fly. Buildings were not destroyed. The police were bystanders, even encouraging bystanders. There were no stand-offs. Hundreds of thousands of Aboriginal people and their supporters came into the streets in seeming anger with Canada and Canadians. But peace broke out. The lightning bolts that were Idle No More brought illumination not destruction. Canadians saw something that they had rarely seen before—conviction tied to culture, hope arising from sorrow, determination wedded to a sense of injustice, family connected to political protest.

Canadians watched Idle No More with an odd mix of wonder, worry, and incredulity. Street protests have again become common in the Western world. This is, after all, the age of G-8 and G-20 protests, the inchoate Occupy movement, various and continuous environmental demonstrations, and mass uprisings in Europe related to the continent's economic despair, particularly among the young. Aboriginal protest is also commonplace. Each year, there are dozens of comparatively minor conflicts, including blockades and demonstrations, with occasional large struggles, like the long-standing standoff at Caledonia, Ontario, and the 2013 shale gas protests at the Elsipogtog First Nation in New Brunswick. But none of these protests foreshadowed or laid the groundwork for Idle No More.

Not much time has passed since the last wave of Idle No More demonstrations swept across Canada. Some observers have already described the movement as a spent force, somehow classifying it as a failed political gambit. After all, these critics might say, the Conservative government of Prime Minister Stephen Harper has not budged from its entrenched positions on key development, environmental, budgetary, or political matters. And the country seems to have moved on. In the winter of 2012–2013, Idle No More conversations engaged the whole nation. A year later, it seemed like a lost cause.

But Idle No More is far from that. It may prove to be the most important and transformative event in recent Canadian history, on par with the rise of women's rights in the 1960s, the sovereignty movement in the Province of Quebec, and the gay pride movements of the 1970s and 1980s. In the decades to come, Idle No More will be analyzed by hundreds of academics in theses, dissertations, and scholarly articles; and it will find pride of place in first-person accounts and journalistic renderings. These works will capitalize on the passage of time, the perspective produced by distance, and the opportunity to collect a great deal of additional evidence.

#IdleNoMore is not a book of the types described above. It is, instead, a personal reflection on a process that I think will redefine Canada and, most certainly, transform Indigenous politics and affairs in this country. It is inspired, as well, by the insights and passion of *The Winter We Danced: Voices From the Past, the Future, and the Idle No*

More Movement, a book that celebrates and shares Aboriginal views from and about the movement.[1] Let me put my thoughts—my bias, if you will—on the table at the outset. I believe that Idle No More *is* (not *was*) a process of fundamental importance. The collective events and gatherings that gained the nation's attention in 2012–2013 represent, in my mind, the largest and most sustained demonstration of Indigenous identity and cultural determination in Canadian history. The movement, powered by hundreds of loosely connected, largely young, and predominately female Aboriginal organizers and activists across the country, represents an assertion of cultural survival and political determination. The people of Idle No More will be quiet no more. Idle No More is far from gone, anything but temporary, and still relevant. It has, in my opinion, unleashed new power, confidence, and determination among Aboriginal peoples in Canada.

#

My first encounter with Idle No More came via the radio. I was driving south from Prince Albert, Saskatchewan, heading back to Saskatoon. At the time, the Conservative government was pushing through its now infamous omnibus bill, Bill C-45, a true doorstopper of a piece of legislation, ostensibly designed to implement the 2012 budget. The program host was interviewing four Saskatchewan women, two of whom later became founders of Idle No More. I don't recall which two of the four founders—Jessica Gordon, Sylvia McAdam, Sheelah McLean, and Nina Wilson—were being interviewed that morning. But I do remember their message, and it was simple: Bill C-45 had gone too far, particularly regarding a series of environmental and First Nations issues. They—the four women—had had enough, and they knew that others shared their views. A teach-in was scheduled for Station 20 West in Saskatoon.

The interview was a low-key item. I thought little of it at the time and expected nothing to come of it. After all, mass movements and even successful political protests are rarely founded on a nuanced analysis of several sections of a massive piece of impenetrable federal legislation. Fundamental injustices bring people to their feet, not subtle rewritings of complex laws. Unease about the shortcomings of federal consultations is hardly the poetry of protest, the antecedent to anger. This protest was about changes to the Navigable Waters Protection Act, a piece of legislation that fewer than one Canadian in a hundred had ever heard of, let alone read, before November 2012. Such is not, I reminded myself, the stuff of revolutions.

Gordon, McAdam, McLean, and Wilson had a name for their gathering—Idle No More—and a clear goal: to articulate western Aboriginal frustration with the Harper government's legislative strategy, particularly relating to Indigenous and environmental issues. In this, they were hardly alone. Many Canadians were, in the fall of 2012, upset about the government's cavalier approach to Parliament. The New Democratic Party and the Liberal Party of Canada were in high dudgeon about the prime minister's determination to usher through sweeping changes under a single piece of legislation. Editorial writers and columnists across the country bemoaned the abuse of Canadian democratic traditions.

Idle No More. I remember thinking that the name was odd, when I first heard it. But then, like virtually all other observers, I also assumed that this protest—small, localized, and unfunded—would disappear overnight. It did not disappear. Within a few days, Idle No More had garnered nationwide attention. A couple of weeks later, Idle No More was known around the world. Virulently anti-Harper and anti-government at one level, it was also culturally rich, its participants articulate and passionate.

#

Idle No More is a highly significant movement whose full social impact and influence on Aboriginal and non-Aboriginal relations in Canada will unfold over decades, not months. I struggle to understand the movement, even as I admire its strength, peacefulness, and transformative potential to mobilize and empower Indigenous peoples. As a non-Aboriginal man who watched from the sidelines and did not participate in any of the organized activities or demonstrations associated with Idle No More, I am, in many ways, far removed from the centre of the movement.

I have, however, worked on Aboriginal issues for decades. One of the most influential events in my life was the 1973 publication of *Together Today for Our Children Tomorrow* by the Yukon Native

Brotherhood; it was the document that launched the Yukon land claims process and started the radical transformation of the Canadian North. I was in Grade 11 at the time, attending F. H. Collins High School in Whitehorse. My first publication—a letter to the editor of the *Whitehorse Star*—was a brief commentary on Aboriginal land claims. I wrote that the government should sign with the First Nations, not expecting it would take twenty years to get to the point of signing. I subsequently studied Aboriginal issues at university and have written about Aboriginal concerns, served as a consultant with Aboriginal organizations and governments, taught university courses on Aboriginal topics, and had hundreds of conversations with Aboriginal leaders, students, activists, and community members. I do not like being described as an "expert" on Aboriginal affairs. I am, instead, always a student, and I have been blessed by the willingness of many Aboriginal people to share their stories, experiences, and perspectives with me.

#

IdleNoMore has two origins. The book started with the arrival in Saskatchewan of Bruce Walsh, the newly appointed director of the University of Regina Press. I was re-introduced to Bruce, a renowned marketer of books, through a mutual friend, Aurèle Parisien, a professional editor, cultural critic, and Renaissance man of the highest order. Recently arrived at his new post and visiting me in Saskatoon, Bruce made it clear he was eager to revitalize academic publishing in Canada. In the spring of 2013 he asked me a simple question: "If you could write one book for the University of Regina Press, what would it be about?" "Idle No More," I answered, without hesitation, not because I knew I had all the answers about this strange and remarkable movement but because I had so many unanswered questions. The contract arrived in the mail a few days later. It turns out that he was not kidding. Bruce also insisted on the book being ready within a year.

However, I didn't set to work straight away. Instead, my decision to proceed came a few months later, over dinner with friends Mike Rudyk and Cherish Clarke in Whitehorse. I knew Mike from our work together on a series of television documentaries for Northern Native

Broadcasting. He was now working as a cameraman for CBC Television in Whitehorse. His wife, Cherish, is a talented young Aboriginal woman, a dancer and singer, a cultural leader among the Taku River Tlingit First Nation. These two are the kind of young Aboriginal people, well-educated, determined, and committed to their community, who are redefining the country from the inside. As we ate and chatted that evening, our conversation quickly turned to Idle No More.

Cherish, it turns out, was a local organizer for Idle No More events. She became a primary spokesperson for the movement in the Yukon, speaking to the press and to the crowds gathered at the Whitehorse meetings. The experience was empowering. Cherish has been politically active for some time, serving as the president of the Liberal Party in the Yukon and as the co-chair of the Aboriginal Peoples Commission of the Liberal Party of Canada. She is precisely the kind of young, engaged, powerful, and determined Aboriginal person who is working at the community and regional level to re-imagine the future of Indigenous peoples in Canada.

Cherish related that she had mixed feelings about her experience organizing Idle No More events. She was empowered by the participation of young people and inspired by the wisdom and determination of the Elders. She took delight in the support Idle No More received from a small number of non-Aboriginal people. But she felt real pain from the attacks directed at her by critics of the Idle No More gatherings. Cherish experienced great pride in the peaceful and constructive nature of the events, and she had trouble comprehending how some people could be so furious at First Nations people for presenting their case to the community at large. More than anything, the angry words directed at her personally reminded her of the depth of anti-Aboriginal sentiment held by some Canadians.

That evening with Cherish and Mike reminded me of something very important: politics and political movements start and end with people. Ideas, words, documents, and policies are all part of the political process, for Aboriginal people and for others. But politics spring from lived experience, not simply from political structures and organizations. Cherish and Mike live in one of the most promising corners of the country in terms of Aboriginal aspirations and conditions. With the Yukon's modern treaty—The Council for Yukon First Nations Umbrella Final Agreement—as a base, the territory is transforming the way Aboriginal and non-Aboriginal people live, work, and interact. I grew up in Whitehorse and consider myself fortunate many times over to have been raised there; the Whitehorse that Cherish and Mike live in is a dramatically different and, in my opinion, better place than the town of my youth.

But the world for First Nations peoples in the Yukon—and in all of Canada—is far from perfect. Systemic cultural and economic struggles overlay personal crises and challenges. The resurgence of Indigenous cultures of which Cherish and Mike are part is offset by continued language loss, private tragedies, and poverty. To Cherish, in particular, Idle No More was an overwhelmingly optimistic process. Political protest was part of the movement, to be sure, and Cherish's frustration with the Government of Canada was evident to me that evening in her detailed critiques of legislation and policies. But Idle No More, to both Mike and Cherish, transcended politics, in both the small "p" and large "P" sense of the term. The movement was an assertion and demonstration of Aboriginal culture—even more, a celebration of cultural survival.

Cherish Clarke and Mike Rudyk are remarkable individuals, gifted with the talent and determination to put their ideas into action and the courage to display their values and commitments in public. They would be the first to point out that they are far from alone, and both argue that the brilliance of Idle No More lies primarily in bringing hundreds of young, powerful, and passionate Aboriginal Canadians into the public realm. The character and commitment of Aboriginal people—Cherish and Mike multiplied hundreds of times—is the real story of Idle No More. Forget, if you can, the high-profile elements of the Idle No More movement: the protests in Ottawa, the meetings with Prime Minister Harper, and subsequent efforts by Aboriginal and non-Aboriginal activists to co-opt the name and power of Idle No More for legitimate, but narrower, purposes. Do not look for the meaning of Idle No More in the halls of Parliament or on the editorial pages of the nation's leading newspapers. Instead, connect the movement with an individual like Cherish Clarke—a dancer, singer, activist, and marvelous young Aboriginal person who simply wants a better life for her family and First Nations people in her community and across Canada. Find the real story of Idle No More in the hearts and minds of tens of thousands of Aboriginal people in Canada who are determined to take control of the future, to reassert identity, and to celebrate cultural survival.

#

As readers will quickly see in what follows, my emotions relative to the movement, like most non-Aboriginal Canadians, have run the gamut. I was nonplussed by the launch, confused by the episode with Chief Theresa Spence, distressed by the January 2013 struggle between the Prime Minister's Office and the Assembly of First Nations, amazed by the resurrection of the spirit of Idle No More in the early months of 2013, stunned by the tenacity of young Aboriginals heading off on long marches to Ottawa, saddened by the lack of non-Aboriginal interest in these formidable journeys, intrigued by the complex and multifaceted messages in the rallies, and puzzled in the extreme when the promised demonstrations of "Sovereignty Summer" in 2013 fizzled out.

It is hard to explain a movement that was, intentionally, leaderless, inspired by remarkable founders, suffused with a decolonization critique, peaceful, largely comprised of young people, and far more cultural than political. Idle No More's rise and sudden fall seems, on the surface, to be like the amorphous and ultimately sadly irrelevant Occupy movement. The range and diversity of the rallies, however, bear no resemblance to any comparable movement in Canadian history. At the same time, the absence of a coordinating body and internal organization seems to doom it to political oblivion.

I must say that the general, non-Aboriginal Canadian response to the movement was not a surprise to me. For every person who has found common cause with the movement's environmental message and who supports Idle No More's cultural spirit, there are many others who mock the movement's name and express nervous fear about the scale and spontaneity of the uprising. As well, during Idle No More's upsurge, the media struggled to make sense of this emerging movement that lacked a manifesto, a fixed leadership, or deliberate intent and management.

In the pages that follow I will offer my view of what happened, gleaned from hundreds of YouTube videos, thousands of Facebook postings, and tens of thousands of tweets, newspaper accounts, and other evidence of a movement that refused to follow the rules of both Canadian politics and global protest. For now, however, let me tell you what I think Idle No More was and was not. Some writers, such as Judy Rebick, have compared Idle No More to the Black Power movement in the United States and the struggles for gay rights and women's rights across North America. There is something to be said about these connections. The gay rights movement shares Idle No More's elements of pride and assertiveness, but it sprang from the reality of deep oppression and the outright suppression of homosexuality. The women's movement arose from a long history of marginalization, and the tactics bear some resemblance to Idle No More, but what Idle No More lacked in structure the women's movement offered in empowered leadership and organizational strength. The Black Power movement was spontaneous and lacked formal direction, but it was much more violent than Idle No More, which had peacefulness at its core.

Idle No More coalesced at a time of rapidly growing confidence among Aboriginal peoples in Canada. A series of political arrangements, including the constitutional entrenchment of Aboriginal and treaty rights in 1982, and dozens of favourable court decisions, from Sparrow and Calder to Marshall and William, have given real and substantial powers to First Nations.[2] Moreover, tens of thousands of First Nations, Inuit, and Métis young people have been attending colleges and universities, discovering common cause on campus and a lively critique of Canada in many of their classrooms, often as a result of the growing number of Aboriginal scholars and teachers. Many Aboriginal groups have money—the nosh that drives the power system in Canada—from recent land claims agreements and other settlements. As the court victories have mounted up, as corporations have begun collaborating with Aboriginal communities, as successful Indigenous businesses have risen to prominence, as governments have made concessions to gain support for development projects, Indigenous peoples in Canada have realized that a power shift is under way. In 2010, when Canada signed the Declaration of the Rights of Indigenous Peoples (adopted by the United Nations in 2007), Aboriginal peoples in Canada saw that the whole world had embraced not just their rights but their very existence. If few non-Aboriginal Canadians paid much heed to this declaration, for Aboriginal people it meant a great deal.

Another contributing factor to the Idle No More movement is the collective and individual memory evident in Aboriginal communities: the people remember the stories of their parents and grandparents. In one of the most profound expressions of the power and effectiveness of collective memory, Aboriginal people have demonstrated a shared understanding of the oppressive effects of the Indian Act, the destructive influences of residential schools, and the lingering and painful impacts of systemic racism and discrimination. They know, even as Aboriginal achievements accrue, that many in their communities have suffered—and will continue to suffer—grievously. Refusing to turn their backs on their relatives and neighbours, these Aboriginal people seek to transform their personal accomplishments into collective rewards.

To be sure, Aboriginal Canadians were, by 2012, angry in many ways. They were furious at what they perceived to be disrespect from governments and non-Aboriginal people generally. They were angry at the poverty and social distress that plagued many communities. They were frustrated that non-Aboriginal people resisted rather than celebrated their rights, now entrenched in Canadian law. Many were upset with their community and regional leadership and wanted more and better governance within Aboriginal organizations. Despite what many Canadians think, Aboriginal peoples have displayed more distress about corruption and mismanagement in their leadership than any other group in the rest of the country.

But Aboriginal pride was also at the core of the Idle No More movement. Perhaps, I have wondered, it is as simple as this: learning the history of their peoples, both locally and nationally, Aboriginal Canadians came to realize that their very survival, including the persistence of their cultures and values, was one of the greatest success stories in this country's history. In 2012, they knew what happened in the past. They knew the realities of the present. And then they looked around. They saw young and old Indigenous people proud of their cultures, eager to preserve their languages, and determined to press for their rightful place within Canada. When they considered the history of oppression and cultural destruction in their communities and the resilience of Aboriginal cultures across the nation, they could hardly be anything but angry, and proud, and more than a little determined.

This is where non-Aboriginal confusion about the movement comes in. During the first six months of the rallies and celebrations, non-Aboriginal people kept asking what it was that the First Nations, Inuit, and Métis peoples wanted. But that was just it. With the exception of the defeat of the omnibus bill, they were not asking for things. There was never going to be a list of demands or a set of specific complaints, although individuals and groups across the country offered powerful critiques of the nation, its policies and socio-economic systems. In fact, Idle No More was not meant for non-Aboriginal Canadians. It was not an attempt to persuade, convince, or direct political change.

Idle No More, it seemed clear as time went on, was by Aboriginal people, for Aboriginal people, and about Aboriginal people. For the first time in Canadian history, non-Aboriginal Canadians were relegated to the sidelines. This was not a hundred mini-Okas or mini-Caledonias, two events that pitted Aboriginal against non-Aboriginal people. Idle No More was a series of Aboriginal gatherings; other Canadians were welcomed as spectators and supporters. Herein lies its magic and power. It was the largest and most sustained public demonstration of Aboriginal confidence, determination, pride, and cultural survival in Canadian history. And what a remarkable series of events it was during its inaugural year.

#

L et me end this preface with a story. Early in 2014, I attended a government meeting with fifteen or so politicians and senior officials. The topic—a standard one in much of Canada—was how to produce greater Aboriginal engagement in resource development. The meeting was surprisingly upbeat in that everyone in the room (although some a tad reluctantly) agreed and recognized that First Nations participation was essential. On the several occasions that speakers referred to Idle No More, the reference was greeted by knowing nods from around the table. It was clear that the national conversation had shifted, that the spirit and values of Idle No More represented the new normal in Canada; governments and others quickly realized that Aboriginal assertiveness was the reality going forward. Idle No More had refashioned Canada.

There are those who have been quick to call Idle No More a failure, to describe the movement as poorly organized, unfocused, and without a real point. This view of the movement is wrong on all accounts. Idle No More was stunningly successful and has already shown remarkable staying power, albeit in unexpected ways. Idle No More captured and then unleashed the transformative power of Aboriginal Canada. It showed Aboriginal people that they had real and lasting power. It demonstrated that Indigenous Canadians had a common cause. It changed the vocabulary and the spirit of Aboriginal youth. In November 2012, I was bewildered by the speed of Idle No More. In the fall of 2014, I am amazed at how it has reshaped Canada so quickly. A movement allegedly without a purpose, seemingly without real leadership and organization, and consisting of more drumming and singing than manifesto writing, has most assuredly set this country on a different course.

Canada is changed, Aboriginal Canada is changed, and the country is not going back.

The Founders of Idle No More, from left
to right: Sheelah McLean, Nina Wilson,
Sylvia McAdam, Jessica Gordon.
Photo: Marcel Petit of m.pet productions

ONE

MOBILIZING AN AWAKENING

I n 2012, the level of frustration in Canada was growing. The Conservative government, led by Prime Minister Stephen Harper, had introduced another omnibus bill, Bill C-45, ostensibly to implement the 2012 federal budget. Harper's government had done the same the previous year, lumping dozens of seemingly unrelated items into a single piece of legislation. Each of these bills attracted many critics, but the cacophony lacked focus and smacked, to the external observer, like a relentless series of self-interested complaints. The 2011 outcries across the country fizzled out, pretty much precisely as the Conservatives had hoped and expected.

The 2012 protests seemed destined for the same fate. The 450-page document that is Bill C-45 stuck out in multiple directions. Amendments to the Indian Act would give bands greater freedom to utilize their land. Members of Parliament and civil servants were required to pay a higher share of their pension contributions.[1] Changes to Employment Insurance gave Cabinet more control over program funding, and changes to the Environmental Assessment Act continued the process of "streamlining"—some would say fast-tracking—procedures. There were also shifts in the regulation of wheat; improvements to small-business tax credits; funding for a bridge between Windsor, Ontario, and Detroit, Michigan; changes to the management of hazardous wastes; and new regulations governing Maritime labour.[2]

The document was hefty, complex, and impenetrable for the average citizen. Political revolutions usually centre on clear and obvious targets: tax increases, program cancellations, major changes in government legislative commitments. Bill C-45 seemed, at worst, like death by a thousand policy cuts, a provocation aimed at many and diverse interest groups and highly unlikely to spark a vigorous national debate. This was Ottawa at its most convoluted. To critics of the Conservative government, the bill was an act of a political bully, forcing legislation that warranted detailed examination and debate onto an unwary country.

Supporters saw it differently. The majority government was committed to cutting the size of government, improving administrative and regulatory efficiency, and implementing the broad agenda set out during the 2011 federal election campaign. To the Conservatives and their fans, Bill C-45 was a piece of legislative housekeeping, tying up relatively small ends and moving forward with initiatives that the government wished to implement expeditiously. Before the middle of November 2012, most Canadians took the bill as the unstoppable and not particularly noteworthy action of a majority government that was eager to get on with business.

By November 2012, the Aboriginal complaints about certain pieces of the omnibus legislation—particularly the changes to band control over land and environmental regulations—seemed minor compared to the massive challenges facing Aboriginal peoples across Canada. There were many good reasons for First Nations, Métis, and Inuit peoples to be upset about their position within Canada, ranging from education and health outcomes to the over-representation of Aboriginal people in prisons and difficulties with treaty and Aboriginal rights implementations. Bill C-45 seemed, even to long-time observers of Aboriginal affairs, like a minor irritant at best, and for most people, insignificant.

Four Saskatchewan women—Jessica Gordon, Sylvia McAdam, Sheelah McLean, and Nina Wilson—however, started talking about the legislation shortly after it was introduced into the House. To these women, the bill threatened to further erode Indigenous rights. They were frustrated by the government's policy and worried about the environmental and Indian Act provisions of the legislation. They were also disappointed by the lack of consultation with Aboriginal

Canadians. At first, their actions and behaviour paralleled discussions played out over dining room tables, in offices, and in pubs and cafés across the land. People complain about government. They get angry over new legislation. They have better ideas than the government and policy makers and wonder why their wisdom is ignored.

Gordon, McAdam, McLean, and Wilson decided to do something. This, among all the things that happened over the coming months, was the most radical step. Few Canadians outside of partisan politics step forward and turn their complaints and frustrations into public action. These women, however, organized a gathering in Saskatoon, Saskatchewan, to take place on November 10, 2012. They described it as a "teach-in," an airing and sharing of views about the government's plans. Drawing a crowd for a non-partisan political event is no easy feat, although it is perhaps easier in the highly engaged political environment in Saskatchewan than in other places. The Aboriginal twist to the protest may also have given the teach-in greater currency; the First Nations and Métis political environment in the province has long been highly charged.

To draw an audience, the organizers set up a Facebook page, hoping that social media would help bring a crowd to the teach-in at Station 20 West, a Community Enterprise Centre in the predominantly Aboriginal community of Saskatoon West. Priscilla Settee, a member of the Cumberland House Cree Nation and a professor of Native Studies at the University of Saskatchewan, booked the space for the gathering. The organizers called the event "Idle No More," a declaration of the women's determination that they—and anyone who wanted to join them—would not sit silently while the Government of Canada transformed the foundations of environmental and Indigenous law. Their Facebook page was succinct and without an explicit mention of Aboriginal issues. The Facebook events page, which attracted more traffic than the number of attendees at the meeting itself, announced the upcoming event—one of considerable, but unknown, promise:

> This is a grassroots movement for solidarity which welcomes all community members!

> Location: Station 20 West, Saskatoon, SK.
> Actions to take place:

1) Information on Bill C-45
2) Forums to voice questions/concerns
3) Petition demanding that Bill C-45 be stopped

A rally to oppose the omnibus Bill C-45 which will give far reaching and far sweeping powers to Aboriginal Affairs Minister. This bill also gives OIL and nuclear companies room to devastate the land and environment even further. Due consultation is needed in matters that affect all people.

Our silence is consent![3]

Through Facebook, invitations were distributed to almost 3,800 people. Of that sizable number, 357 people indicated that they intended to come to the rally. Another 216 said that they might attend. This was not enough to fill a concert hall, to be sure, but there was a decent indication of interest for a nuanced and complicated political event. Moreover, the event was open to all comers, so the Facebook replies were more a sign of intent than a final tally.

Supporters of the event pushed invitations out electronically, especially via Twitter. Jessica Gordon tweeted on October 30, 2012, "Awesome day of laying the groundwork for rally and petitions opposing #omnibus #billc45 re #indianact please find our fb group #IDLE NO MORE."[4] On November 4, Gordon followed up with a critical note to Shawn Atleo, National Chief of the Assembly of First Nations: "@shawnatleo wuts being done w #billc45 evry1 wasting time talking about Gwen stefani wth!? #indianact #wheresthedemocracy #IdleNoMore."[5] Gordon kept spreading the word with additional tweets that same day, reaching out to individuals and connecting with other groups, including a number focusing on Aboriginal issues:

@EllenGabriel1 ready to fight #IdleNoMore need to #wakeup our #grassroots

@jake_dakota @mfiddlercbc I've started a group #IdleNoMore rally to oppose #billc45 first step in mobilizing an awakening.

Mobilizing an awakening #IdleNoMore rally to oppose #omnibus #billc45 first step to larger #treatyrights #indianact #missingmurderedwomen

Others, including Tanya Kappo, a woman from Sturgeon Lake Cree Nation, Treaty 8 territory—who would become an active member of the movement and who was a friend of Sylvia McAdam—also used Twitter to spread the word: "Rally against Bill C45, specifically Indian Act changes. Saturday, November 10 at Station 20 West, Saskatoon, SK. 12pm–2pm."[6]

A poster was circulated electronically. Not unlike any one of hundreds of such protest announcements circulating in communities across the country each year, it highlighted the event's focus on environmental issues, Indigenous rights, and the authoritarian actions of the Government of Canada.[7]

The event organizers reached out before the November 10 gathering to generate support for their campaign. On November 7, 2012, Jessica Gordon notified supporters that a petition would be circulated before and at the rally, which would be presented to the House of Commons, and that e-mail addresses of MPs involved in reviewing the bill would also be made public. She wrote that the petition and e-mails sent to MPs would help "create a change in the dialogue and decisions," and she urged people to "[f]lood the emails of the conservative MP's who will be reviewing changes to your rights. Tell them you do not agree with the budget implementation Bill C-45 . . . MP's Jean Crowder, Elizabeth May and Carolyn Bennett are good allies and along with others sit on the Standing Committee of Aboriginal Affairs. It's your right and they welcome your concerns."[8]

Nina Wilson offered a similar call for support when she was interviewed on November 19, 2012, at the Indian and Métis Centre in Winnipeg by Trevor Greyeyes, a freelance writer. Responding to a question on what their hopes were, Wilson replied:

The grassroots people . . . are hoping that we can get some talks going. We're also hoping that we can get more people inspired and motivated to speak and to not be afraid to learn . . . The Bill itself is really complicated . . . I can't imagine anybody would want to sit down and read that . . . just for the sake of reading something. So, we're trying to help people . . . to get their voices back so we can . . . have more of a First Nation voice and not just First Nation but an Indigenous voice and a grassroots voice because it [Bill C-45] affects everybody.[9]

Most of the local media paid little attention to Idle No More during the lead-up to the event. However, reporter Ashley Wills, from News Talk 650 CKOM in Saskatoon, reported on the impending rally, noting that the group was worried about how the bill was being rushed through Parliament and was thus "taking a stand," especially against proposed changes to the Indian Act and environmental protections. As Sheelah McLean told Wills, "We feel that we need to do something to slow this bill down . . . We also need to point out the fact that there are changes to Indigenous people's lives that they have had absolutely no consultation about . . . It is definitely taking away protections from our water, from our environment and from our land. It's opening up our natural resources to corporations and companies; these are things that previously had protections."

McLean noted that it was illegal for Aboriginal peoples not to be consulted about proposed legislation affecting the Indian Act, and she stressed that the bill would give "more power to the Minister of Indian Affairs to determine what happens on Indigenous lands . . . I think the biggest problem is, if this is going to be beneficial for Aboriginal communities, why aren't they being consulted on it?"[10]

Wills noted where the rally would be held, and she emphasized that MPs had six days to review the bill.

THE LEADERS OF A LEADERLESS MOVEMENT

The organizers behind Idle No More set the movement apart from most other protests and social movements. The four women—Jessica Gordon, Sylvia McAdam, Sheelah McLean, and Nina Wilson—may well be the most unassuming and spotlight-avoiding leaders of a significant social movement in Canadian history. It is the norm for protests to coalesce around a key individual or group, typically charismatic, high-profile, and outgoing individuals who understand that they embody the values and expectations of a broader social group. These four are nothing like that. They are Indigenous and non-Indigenous, motivated by what they viewed as aggressive government action and what their website described as a "legislative attack on First Nation people and the lands and waters across the country."[11]

Although the founders made the list of the top one hundred global thinkers of 2013, identified by Foreign Policy in its annual poll,[12] the organizers have deliberately avoided the limelight and have consistently indicated their desire for Idle No More to be understood as a collective and spontaneous action, as opposed to a response to the organizers' efforts. They have given a surprisingly small number of media interviews and have typically turned attention to local event coordinators. Nonetheless, it is useful to understand a little more about the four remarkable individuals who decided that standing idly by in the face of unwelcome government intrusions on Aboriginal and Canadian interests was unacceptable.

Jessica Gordon, a Cree/Saulteaux woman from Pasqua, Saskatchewan in Treaty 4 territory, has had a long history of community engagement before she became involved in the Bill C-45 protests, working with groups like the Saskatchewan Urban Aboriginal Strategy.[13] She has a background in business administration, and has completed studies at the University of Regina and the Saskatchewan Indian Institute of Technologies, and she also has extensive experience in the not-for-profit sector.[14] Like the others in the organizing committee, Gordon was committed to rallies that were "peaceful, casual—not causing any trouble to the population."[15] Gordon was the original digital "face" of the rallies, drawing people to the event with #idlenomore.[16]

A *nêhiyaw* (Cree) woman from Treaty 6 territory in northern Saskatchewan, Sylvia McAdam was born on the Big River Reserve and is a direct descendant of one of the signatories to the original Treaty 6. Trained as a teacher and lawyer, fluent in Cree, McAdam is strongly engaged with First Nations communities, living on the Whitefish Lake Reserve.[17] She received an undergraduate degree in Human Justice from the University of Regina and an LL.B. from the University of Saskatchewan. She has written and taught on First Nations culture and spirituality, and has published a book, *Cultural Teachings: First Nations Protocols and Methodologies*, for the Saskatchewan Indian Cultural Centre in Saskatoon and the First Nations University of Canada.[18] Her training in the law and her interest in Indigenous traditional practices and territories contributed to her being in a position to mount a powerful critique of Bill C-45.

Sheelah McLean, the only non-Aboriginal of the four women, was born and raised in Saskatoon, Saskatchewan, a third-generation member of the settler community. She is a doctoral student at the University of Saskatchewan, and has taught both as a high-school teacher and a university instructor. She has a Bachelor of Arts, Bachelor of Education, and a Master of Education with a specialization in Native Studies and Critical Theory. She has been active with Students Against Racism. Her master's degree, in Educational Foundations, focused on "colonization, racialization, and the effect of these forces on communities."[19] McLean, and others involved in the first meeting and early activities, highlighted the influences of University of Saskatchewan faculty, particularly Dr. Verna St. Denis, professor in the Department of Educational Foundations in the Faculty of Education, and Dr. Priscilla Settee, professor in the Department of Native Studies. McLean was drawn to the teach-in through discussions with Sylvia McAdam, Nina Wilson, and Jessica Gordon. As McLean later commented in an *Arts & Science Magazine* article in the spring of 2013, "I knew Sylvia because I'd asked her to speak at a refugee rights rally I organized. She was impressed with its energy and contacted me to do the same against Bill C-45."[20]

Nina Wilson, of the Three Pole People (Nakota, Dakota, and Lakota) and Plains Cree, is from Crooked Lake Agency, Kahkewistahaw First Nation in Treaty 4 territory in southeastern Saskatchewan. She was a graduate student at the University of Saskatchewan in the fall of 2012, and later went on to graduate school at the University of Manitoba.[21] She was drawn into the original teach-in through discussions with Sylvia McAdam. She came to the Idle No More movement with a long history of activism. As she noted, "I am always working on things. Always. I guess to live the messages, to live in solidarity with the people, and live with unity, and live with the history, and carry that with me every single day so that there is something for our children to have a good sense of who we are. I am very lucky to have influence and so being able to do that, I do it from the very best place that I can."[22]

Idle No More's rally to oppose Bill C-45 took place at Station 20 West on Saturday, November 10, 2012, from noon until 2 p.m. The purpose was clear: raise concerns about the bill, promote a petition calling on the government to back down, and build a community of like-minded Saskatchewan residents upset with the federal strategy. About forty or fifty people attended, well short of the number who responded positively on Facebook (a common occurrence in social media mobilization). The rally had all of the elements of a meeting of scholars, activists, and community members. The speakers at the event included Sylvia McAdam and Sharon Venne, a Cree lawyer who helped with negotiations related to the United Nations Declaration on the Rights of Indigenous Peoples. There were two New Democratic Party MLAs: David Forbes, representing Saskatoon Centre, and Cathy Sproule, from the Saskatoon Nutana constituency. They were joined by others, including: community activist, Max Morin; Khodi Dill, a Bahamas-born, spoken-word poet, artist, and University of Saskatchewan graduate student; and Erica Violet Lee, a *nêhiyaw* (Plains Cree) undergraduate student from the University of Saskatchewan and the cultural coordinator for the Indigenous Students' Council.

The full details of the speeches are not available. Khodi Dill's speech, however, was distributed on YouTube. Dill, who said he was a "non-Aboriginal person but [there] in support," had some strongly worded questions about the bill and the government that wanted to implement it:

> If our government values the environment, then why is it bundled into this omnibus implementation bill? If they value the environment, why are they removing protection? Why are we now only protecting one per cent of waterways in this nation? If the government values our First Nations people, then why are significant changes to Indian Act legislation again bundled, almost hidden, within this budget bill? Why was there no consultation, informed consent? And why was there no due diligence if they value First Nations people?

He also read from a poem he composed "in the style of a poet named Gil Scott-Heron who wrote [...] 'The Revolution Will Not Be Televised.'" Dill said that his poem was written "from the point of view of the Government of Canada, historically, currently, to the First Nations people of Canada," and it includes the following striking images and challenging assertions:

> . . .
> See white is the new good,
> And brown is the new bad.
> White is the new happy,
> And brown is the new sad.
> So sign this paper, sign this treaty,
> We'll keep you around and keep you needy.
> Yes sign this treaty, sign this paper

And brace yourselves for the silent caper.
The genocide will not be televised.

. . .

You will not be able to catch it on CTV,
So the next time Lloyd Robinson tells you
That that's the kind of day it's been, don't listen.
Just ask yourself, whose story is missing,
Whose rights are missing, whose women are missing,
Whose women are missing, whose women are missing?
The genocide will not be televised,
Will not be televised, not be televised.

The genocide will be no re-run brothers and sisters,
The genocide will be live.[23]

The setting of this first gathering was modest. The audience was small. At this point, Idle No More was little more than a slogan associated with a teach-in in Saskatoon. But even in the earliest of days, before the media paid attention to the gathering prairie storm, words of determination spoke even more eloquently than political statements and anti-government arguments.

Like Dill, Erica Lee was critical of Bill C-45. She criticized John Baird for calling Bill C-45 the "Jobs and Growth Bill," wondering who in Canada would benefit from it: "it's certainly not Aboriginal people, it's certainly not poor people, and it's certainly not any of us in this room at all." Lee also felt that the bill would destroy "environmental policy, or whatever remains of it, by dramatically cutting environmental assessments and putting power in the hands of businesses," and she went on to discuss how Aboriginal peoples have historically been treated by the Government of Canada and how she believed Bill C-45 would affect Aboriginal peoples:

> Canadian governments are fantastic at ignoring and delegitimizing Aboriginal grassroots movements. That's why we still teach Canadian history in schools as the peaceful transfer of Aboriginal lands to the Queen via treaties, when it was actually involved with starvation, genocide, rape, and coercion of Aboriginal peoples by

the Government of Canada. That's why we still repeat tired phrases like, "they don't pay taxes," "they're all on welfare and they're all drunken criminals," "if only they'd work a little harder," and "we just need to give First Nations people transparency and accountability in their governments because they can't govern themselves." Meanwhile, there is no mention of the government role in the continued poverty, racism, and hatred against Aboriginal people that we have all encountered. So, I could say that we as Aboriginal people need to rise up together and fight back against the government.

Then, Lee personalized her activism, and in doing so, set up a challenge to other students like her. She said: "I'm in a political studies class right now, and I was thinking the other day about how we sit there and we learn about structures, we learn about government, we learn about it like it's history and facts. But we're never told to go out and do something, and it's because we're not supposed to. We're just supposed to sit there and learn, repeat what we're told . . . and never question what the government we're learning about is actually doing to us as people, as students."

Lee was not the first, nor the last, of the Idle No More speakers in the coming months to call out young people for their complacency and encourage them to support the cause of the marginalized. As she said that day at the teach-in, "Let's not discuss this bill in terms of its effect on Aboriginal Canadians alone, or what Aboriginal Canadians can do to fix this situation because that will get us nowhere. We are all at risk when treaty rights are violated. We are all at risk when our government chooses to pass legislation without consent, while stifling protest . . . I don't know if you know this but not just Aboriginal Canadians need to drink water. We need to wake up and realize that environmental conservation and land rights are not special interest issues."[24]

The organizers of the Station 20 West event distributed a petition to band offices, community groups, and others, asking them to sign up followers and help produce a petition that would be forwarded to the House of Commons.[25] Other petitions were circulated via Facebook and other online methods, seeking to draw as many people as possible into the protest against Bill C-45. At this early stage in the movement, take-up was not immediate. The first YouTube videos did not go viral and attract hundreds of thousands of viewers like the latest Justin Bieber escapade. The meeting was low key, and the eloquence and passions of the speakers did not immediately resonate outside the small circle of people who attended the Saskatoon meeting.

The two highly engaged MLAS—NDP members David Forbes and Cathy Sproule—speaking about a matter of national politics, made the event seem very local. The CBC and the Saskatoon *Star Phoenix* did not even cover the meeting immediately. However, Mark Bigland-Pritchard, an environmental engineer and a worker at Turning the Tide bookstore, who attended the event, wrote, "Many thanks to the organisers and to all the speakers, both those who were booked and those who spoke in the 'open mic' period. Something important happened today—indigenous and settler people working together to build the resistance. I am excited to see so many grassroots indigenous leaders emerging, and I look forward to lots of cooperation in the future."[26] And Miki Mappin, a Saskatoon-based artist who was born in South Africa, was similarly impressed, posting a comment on the Idle No More Facebook events page: "Especially inspiring were the young, articulate and passionate women who spoke. This is what is going to fire people up and change the world!"[27]

Hindsight tells us that the gathering on November 10, 2012, was transformative, despite the fact that not a great deal that occurred during that first meeting could hint at what would come. But, in fact, there were some signs of something different happening that afternoon, including: the shift from a general critique of Bill C-45 to an indictment of government management, or mismanagement, of Aboriginal legislation and programming; the prominence of women in the organizing group; the integration of Aboriginal and non-Aboriginal perspectives; and the active engagement of young people, as captured in the speeches by Dill and Lee later posted to YouTube.

It is easy, now, to highlight the organizers' use of Facebook, YouTube, and Twitter as a sign of a protest movement engaged with new media, and yet this was scarcely an innovation in 2012. Barack Obama had been elected President of the United States in 2008 due, in part, to the effective use of new media, and Republicans in the United States and the Conservative Party in Canada had capitalized on the new technologies to spread their word. Social media gave an emerging group ready access to large numbers of people and added to the small set of tools it had at its disposal. But the message about Aboriginal determination, combined with a real audience made strong by young people—Aboriginal and non-Aboriginal alike—put a foundation under the November 10 gathering that social media, alone, would not have been able to accomplish.

So what brought a few dozen to the small and poorly media-covered meeting at Station 20 West in Saskatoon that November weekend? The movement's founders believe that Bill C-45 was the trigger. For example, on November 3, 2012, prompted by her feelings regarding the omnibus bill, Jessica Gordon left the following comment on the Facebook events page:

> I've never really followed, been involved or been passionate about "Canadian Politics," heck I even made a conscious effort to stay away from "First Nations Politics" after I realized that thinking about it wouldn't allow me to fall asleep at night. Although, now in the past couple weeks after becoming aware of upcoming unconstitutional and undemocratic laws about to pass regarding NOT ONLY First Nations people but the rest of Canada as well, it would seem that the restless sleeps, the virtual constant reading of articles, legislation, other people's opinions and so on is nothing compared to what may come when our rights are compromised. My intention is not to bash a certain political party, politician/lobbyist, corporation or individual. My intention is to become aware, share and try my best to make a change or right some wrongs. I have the choice to be silent even though I have a burning urge to scream OR, I have the choice to, not only voice my concerns but to also do something about it. There is no way I could be ok with telling my kids and future grandkids that I did nothing to make a better place for them. What will you tell yours?[28]

After the November 10 meeting, Canadian media began to focus on the bill and what it would mean for Canadians. The omnibus bill was a cumbersome document, its major shortcomings difficult to pin down. For some, the major problem lay with the changes proposed to the management of First Nations lands. Specifically, Bill C-45 loosened the provisions governing the leasing of reserve lands. As the Aboriginal Peoples Television Network reported on November 21:

> First Nation band councils would no longer need majority community support to lease out parcels of reserve land under proposed changes to the Indian Act contained in the Harper government's omnibus budget bill. The proposed changes are raising concern among some prairie First Nations who say the Harper government is unilaterally changing the laws impacting reserve lands in defiance of the treaties and without any consultation. Aboriginal Affairs Minister John Duncan, however, says . . . "It has nothing to do with selling off, surrendering lands. It has everything to do with allowing First Nations a much quicker and simpler process to designate lands they want to turn to economic development purposes, for leasing purposes."[29]

Sylvia McAdam argued that the proposed legislation was "contrary to everything Canadian citizens believe in," for it made it easier and faster to remove lands from First Nations control, a process designed to serve business interests rather than the people.[30] A few days after the November 10 teach-in, the *Slave River Journal* noted that other Aboriginal leaders agreed:

> "This is unacceptable. They have made a unilateral decision to remove the protection of waterways without adequate consultation with First Nations and communities that rely on river systems for navigation and cultural practices protected under treaty," stated Eriel Deranger, ACFN [Athabasca Chipewyan First Nation] spokesperson. Deranger said the changes will give a "green light" to the oil sands industry to destroy

waterways of cultural and biological significance on AFCN territory . . . . "I am seriously concerned this is an indication of corruption in our current government," said ACFN Chief Allan Adam.

The article further quoted Adam who added that the bill creates "more loopholes for industry to continue annihilating our lands."[31]

The challenge for opponents of the omnibus bill lay in getting the public to focus on specific provisions and not on the whole piece of legislation. For First Nations observers, as Deranger, Adam, and others noted, the devil truly was in the details. Like the four founders of Idle No More, many people were not content.

Within a few days of the first teach-in, echo-events began to occur across the province, demonstrating that the interest in the cause extended beyond the small meeting at Station 20 West. First Nations and Métis people across Saskatchewan were the first to take to the streets. As Nina Wilson wrote the night of the first event in Saskatoon, "I am very touched by the pictures, the videos . . . and the spirit of this intention . . . we are all in this together." She also posted that she "heard a comment in a class last week, a woman stated she was from a 'landless people' . . . that just made me feel so much urgency, we are all treaty [people] means something."[32] One of the movement's organizers also posted information about the Saskatoon public hearing to be held on November 21, 2012, at the Saskatoon Indian and Métis Friendship Centre. This hearing would give people the opportunity to meet with members of the Standing Committee on Human Rights.[33]

At a First Nations University meeting, held in Regina on November 17, a long list of speakers addressed the crowd: Kevin Wesaquate, an artist from Piapot First Nation; Kevin Daniels, a Regina scriptwriter; Julianne Beaudin-Herney, artist in residence at the University of Regina; Sarah Koi, a Cree woman born in Vancouver; Regina community activist Jaqueline Anaquod; Solomon Cyr, a communications specialist and executive assistant to the George Gordon First Nation; Ralph Goodale, long-serving Liberal Member of Parliament; and Gord Barnes, of Amnesty International. A North Battleford event, held the following day, featured talks by Colby Tootoosis, a leadership professional from Poundmaker Cree Nation; Sylvia McAdam; Marius

Paul of the Dene Nation and the Committee for Future Generations; and Chief Eddy Makokis of the Saddle Lake Cree Nation in Alberta.[34]

The small meeting at the Indian and Métis Friendship Centre in Winnipeg, held on November 19, included Nina Wilson. While there, she spoke with Trevor Greyeyes for his web-newscast about the embryonic movement: "We started in Saskatchewan. There were just a few ladies that were just, you know, concerned. We were seeing things in the media that . . . we were starting to pay attention to. . . . From there it spread. So, now we've had these rallies to inform people and to have the grassroots voice in Saskatoon, Regina, North Battleford, there's talk about Prince Albert and now here in Winnipeg."[35] A Prince Albert event went ahead at the Margo Fournier Centre on November 24.[36] The speakers there included Jessica Gordon; Michelle Sanderson, a singer from the Peguis First Nation; Michael Gatin, of the Saskatchewan Teachers' Federation; Kevin Joseph, columnist for the *Prince Albert Herald*; Jessica Iron Joseph, a freelance writer from Prince Albert; and Colby Tootoosis.

On November 25, 2012, Jessica Gordon wrote about elevating the intensity of the critique of government policy and the omnibus bill, letting people know that the petition was signed by hundreds online and off during those rallies held in Saskatoon, Regina, North Battleford, Winnipeg, and Prince Albert, and that other rallies were in the works:

> I feel now is the time to set out on a new plan of action! We must start mobilizing a national day of action as soon as possible so our brothers and sisters may participate in this great movement! The House of Commons breaks for Xmas on [December] 14th. It is our plan now to mobilize people from across Canada to visit MP offices, industry corporations, legislative buildings in an act of solidarity to oppose [government] bills and legislation that do not respect free prior and informed consent while asserting our sovereignty. We feel coordinating efforts and campaigns would not only show our support to these causes but also speak volumes in numbers of our grassroots voices. . . . We would like this to be a coordinated effort amongst all groups and a mutual sharing of support, recognition and solidarity![37]

It is vitally important to note what did *not* happen next. One would expect that, presented with a significant cause and some evidence of public interest, and possessed of real drive and determination, Gordon, McAdam, McLean, and Wilson would now establish a more formal group or perhaps link to an existing Aboriginal organization. One would expect that, perhaps now, a manifesto be drawn up, a plan made for regional or national mobilization, some central administration and some fundraising begun. The original organizers, however, did none of the above. Having lit the fire, they continued in their personal efforts to fan the flames, speaking to groups, and, eventually, travelling the country in support of the cause. But they did not connect their activities to existing Aboriginal political protests or reach out to the established Indigenous organizations. Instead, they distanced themselves from the existing Aboriginal leadership and structures, and did not formalize any arrangements or assert personal control.

Idle No More was not designed to join with existing Aboriginal political activities but rather to empower the Aboriginal people of Canada and their supporters. As an oft-repeated statement, starting to circulate on the Internet, noted: the "face and leaders of Idle No More are the grassroots people." Many of the people who stepped behind the Idle No More banners had harsh words for Aboriginal politics and politicians and made it clear that their frustrations were focused on the broad status quo, not just the Harper government. The organizers issued a call to action, laying out their vision for a widespread response to the existing government system but also making it clear that they wanted to embolden Aboriginal people to speak their minds about the issues that mattered to them and their communities. As they noted in a mid-December press release:

> When we stand strong and believe in our ways and assert acts of Nationhood, it does not matter what amount of legislation the federal government introduces or passes because it is not with our consent and therefore, is not applicable. Stand strong and believe in the spirit and intent of our Treaties as that's what our ancestors are calling us to do. We must continue to assert acts of Nationhood premised on ancient ways and teachings that

were given to us in our original instructions by Creator when we were placed here on Turtle Island.[38] We encourage·people to advocate for our Mother (the land), the Water (giver of life) and those generations that have yet to come. We must keep that warrior spirit alive and continue the advocacy efforts as there are other Bills in parliament and our energies must be directed towards fighting against them. We will continue to rise up and make our presence known across Turtle Island, the land that is rightfully ours as Creator put us here. Stand Up and Rise UP—this Fight is NOT Over. We need you all in this—we shall PERSEVERE![39]

By the end of November 2012, the Idle No More movement had grown beyond the original teach-in, finding decent audiences and generating some media interest on the prairies. The four founders had demonstrated their knowledge of both the government's strategies and the aspirations of Aboriginal people in Canada. They had shown real commitment to the cause but an equal determination not to become the dominant face of the protest movement, whatever it might become. While Bill C-45 remained front and centre—the focal point for frustration and organizing—the founders had articulated a much broader sense of unease, exasperation, and hope amongst First Nations and Métis communities on the prairies. They tied their anger over the Government of Canada's legislative initiatives to their struggle to ensure the integrity of treaties, respect for Aboriginal governance, and protection of their traditional lands.

As recorded on the Idle No More Saskatoon Facebook page (created on December 24, 2012), event organizers were calling

on all people to join in a revolution which honors and fulfills Indigenous sovereignty which protects the land and water. Colonization continues through attacks to Indigenous rights and damage to the land and water. We must repair these violations, live the spirit and intent of the treaty relationship, work towards justice in action, and protect Mother Earth. All people will be affected by the continued damage to the land and water and we welcome Indigenous and non-Indigenous allies to join in creating healthy sustainable communities. We encourage youth to become engaged in this movement as you are the leaders of our future.[40]

It had become an eventful November. After the first teach-in in Saskatoon, *TheStar.com* reported that intense activity through social media sites, such as Facebook and Twitter, erupted.[41] The activity continued to intensify into December. Rebecca Lindell from *Global News* reported that data gathered between December 16 and December 23 showed an increase in the number of tweets from 6,333 tweets (1,751 sources) to a peak of 32,128 tweets on December 21, the Idle No More National Day of Action.[42] An early analysis of the movement's social media presence was captured by analyst Mark Blevis. He reported that, during the first two months between November 25, 2012, and January 19, 2013, there were 113,409 unique tweeters issuing 867,614 tweets, with January 11, 2013, as the most active day.[43] From quiet beginnings, something truly impressive had been launched.

###

Idle No More was thus under way. While it is wrong to suggest that Aboriginal people in Canada had been silent or even quiet before the movement began—the last forty years have been noisy ones, after all—it was clear even in the early days that Idle No More was something unique in Canadian history. Commentary on the emergent movement consistently tied its activities to the omnibus bill and contemporary federal government policy. But this view understates the degree to which Idle No More was a long time in the making and had much more staying power than most Canadians expected. The trigger may have been the Conservative government's omnibus bill of 2012, but the mass movement that became Idle No More emerged out of broader and deeper forces that have shaped, impinged upon, constrained, and harmed the lives of Indigenous peoples across the country.

Sylvia McAdam, speaking on Parliament
Hill on December 21, 2012. Next to her,
Perry Bellegarde, Chief of the Federation
of Saskatchewan Indian Nations.
Photo: Nadya Kwandibens / Red Works Studio

TWO

THE ROOTS OF ABORIGINAL ANGER AND HOPE

dle No More did not come out of thin air. The meetings, rallies, singing, and drumming that swept across Canada in the winter of 2012–2013 have deep roots in Canadian history. Aboriginal Canadians have been profoundly sad for a long time. The majority of Aboriginal Canadians harbour deep frustrations with the country and, it must be said, with non-Aboriginal Canadians at large. Although conditions have improved considerably in recent decades, discrimination and racism remain a very real part of Aboriginal people's reality in Canada. That our nation's embassies are graced with impressive works of Indigenous art or that Aboriginal ceremony has become an increasingly common part of Canadian celebratory life does not change the lived experience of thousands of First Nations, Métis, and Inuit peoples across the country.

Despite the situation, Aboriginal Canadians are an intensely hopeful people. Even though they have been forced off their lands, marginalized in their home territories, impoverished, controlled by paternalistic governments, and often reviled simply for their "Indian-ness," they maintain a surprisingly optimistic outlook on their future.

Aboriginal people still show up at the negotiating tables. They share their stories, cultures, and ceremonies with continued grace. They seek justice in Canadian courts and not through acts of violence. Aboriginal communities, even in the midst of their despair and crises, support their Elders, maintain traditions, and protect their traditional lands. The story is not that there have been outbursts from time to time—blockades, protests, insurrections—but rather that there have been so few of these, and far between. Canadians have spent too little time wondering why Aboriginal people, who suffer such hardships and so many dislocations, have been so nonviolent, so rarely disruptive, and so persistent in their pursuit of real solutions. Strong despite the effects of colonialism, determined despite decades of contact and oppression, Aboriginal people remain resilient, determined to claim their rightful place in Canadian society.

The rallies that began to spread across Canada in the winter of 2012 were a logical outgrowth of the generations of contact, conflict, and attempts at reconciliation. They were, in pretty much equal measure, demonstrations of determination and frustration, hope and anger, optimism and despair. The range of emotions and reactions cannot be explained by the response to Bill C-45, the frustration with the Harper government, or any specific experience, politician, or event. Idle No More began with frustration about the omnibus bill, but it was fuelled by several hundred years of the Aboriginal experience with settlers, as well as the combined passions, disappointments, and dreams of thousands of Aboriginal people from coast to coast to coast. Idle No More was more an outcome than a cause, a manifestation of deep Aboriginal unease more than a spontaneous reaction to the events of 2012. To understand what happened in that busy and dramatic period, one has to appreciate the aspirations and hopes that have been resting uneasily in Indigenous communities for many years.

Let's be clear about the unpleasant truth about the lived experiences of Aboriginal Canadians. As a non-Aboriginal Canadian, a person of middle-class privilege, and a beneficiary of the opportunities available to the generation that came of age in the late 1960s and early 1970s, I was a close but removed observer of the reality of Aboriginal life. I was raised in Whitehorse, Yukon, living in a large government house that sat atop the clay cliffs on the west side of the famed Yukon

River. If you walked to the edge of the cliff, the Whitehorse Indian Reserve (since relocated) lay a kilometre or so below, bordered by the swampy lands next to the Yukon River, the city's industrial area, and the clay cliffs. A few rows of government-built homes, small and crowded, were laid out in suburban style below us. When the temperature got really cold—below –30°C—some of the people would go out in the middle of the night to cut wood, a quick means of letting those of us atop the hill know it was freezing outside. We did not have much contact with the First Nations children and families who lived below. Our elementary school in Camp Takhini was overwhelmingly white, drawn largely from the families of highway workers and government employees.

One point of contact we had with kids from the reserve related to bicycles. Kids climbed the cliffs from the reserve, grabbed the bikes from around our houses, and threw or rolled them down the clay banks. Several times I looked over the cliff and saw one of our bikes or those of our neighbours in the trees at the bottom. It was a hard slog to get down the hill and pull and push the bike back up the steep incline. This was irritating but hardly a crisis. Serious vandalism in or thefts from the Camp Takhini area were extremely rare.

I told this story about the bikes at an economic development conference in St. John's, Newfoundland, in September 2013, using it to illustrate the significant gap between the lives of Aboriginal and non-Aboriginal northerners and received the expected laughs at the poetic justice of the bike episodes.

At the end of the talk, two First Nations people from the Yukon approached me at the podium. The lady laughed cheerfully at my story and told me that several of her friends on the reserve had pulled off a few heists. The man, a friendly and gregarious fellow, introduced himself. "I was one of those who got your bikes," he said with a chuckle. "You white folks weren't very bright about your bikes." We reminisced for a while, enjoying the fact that we could make fun of an episode that, at the time, demonstrated to both of us the gulf between our families and our lives.

Contact was limited. A small number of First Nations students were in my elementary school classes, and a few Aboriginal people came to our church. The Anglican summer camp near Carcross, an hour south of Whitehorse, operated next to a large residential school, but our contact with the students living there over the summer was limited to a couple of remarkably aggressive—and exciting—baseball games. A late-1960s visit my ski club and I made to Old Crow, a remote community well above the Arctic Circle, provided us with a surprising introduction to a population strongly connected to the land, cut off from the world of television and material wealth, but friendly and active. A snowball fight, launched by an elderly lady who laughed uproariously when her missile clipped one of us on the head, soon involved the entire community in one of the funniest and most enjoyable encounters between Indigenous peoples and newcomers one could imagine.

The pattern of proximate separation continued in high school. Our Grade 8 class was almost 30 per cent Aboriginal. By Grade 12 graduation, only a handful of Indigenous students remained. Most of the best basketball players were Aboriginal—one of the few positive legacies of months in residential school—as were many of the most talented cross-country skiers. But outside of sports, contact between Aboriginal and non-Aboriginal students was limited. Not invisible and not sharply protested when it happened, just limited. So it was in the workforce. First Nations people rarely had front-line retail and service jobs in town. Not many worked for the government or in the private sector. Native and non-Native people just lived separately, occupying very different spheres and living markedly different lives.

Aboriginal and non-Aboriginal Yukoners, however, actually connected more than most Aboriginal and non-Aboriginal people in the rest of Canada. As recently as the 1960s, most Aboriginal people in Canada lived on reserves, or in one of the squatter settlements in and around towns, cut off from the non-Aboriginal majority in the cities and major towns. Few worked in retail and even fewer had professional jobs in the city. And yet, despite the fact that Whitehorse was small enough for regular contact, real understanding between the two groups eluded most Yukoners. First Nations and non-status people in the territory started organizing in the 1960s, frustrated by their lack of control over their traditional lands and the growing welfare dependency. The Yukon's non-Aboriginal majority reacted with dismay to the launch of the Yukon Native Brotherhood's land claim in 1973. Many angry words were shared in the aftermath of the assertion of Aboriginal rights.

I left the Yukon in 1974 to attend university in Vancouver. Intellectual wanderlust eventually led me to the study of history and a master's degree at the University of Manitoba—focusing on the fur trade in the Yukon—and a Ph.D. at the University of British Columbia, where I worked on Native-white relations in the Yukon. Having set my professional sights on an academic career, I researched, wrote about, and taught Aboriginal history and northern issues, maintaining as much contact with the Yukon as my other commitments permitted.

An unexpected opportunity emerged shortly after I joined the University of Victoria as a faculty member. I was contacted by George Henry, a high-school friend and filmmaker and one of the people behind the creation of Northern Native Broadcasting Yukon (NNBY). NNBY was an Aboriginal-controlled radio and television company based in Whitehorse. With George and his colleagues at NNBY, I worked on a series of documentaries, including a 1988 film on residential schools, *The Mission School Syndrome*, and I found myself in the middle of Aboriginal debates about history, politics, and cultural aspirations. It takes nothing away from my ten years of post-secondary education to say that the five years working, off and on, with NNBY gave me an intense understanding and engagement with First Nations issues in a way that the academy never could.

One event in particular stood out. NNBY had flown in some first-rate Canadian video producers as part of a staff-training exercise. Each group of four or five staff members was charged with making a public-service advertisement on an issue of importance to Yukon First Nations. A while later, we gathered to watch the short clips. The first few were nicely done, professionally shot, straightforward, and ready to go to air as part of the Needa (Your Eye) program. One, however, produced some challenges. It was a clear message about a difficult, jarring subject: suicide. The images used for the advertisement were stark, a hand fumbling with a cigarette, a rifle lying on the table in front of an ashtray. Somber music. The hand reaches for the rifle and chambers a shell. Fade to black with a short voice-over, pleading something to the effect of, "Don't do it! Speak to an Elder." The audience watched in silence, the air heavy with emotion. The production team quickly introduced a second version with a different ending. As the hand reached for the rifle, another hand came from the side, gently took the gun, and the voice said, again, "Don't do it! Speak to an Elder."

The imagery was startling and the message powerful. Everyone agreed that either one was first-rate and should be used. At least one of the southern producers had questions and suggested that NNBY get professional advice from the Yukon's suicide-watch agency. They came to meet with us a few days later. I still have vivid memories of the setting. We gathered in a circle. My oldest son, then eight or nine, sat on my lap. The government officials started by outlining why they thought the video was not suitable: namely, it might lead someone to commit suicide, a horrible prospect. Discussion ensued.

After a few minutes, a middle-aged woman spoke up, a Native-language announcer who rarely joined in discussions: "Have you had anyone die?" she asked. The two female officials explained that, in the course of their work, they had encountered many sad events. "I meant in your family," she countered. They admitted, thankfully, that they had not. The announcer then described a death by suicide of a relative. Tragic. And then it started. The woman sitting next to her, unprompted, told her story. Then another, then another, and then another. Around the circle the stories went, skipping quickly over the non-Aboriginal folks who had few examples to contribute. Some twenty to twenty-five Aboriginal people had a personal connection to suicide, some still raw with immediacy, others with the painful edges eroded by the passage of time. The video did not air, despite the wishes of the majority of the Aboriginal workers at the station.

That circle talk, more than any in my life, brought home to me the fundamental gap that exists between Aboriginals and other Canadians. The folks in the circle were my professional colleagues and, in a couple of cases, long-time friends. Yet they had never shared these stories with me. The act of suicide was not the only important part of the stories. The speakers spoke of a sadness that began long before the terrible tragedy of self-inflicted death, a sadness that is the result of a colonial legacy that has too often manifested itself in broken lives, jail sentences, violence, drug abuse, discrimination, cultural loss, identity crises, and the like. This troubling afternoon stays with me, a constant reminder of the different lives of Aboriginal and non-Aboriginal people.

Five years after this episode, in 1992, when I was working at the University of Northern British Columbia (an experience that brought me into extended contact with First Nations from across the North), I had a more personal encounter with the reality of Aboriginal life. My colleague, a quiet and highly professional Aboriginal woman, had strong family connections in north-central British Columbia. Over the course of our first two years together, she experienced a series of violent deaths among her extended family, ranging from a boating accident, a drunk-driving incident (a relative was killed by a drunk driver), a single-vehicle accident, a suicide, and a hunting incident. Far too often, she was called away from work to attend to family responsibilities, both immediate and longer term, resulting from the deaths. She remained cheerful and upbeat throughout, although I don't know how. This was, quite simply, the reality of her community and family life. It bore no resemblance to mine.

So, when tragedy struck the family of another Aboriginal friend of mine, this time living in a prairie city, I had some broader context to help me understand what was happening—not that it helped. The young woman, a fantastic artist and performer, a great student, and an ebullient personality, was perhaps the last Aboriginal person one would think would take her own life. She was in university and on the path to a good life and career, it seemed. She could have had a future in fine arts or, like her mother, become a community advocate. She was confident but not arrogant, talented but not aloof, community-oriented but comfortable in the city at large. But she was deeply troubled by the unsubtle racism she experienced in the city; when walking with white friends, she would be the one pulled aside by the police to be questioned about why she was walking on the east side of Saskatoon, an area with a small Aboriginal population.

At the time, she was working at a retail store. Her former boyfriend, with whom she was still close, went to pick her up from work one day. He wandered the store waiting for her, and he was accosted by the staff, who accused him of shoplifting. She came to his defence only to find herself drawn into the circle of accusation. It turns out her coworkers thought she was serving as the lookout for her friend. They had no evidence of shoplifting, for the simple reason that he had not been stealing and never had, but they fired her anyway. A short time later, after writing heart-wrenchingly thoughtful letters to family members and friends, outlining the endless pain of living in a racist world, she overdosed on pills and died. Her mother was devastated by the loss of her brilliant and beloved child, which embodied for her the reality of being Aboriginal in twenty-first-century Canada.

Aboriginal teen suicides are seven to eight times more common than non-Aboriginal teen suicides. The pain and hurt behind these acts and experiences is much more widespread than most Canadians can comprehend. As I watch, work with, research, and write about Aboriginal life in this country, I have come to witness how pervasive the hardships are and how the external signs of success—high-school graduation, college and university degrees, professional work, Native-run businesses, self-government, political recognition, legal victories—do not come close to removing the dark stain of Canadian racism and historical injustices that still colour and spill out over the land.

But there are many promising developments, as well. Over the last thirty years, my view of the world has continued to be shaped and reshaped by my engagement with Aboriginal peoples: students at universities, Indigenous political leaders and administrators, government officials responsible for Aboriginal affairs, as well as exposure to Indigenous issues from New Zealand to Russia, Japan to Norway. I was profoundly moved by the emergence of the modern land claims process in the Yukon, the determination of students in remote communities in northern Manitoba to complete their degrees through Brandon University, the efforts of Kim Recalma-Clutesi, Bill White, and other First Nations people to create a safe place for Aboriginal students at the University of Victoria, of First Nations in northern British Columbia to be a central part of the newly created University of Northern British Columbia, of the passion of the Maori faculty and students of the University of Waikato in New Zealand, and the surprising and rapid response of Maritime First Nations to legal victories in the late 1990s.[1] I marvelled at the dedication of First Nations and Métis students, faculty, and staff to ensure that the University of Saskatchewan became their university in thought and action, and the growing complexity of Aboriginal approaches to the Canadian courts. Over the course of two decades, I watched from afar as Indigenous peoples the world over tackled the seemingly unachievable goal of creating a United Nations document on Indigenous rights, and then brought the nations of the world on board in crafting it, finally passing the United Nations Declaration on the Rights of Indigenous Peoples on September 13, 2007.

Canada held out for a time, not signing on until three years later, in 2010.

CREATING SPACE AT THE UNIVERSITY OF VICTORIA

First Nations peoples are prominent in British Columbia. Their artistry is evident in totem poles and longhouses, dancing and button blankets. Land claims negotiations and Aboriginal treaty and land rights play a crucial role in provincial politics. At British Columbia's universities, Aboriginal topics attract a great deal of student interest and the research undertaken by Indigenous peoples is some of the best in the world. However, it was not always thus.

In the late 1980s, I worked in the Department of History at the University of Victoria. Because of my classes on northern history and Indigenous-newcomer relations in Canada, my courses attracted many Aboriginal students. University professors have an opportunity to impart knowledge to and share insights with their students. Fortunate university lecturers capitalize on the chance to learn from and with their students. At the University of Victoria, I had just such an opportunity, one that transformed my attitude to work, scholarship, and Aboriginal-newcomer relations.

Early on, two prominent Aboriginal students—Kim Recalma-Clutesi and Bill White—approached me about helping them establish a Native students' society. They did not need much help on the logistical front as they were accomplished organizers. They quickly opened my eyes to the unique situation facing Indigenous students on campus: financial challenges connected to delays in receiving government grants processed through band offices, family and community crises, and difficulties for students experiencing the transition from remote villages to an urban campus. The university also engaged in a debate about the institution's initial reluctance to allow First Nations graduates to wear button blankets at their graduation ceremonies.

Two developments stood out. The First Nations students were frustrated with the lack of on-campus attention to Aboriginal culture. So, working with few resources, they decided to organize a large cultural event for the university community. They recruited singers, dancers, and speakers from across Vancouver Island and then booked the largest venue on campus—a declaration of their unfailing optimism. Their event was masterful, offering an excellent representation of vibrant and resilient cultures. Equally important, the hall was filled nearly to capacity. Nary a political word was uttered that night. The students emphasized Indigenous spirituality, culture, and social values, not land rights and treaty processes. It was, in the end, a turning point in the university community's relationship with Aboriginal peoples. Within a few months, the university appointed Bill White as an advisor on Indigenous affairs and protocols, laying the foundation for the institution's future collaboration with First Nations.

At the same time, Kim Recalma-Clutesi pushed quietly for a more comprehensive approach to learning from and with First Nations peoples. With support from the provost, Dr. Sam Scully, a special course was organized on the cultures and histories of the First Nations on Vancouver Island. The format was straightforward. The first half of each class involved presentations by and discussions with Aboriginal Elders and community leaders, typically on a specific topic. The second half involved University of Victoria faculty members who provided an academic overview of the topic covered by the First Nations speakers. The idea that Kim brought forward was to be mutually respectful: to grant Aboriginal wisdom and cultural knowledge the kind of authority accorded to Western-style scholarship and teaching styles. The course was amazing, presenting different voices, experiences, and perspectives and challenging students to step beyond their academic comfort zone and listen to Aboriginal leaders in new ways. This was not the first course like this in Canada; several universities had Native Studies programs by this time and the format was familiar in these institutions. For University

of Victoria, and certainly for me, however, this was a new beginning, and the course provided valuable insights into new
ways of sharing and respecting Aboriginal culture and wisdom.

My time at the University of Victoria, and specifically the
opportunity to work with the First Nations students and their
emerging organization, was crucially important to me. The
challenges facing Aboriginal students are formidable; in one
Vancouver Island school district, for example, Native students
have been automatically streamed into non-academic English
and Math courses, making them ineligible for university entry.
But the passion of the First Nations students I came to know—
passion and determination in the face of difficult barriers to their
academic and personal successes, and to the informal con-
straints on Aboriginal knowledge, learning styles, and perspectives—was incredibly enlightening. The First Nations students
made it clear that they expected and wanted a better future,
but they also demonstrated a willingness to share knowledge
and learning in a manner that seemed out of step with the oppression they experienced in contemporary Canadian society.

Aboriginal issues have never been an abstraction, for I remember
well my early years in the Yukon and the time I have shared with
hundreds of Aboriginal students, faculty members, community leaders, officials, and politicians over the years. The Aboriginal people I
have met in leadership roles and in colleges and universities demonstrate a remarkable commitment to improving the lives of Aboriginal
peoples. If only, I have thought many times, Canadians could see the
passion and sustained effort by Aboriginal peoples to improve their
communities, then many of the offensive stereotypes about Indigenous peoples would quickly disappear. There is anger and frustration
in Aboriginal communities, to be sure, but underlying these feelings
are optimism and the hopeful belief that determination and effort
will make a real difference for them and for the entire country in
the future. The non-Aboriginal response to Indigenous conditions is
also not as consistently mean-spirited as much commentary would

have it. I have been in meetings with church leaders and members trying to rebuild their relationship with First Nations after the dismantling of confidence in Christianity and Christian representatives. Further, in my discussions with government officials and politicians rethinking policies, I see many good-intentioned people determined to work with Aboriginal people to create better and more sustainable opportunities.

But the disconnect between Aboriginal and non-Aboriginal Canadians continues. For most non-Aboriginals, the stories in the newspapers—about epidemic suicide, reserve poverty and violence, health and housing crises—are not generally reinforced by personal experience. Few southern Canadians have been to isolated, northern, and remote communities. Attawapiskat—the long-suffering northern Ontario community drawn once more into the limelight by Chief Theresa Spence in the winter of 2012—is as much an abstraction to most Canadians as are Somalia and Haiti, places of hardship and suffering that are far removed from the lived realities of most Canadians. More than that, non-Aboriginal Canadian stereotypes of Aboriginal people live on: lazy and drunk Indians, corrupt chiefs, decrepit reserves, and dying if not dead cultures. And so does anti-Aboriginal racism: offensive jokes, harsh assumptions, and critical comments about dependency on government spending and the inevitable demise of Indian reserves.

Not being Aboriginal, I struggle to understand how Indigenous peoples in twenty-first-century Canada feel about their lives, communities, futures, and place in the country. Aboriginal people speak up more freely in public than they did twenty years ago; there are articulate and determined political leaders who describe Indigenous realities, and Aboriginal writers, filmmakers, singers, and visual artists document First Nations, Inuit, and Métis conditions and concerns. Over time, I have come to understand Aboriginal realities better and to worry about the odd, uneven, and uncertain relationships between Indigenous and non-Indigenous peoples. We share this place Aboriginal people often call Turtle Island. We experience each other, but real understanding remains tragically elusive.

My north-centred and largely western Canadian experiences are not the norm for non-Aboriginal Canadians, both because of my northern upbringing and because of my professional experience with

Indigenous peoples. I also lived for three years in New Brunswick and six years in southern Ontario, gaining perspective on the very different realities of southern and eastern Aboriginal peoples. Across the south of the country, Indigenous peoples and non-Indigenous peoples typically live much farther apart than those in the territorial North. The cities and major towns of the southern portion of Canada are primarily non-Aboriginal spaces. First Nations, Métis, and Inuit peoples lived separately, often in isolated and remote locations. There are points of proximity, particularly in the Canadian West, where First Nations reserves sit next to or close to major towns and cities, but even here contact is limited. After the Second World War, Aboriginal people showed up at rodeos and agricultural fairs—at the latter, displays from Indian residential schools were prominent—and later, at hockey and basketball tournaments, but economic and social integration were minimal.

It is hard to find the right metaphor to capture the essence of Aboriginal-newcomer relations in the post–Second World War decades. Racism and discrimination were rampant but far from uniform. Violence between Indigenous and other Canadians has been remarkably rare since that time. Aboriginal peoples generally lived separately, but the movement into the towns and cities accelerated. In the 1960s and 1970s, few Aboriginal people worked in office or front-line jobs, but a growing number began to work in the mainstream economy, particularly in the resource sector. The standard stereotype of this era depicts Aboriginal people turning quickly to dependence on government welfare payments; in part, this is true, but it is far from an adequate description of the reality of the Aboriginal experience across the country.

It is far from perfect, but a metaphor that may capture the spirit of the Aboriginal and non-Aboriginal relationship in Canada in the latter half of the twentieth century is found in an odd geographic situation in the Waterloo region of Ontario. There are two roads there—Erb and Weber—that cross each other four times as they wind their way through Kitchener and Waterloo. In an awkward and inconsistent way, the streets run parallel for most of their length, cross unexpectedly, and then run alongside each other again. So, too, Aboriginal and non-Aboriginal Canadians live alongside one another, sometimes crossing paths. Social and economic spaces are close, but distinct, and on a variety of occasions, Aboriginal and non-Aboriginal peoples come together for ceremonies, in educational and work sessions, casually on the streets, and in court and legal systems. It's an odd relationship that has continued for much of the post-war era.

#

However important to understand, the social geography of the Aboriginal–non-Aboriginal relationship in Canada does not alone explain the roots of Idle No More. Wrestling with the challenge of connecting historical processes to a widespread contemporary event leads to the temptation to offer a history lesson, following the now well-known stepping stones of the transition of Aboriginal people from valued military and diplomatic allies to wards of the state, through the creation of reserves that kept First Nations apart, to residential schools that tried to assimilate them into the Canadian mainstream. There are many events, processes, rules, and regulations that could be canvassed in detail as a way of laying an explanatory framework for the passionate outbursts of 2012, including: the Indian Act that controlled and limited the freedoms of First Nations people; notions of cultural and religious superiority that convinced governments to regulate such crucial Aboriginal traditions as the potlatch; Indian Agents, who selectively doled out passes that controlled who could leave the reserves; regulations that prohibited First Nations from hiring lawyers to press their claims and, for a time, refused to allow First Nations to meet for the purposes of lobbying or protesting government policy; treaties that were signed with ceremony and seeming commitment by all but that lay unfulfilled and poorly implemented. And so it goes, step by difficult and discriminatory step: not having the right to vote in elections until well after the Second World War; women losing their Indian status if they married a non-Aboriginal (and non-Aboriginal women gaining status if they married an Indian man); requirements that First Nations surrender their Indian status through enfranchisement if they entered a profession or wanted to start a business or own land; the list of injustices is long.

The unfair treatment poured forth with numbing familiarity. Forty years ago, one might complain that few Canadians knew of the pattern of mistreatment. That ignorance no longer holds, thanks in part to the presentation of new perspectives and interpretations of Aboriginal history in the schools and broad coverage in the media and popular culture of the impact of government actions on Indigenous peoples. Despite its shortcomings, the federal government's apology for the residential schools was a potent symbol to Canadians that the Government of Canada had acted in a profoundly destructive way in imposing its will and its culture on Indigenous peoples. Several generations of Aboriginal leaders have articulated the grievances and frustrations of their people to the point that only the deliberately uninformed do not know about the pattern of discrimination and dominance that governed Aboriginal affairs in this country from the mid-nineteenth century on. Indeed, a history lesson is not needed here (although, one is always useful) to make the obvious point that Indigenous people in Canada have good reasons to be angry and are justified in their unleashing of forty years of political protests and legal challenges against the status quo.

These same culturally destructive processes, exacerbated by the consistent gap between the quality of life of Aboriginal and non-Aboriginal Canadians, also point to one of the most demoralizing realities of Canadian life—namely, that Indigenous peoples have internalized much of the despair and anger by engaging in self-destructive and community-damaging behaviour. Rampant drug and alcohol abuse, domestic violence, Fetal Alcohol Spectrum Disorder, and other such prominent social pathologies are an outgrowth of historical processes, not Indigenous cultural norms. Whatever pain and inconvenience non-Aboriginal Canadians have felt through Indigenous protests, including Idle No More, pales in comparison to the costs of historic injustices to Indigenous communities.

Non-Aboriginal Canadians are slowly and uneasily coming to terms with the historical injustices, closing the last residential schools in 1996 and many years, lawsuits, and settlement agreements later, apologizing for them. Indeed, the last four decades have seen the Government of Canada and, latterly, provincial and territorial governments spend billions of dollars to address historical grievances, support Indigenous efforts to overcome historical legacies, and, in the process, perhaps expiate non-Aboriginal guilt about the past. The effort has, in my view, been administratively extensive but collectively more than a little insincere. A growing number of Canadians are angry about rising government expenditures related to Aboriginal communities (most of which go to providing Aboriginal people with services that only occasionally match the standard and quality of those available to other Canadians) and Indigenous legal victories. Canadians, it seems, were more comfortable with Aboriginal rights in the abstract when they were being claimed and contested in the courts, rather than in reality, as they are implemented by governments and enforced by the courts. Put more bluntly, the growing Canadian interest in Aboriginal culture and art does not appear to be matched by widespread support for Indigenous rights, self-government, and autonomy.

Somewhere in the convoluted and too-often destructive history of government intrusions in Aboriginal communities, in the post-1970s efforts to rebalance unfair relationships and persistent discrimination against Indigenous peoples, lies the roots of Idle No More. It is the total impact of government actions—not the specific government programs—that are of greatest importance when considering the roots of the movement. Consider it this way. Not all students at residential schools suffered mistreatment and abuse. Not all Indian Agents used the pass system to control movements of Aboriginal peoples on and off reserve. Not all Aboriginal peoples went without jobs or incomes. Not all non-Indigenous peoples approached Aboriginals with hatred or discriminatory thoughts. Not all Christian missionaries set out to destroy Indigenous cultures. There was no symmetry across Canada, no simple, comprehensive, and uniform approach to Aboriginal rights, policy, and programming.

Instead, what matters most is the cumulative and systematic effect of government policy and racist attitudes on the Indigenous peoples of Canada. The specific policies and government initiatives, or efforts to control an individual First Nation, however damaging these actions may be, cannot explain the full impact of all of the policies, the historical experiences, the daily effects of being marginalized. To be Aboriginal in Canada was to live in a racist system that implied and threatened total control. It meant to be defined, regulated, restricted, limited, and otherwise under the influence of policy documents (the Indian Act), government officials (Indian Agents), efforts to eradicate Indigenous cultures (residential schools), intrusive attempts to change spiritual beliefs (Christian missionaries and residential schools), major limits to freedom of movement (reserves), and routine illustrations of legal and civic inferiority (controls over Indian lands, trust funds, professional participation). However powerful and destructive each initiative might have been or currently is, it is the total impact of all of these forces, actions, and policies that weighs on Indigenous peoples.

Non-Aboriginal people in Canada, working primarily through their federal government, gave themselves the resources, tools, power, and ability to control all aspects of Indigenous life, if and when they wanted. Some Aboriginal peoples, like those in the mid- and far North until after the Second World War, were largely left alone. For many other Aboriginal peoples, particularly those living in settlement areas, more controls were applied earlier in the nation's history. But all First Nations came to realize the power of government and the even more ominous authority of the citizenry at large that stood behind the policies and the bureaucracy.

Non-Aboriginal people have trouble comprehending—because so few have experienced anything remotely like this—what Aboriginal people have lived with for generations and experience in a slightly lesser form through to the present. Discrimination is not unheard of for other Canadians, particularly those new to the country and who have non-European backgrounds, but rarely do they experience the discrimination with the intensity and persistence of that focused on Aboriginal people. Few know the pervasive effect of knowing that others tend to see you through a lens distorted by stereotypes. Few have lived with parents and grandparents whose lives were defined by government intrusions and official oversight, many of whom were robbed of parenting skills by residential schooling. Few have had many basic freedoms—such as the ability to own a home in one's community—denied to them by government legislation. Few have had to work their way through life knowing that a legal document—the Indian Act—defines them almost as much as their personality and family history. Living with hatred, racism, and condescension is demoralizing and oppressive, and tragically it is this reality that has had both immediate and long-term effects on Aboriginal people.

It would seem to make sense to see Idle No More emerging out of poverty and despair, but some of the movement's strength came from the reality that conditions are improving for some Aboriginal people and some Indigenous communities. The power to stand up and de-fend one's interest, it seems, comes in part from the empowerment of individuals and the people at large. The situation in Canada fac-ing Indigenous people is not entirely grim, as analyses of educational outcomes, post-secondary participation rates, employment, income, health outcomes, and the like suggest. There are more than enough serious socio-economic and cultural problems to go around, but as-pects of Aboriginal life are improving. First Nations are doing better, and significant changes appear to keep coming. Having lived through generations of marginalization and subjugation, Aboriginal peoples are experiencing significant gains: major Supreme Court victories from the Calder decision in 1973 to the William (Tsilhqot'in) judg-ment of 2014, the entrenchment of Aboriginal and treaty rights in the constitution in 1982, the creation of development corporations (many of which have tens if not hundreds of millions of dollars in investable assets), cultural revitalization, numerous self-governing communi-ties, modern treaties across the territorial North and in the northern provinces, and many other achievements and gains.[2]

Complex forces, it seems, have fueled Aboriginal protest across the country. Emotions have flared, typically at a local or regional level, through blockades and stand-offs, intensifying dramatically throughout the 1980s and onward: there have been incidents at Burnt Church, New Brunswick; Caledonia, Ontario; Gustafsen Lake, Brit-ish Columbia; the Oldman River, Alberta; Oka, Quebec; Ipperwash Provincial Park, Ontario; and Rexton, New Brunswick. Each of these conflicts has slipped into the national lexicon as a symbol of the real-ities of Indigenous–newcomer relations. The media and non-Aborig-inal people in general fixate on these confrontations, seeing them as the inevitable outcome of the history and politics of First Nations' living conditions in Canada. However important these conflicts may be—each arising out of intense local debates and unresolved legal and historical conflicts—what is, in fact, remarkable is that there are so few of them.

For the past two hundred years, Aboriginal peoples have been marginalized, mistreated, controlled, manipulated, and impover-ished. They lost control of their traditional territories, suffered griev-ous population losses, and watched the non-Aboriginal population use their lands and resources to produce one of the wealthiest nations on Earth. The surprise is not that there are occasional protests and conflicts—and there are many small confrontations, typically over land and resource matters. It is, instead, remarkable that there are so few. Indigenous peoples have often internalized their anger, taking it out on themselves, their families, and their communities. This misdirection of Aboriginal protest is one of the most confounding elements in the history of Indigenous–newcomer relations in Canada.

First Nations in Canada rarely take to the barricades; they eschew the surprisingly easy tactic of closing down highways and rail traffic and almost never engage in acts of violence or civil disobedience. There have been protests on Parliament Hill, marches in front of courthouses and legislatures, and various street gatherings. Political leaders speak loudly, often with real anger, about the injustices of Aboriginal life and the inaction of governments. Aboriginal people in Canada have a finely honed critique of Canadian history and policy, and there are few political groups that do a better job of combining passion, legal and historical understanding, and deep frustration with Canadian realities. But Aboriginal recourse has been to public assemblies, political rhetoric, and the courts. There have been threats of much worse. Former Chief Terry Nelson of Manitoba (as of 2014, the new grand chief of the Southern Chiefs Organization) has repeatedly threatened to shut down the country, but he has not done it. Shawn Brant, a Mohawk activist, has blockaded roads and railways in Ontario several times, but he rarely brings a large number of other Aboriginal people along with him.

Despite the lack of demonstrations and violent outbursts, Aboriginal frustrations are real and deeply entrenched. The pain is substantial, pervasive, and has been directed towards themselves and their communities, rather than to the country at large. The harm of history has rested overwhelmingly on the psyche of Indigenous peoples across the country. There has been an absence of outlets, processes, mechanisms, and leaders that speak to the essence of Indigenous values, aspirations, angers, and needs—that provide a means of drawing Aboriginal peoples together to express their beliefs and dreams, to present a strong and constructive alternative vision for Indigenous futures.

A convergence of social and cultural forces continues to recast the realities of Aboriginal life in Canada. Contrary to what doomsayers have been asserting for years, Aboriginal identity remains strong. While statistical evidence of the decline of Aboriginal language use is compelling—and frightening for the communities involved—the values, traditions, reliance on Elders, and other cultural characteristics remain much stronger than outsiders assume. Forecasts of the demise of Indigenous cultures continue to be overstated. Resilience is grossly underestimated. Take, for example, the movement of Aboriginal people off their reserves, into towns and cities. Geographically, it appears that Indigenous communities are coming unglued. In reality, family and community networks remain strong, with routine sharing of resources, cultural events, and family responsibilities between on- and off-reserve people.

There are other reasons for optimism on the Aboriginal front. Indigenous women have emerged again as a formidable political force, both locally (where they play crucial roles in health, education, and on community boards) and, increasingly, in electoral politics at the regional and national levels. Given that such a large number of Aboriginal people at post-secondary institutions are female, it is likely that the prominent role of women will continue. Several decades of government programming in Aboriginal life and services, from health care to cultural revitalization and local economic development, have generated significant achievements. Add to this the re-empowerment of Aboriginal communities and governments through modern treaties, self-government agreements, special claims settlements, and duty to consult and consultation requirements, and one sees clearly that Indigenous communities today have greater authority, more autonomy, some freedom from the Department of Aboriginal Affairs, significant financial and political resources, and levels of confidence in the collective ability of Aboriginal people to use Canadian legal and political processes to their benefit.

The combination of deeply entrenched grievances, sustained prejudice, and serious community difficulties, with the recent significant achievements and important victories of real re-empowerment has proven to be an extremely powerful mix. Aboriginal peoples in Canada, in these early years of the twenty-first century, can glimpse a very different future for themselves, their children, and their grandchildren. Dreams of Indigenous renewal in the post–Second World War decades have, bit-by-bit, transformed into incremental accomplishments. Improvements in Aboriginal conditions have added to the overall collective Aboriginal confidence in the country, as well as to the growing impatience. Goals that seemed unattainable are now within grasp. It is a potent mixture: anger about the past; profound alienation from the Canadian mainstream; a growing foundation of educational and professional achievements; legal power; and frustration with both Aboriginal leadership and persistent government influence over Indigenous affairs. Then add in: the legal and political victories, mostly over the Government of Canada; growing economic independence; cultural achievements; and the international recognition of Aboriginal peoples in Canada. Out of this emerges Idle No More, a movement born out of this matrix of crisis and empowerment, despair and accomplishment, historical legacies and contemporary achievements.

The desire, quite simply, was to shift the pain and the focus from self-abuse and community frustration to a proper and sustained demonstration of Aboriginal culture, identity, and determination. The collective desire for a different path was overwhelming. Aboriginal people in Canada did not need a reason to be angry; what they needed was an outlet.

They found it in November 2012.

A Round Dance forming on the lawn
of Parliament Hill in Ottawa.
Photo: Ben Powless

THREE

THE ROUND DANCE REVOLUTION

"And I'm wondering, why is it quiet? Why aren't our people talking about this? So, I said to myself, I'm responsible for myself, I'm responsible for my children, and my grandchildren one day that I will have. I am educated now. I can do this. I can come and I can share with our people what it is that I understand from this legislation, and let you know what it is that we're facing. Because whatever we decide to do now, we have to decide it very quickly." —Tanya Kappo, J.D., Sturgeon Lake Cree Nation, Treaty 8[1]

It turned out that the need for a time-sensitive response to Bill C-45 was not the issue or the force around which Idle No More would be galvanized into a global movement. Instead, it would be the cluster of issues, hopes, and sources of frustration brought to the fore by the four founders, and, as it happened, many more women, most with university educations. Pent-up frustrations, unhappiness with traditional Aboriginal and non-Aboriginal politicians, dissatisfaction with "warrior" threats—Aboriginal women ran with the spark that was Bill C-45 and then suffused the Idle No More movement with deep cultural meaning and hope—each individual event reflecting the particular concerns and cultural norms of the region's, locality's, or event's participants.

Sylvia McAdam, moving back and forth between Cree and English in a speech at Sturgeon Lake, Alberta, on December 3, 2012, discussed the prominent roles and responsibilities of First Nations women: "That's how come, at the time of treaty-making, we are always maintaining we never ceded and surrendered land because women did not give that authority to the men to cede and surrender the land, and that still exists today."[2] The newcomers, McAdam explained, had with aggressive intent targeted Aboriginal women: "There was something that the European nation brought over here, and I mean not to offend them, but this is fact; it's found in their documents. When they set out to hunt down foxes, rodents, rats, all these different things, they target[ed] the females; they poisoned the nests of those rats, those foxes, anything they considered rodents. . . . [B]ecause we were [thought of as] not human, they took that mentality and targeted the females, the women of the Cree Nation, of all the other Indigenous nations. And when you target the women, you target the nation, and that's what the Indian Act has been doing."[3]

As she underlined the significance of women to the movement, McAdam encouraged all of her audience at Sturgeon Lake to persevere, to stand up and take part in Idle No More events. And she emphasized the necessity of peaceful protests: "[W]e don't want anyone harmed; this is contrary to our laws."[4] Thus, the movement continued to emerge quietly, with another meeting, in another town, with a similar message to Aboriginal people—and perhaps especially to women, whose marginalization McAdam emphasized at Sturgeon Lake. The message was succinct: stand up, be counted, and let the government know about Aboriginal anger.

Hundreds of times in the past, movements similar to Idle No More have formed, and then they have mostly collapsed and disappeared. The vast majority of these nascent movements began with a bang but were soon swallowed by existing organizations, had their causes taken up by political parties, evaporated after a flurry of media coverage, or simply vanished as the anger dissipated and the energy faded. This is clearly what happened to the Occupy movement, which capitalized on real angst within Western society but dissolved into irrelevance as quickly as it began. Sustaining purpose is challenging. Most social uprisings, having captured the attention of a slice of the public's attention, look quickly for a figurehead or come under the sway of a charismatic leader. Many immediately form an organization, raise funds to sustain the activity, or create alliances and strategic plans to keep things moving forward. Movements like the Arab Spring or the anti-globalization movement never found a single leader capable of guiding a broad social group, nor did they coalesce around a single organization. The early environmental movement branched into several organizations, like Greenpeace and the Sea Shepherd Society, demonstrating a broadly based cause that grew and expanded its strength over time.

Other groups—the gay and lesbian rights movement, for example—combine many different elements, from personal support groups to media campaigns, individual and public demonstrations of the cause, and political lobby groups. The Aboriginal rights and justice efforts in Canada already have had a broad base, with arms extending into many areas of interest, including: Indian Act bands and elected chiefs and councils; traditional Elder and tribal governance systems; non-Aboriginal supporters; international advocacy groups; and Indigenous political, cultural, and professional organizations. The Indigenous rights movements have not lacked for spokespeople or access to the media and politicians. Indeed, it hardly seems as though they need any kind of movement or process to draw their plight to the attention of the Canadian public. But they do.

The manner in which the Idle No More movement leapfrogged elected Aboriginal leaders and the usual groups associated with Aboriginal rights in Canada is a significant part of its story, and, I would argue, its success.

This is not to say that Idle No More organizers completely ignored traditional ways of attracting attention to their cause. The first participants in Idle No More rallies and teach-ins clearly intended to persist, and so they soldiered on. Familiar tactics followed the initial meetings: the supporters calling MPs to lobby against Bill C-45, following up with letters and meetings to political and corporate offices. As well, coordinators called for a National Day of Action to occur on December 10, 2012, the International Day of Human Rights. Named also as the "Idle No More" National Solidarity and Resurgence Day, the National Day of Action was meant to help propel the movement across the country. The day was meant to be much the same as other Idle No More events: peaceful demonstrations, a commitment to collective action, and a determination to bring the Government of Canada to heel. Turning to social media, particularly to Facebook and Twitter, to spread the message, supporters of the movement started to expand from their Saskatchewan base. Among the communities that indicated their plans to participate and organize a day of action event were: Calgary, Edmonton, Goose Bay–Happy Valley, North Battleford, Saskatoon, Thunder Bay, Toronto, Vancouver, Whitehorse, and Winnipeg. Idle No More was taking a bold step, without money, structure, or a formal agenda, but with a growing number of supporters. Early participants spread the word quickly, post by post, tweet by tweet, text by text. The message was clear:

> A NATIONAL DAY OF ACTION!!!!!
> http://www.idlenomore.com/
> Where: In your home town
> When: December 10th
> What: Call or send letters to your MP, Visit MPS'
> Offices, hold Teach-ins.
> Demand that our government be accountable to the
> Treaties and to Mother Earth!
> Our Silence is Consent!!![5]

Although Idle No More was only loosely organized and did not have a top-down structure, it did have a clear value system. All events associated with the movement were to be part of "[a] peaceful call to action requesting acts of solidarity against government and industry actions that use legislation and disregard free, prior, and informed consent to further their agendas in the name of profit and progress disregarding the natural law to live as one with Mother Earth." The organizers appealed to high international principles: "The government and industries have been failing to implement the United Nations Declaration on the Rights of Indigenous People. They have also been ignoring and pacifying the need to be responsible and live as one with Mother Earth. We as a collective must do what we as individuals feel is the best way to show the government and corporations that we will no longer be silent and apathetic to their activities."[6]

Idle No More placed Aboriginal engagement on par with criticizing the government. The call to action also asked participants to remember their Aboriginal roots: "go visit your Elders, your family, tell your stories. Go hunt or fish, take part in your ceremonies, speak your language . . . TEACH your language, guide your young ones, sing your songs and embrace your nationhood in any way you can. Not only on this day but every day. LIVE IT."[7] Word of the National Day of Solidarity and Resurgence (National Day of Action) spread through national and Indigenous networks as Jessica Gordon began tweeting, connecting with prominent Aboriginal spokespeople—like Pamela Palmater, a Mi'kmaq faculty member in Indigenous Studies at Ryerson University and a former candidate for national chief of the Assembly of First Nations, and Taiaiake Alfred, a prominent Mohawk thinker and Indigenous Governance professor at the University of Victoria—as well as Aboriginal organizations, including the Aboriginal Peoples Television Network. Some of Gordon's tweets were sent out to people who were invested in the power structure associated with Indigenous rights, simple invitations to spread the word:

> **Jessica Gordon** @Jessicapgordon 4 Dec 2012
> @RussDiabo #IdleNoMore please help spread the word
> December 10th National Day of Solidarity & Resurgence
> @Taiaiake @Pam_Palmater @aptnnews[8]

Other tweets spread the word to members of the Indigenous rights movement and included a clear critique of the existing Aboriginal power structure in place in Canada:

> **Jessica Gordon** @Jessicapgordon 4 Dec 2012
> @kekinusuqs @aptnnews we have #IdleNoMore national
> day of solidarity & resurgence to do such on the 10th.
> Chiefs support or not[9]

This then is how the call went out though it was not at all assured that anyone would answer it. We know that people showed up, but that response was not guaranteed. Check out telephone poles and bulletin boards in urban centres, where splinter groups and protestors routinely post signs calling for collective action. Most disappear without a trace, the posters fading and aging over time until someone, with a sense of mercy, rips down the failed attempts at widespread protest. It was more likely in December 2012 that the attempt to coordinate spontaneous uprisings in more than a dozen communities would splutter and die, with mediocre turnouts and less than impressive outcomes. There was, after all, no real money, no paid organizers, no cross-country network, no advertising budget for getting the attention of the right people to make it happen.

Saskatoon, however, was ready for the National Day of Action, not surprisingly. Indeed, the city has a large and active Aboriginal population, a reputation for public activism, and the University of Saskatchewan, an institution with a strong track record for engagement and leadership on Indigenous issues. Equally important, as the point of origin for the movement, Saskatoon had a prominent place in the planning of Idle No More activities. Young people organized the event, designed to draw attention to the Government of Canada's legislation and to convince participants to connect with Idle No More. On December 10, 2012, several hundred people showed up at the Rainbow Community Centre and marched to the office of local Conservative MP, Kelly Block, before re-forming in a room in the Ramada Inn that quickly filled to overflowing. Chief Simon Bird of the Federation of Saskatchewan Indian Nations kept the focus on the people: "On behalf of the Federation, we just want to make sure that we're not taking any credit away from the grassroots because this is a grassroots movement."[10] Colby Tootoosis, the Nakota Cree councilor from Poundmaker Cree Nation in Saskatchewan, spoke passionately: "Never in all of our history are we more at risk, are we more in danger of becoming strangers in our own land, and that's not an option. This is a great opportunity for us to really humble ourselves, and to begin to re-evaluate who we are as Indigenous people."[11] Milton Tootoosis, also from Poundmaker and an economic development officer attached to the Office of Treaty Commissioner in Saskatchewan, celebrated the prominence of youth: "I saw a lot of young people walking that street, holding those signs, screaming. It's really powerful to see!"[12] In early November, Saskatoon was the site where the torch had first been lit. Now, one month later, it was the place keeping the torch alight.

On the same day, thousands of kilometres to the east in Happy Valley–Goose Bay, Labrador, the Friends of Grand River / Mistashipu drew a dozen or so people to a much smaller event.[13] Here the focus was primarily on questions of the environment and the dislocation of Indigenous peoples. Protestors greeted passing cars with placards, proclaiming:

> Colonization is alive & well in Labrador. Save Muskrat Falls. Stop the rape!! Protect Labrador.
>
> MP [Peter] Penashue, Overspending? Conflict of Interest? ACCOUNTABILITY!!
>
> Our land, our people demand respect.

The Happy Valley–Goose Bay meeting was significant because it not only showed concern about the omnibus bill—Idle No More's national spark—but it also gave voice to urgent regional concerns. This is where the movement encountered a shift, a move on the part of individual organizers and communities to allow the Idle No More movement to support a multitude of voices, concerns, hopes, and dreams. Instead of stalling under the pressure of so many voices, the movement flourished as a result of them, as the coming months would prove. The video report of the Labrador event carried undertones of the broader national campaign, to be sure, but it did so with a decidedly local feel:

> Provincially, we feel we are not being heard as Muskrat Falls and area continues to be destroyed, Public Utilities Board oversight removed, and all independent studies skewed to the "Nalcor [Energy]" way of thinking! People's rights and Aboriginal concerns are being dismissed! . . . Rural and remote northern areas are being treated as the playground for politics and big development! . . . It seems this government both federal and provincial . . . [is] on a fast track to destroying all our beauty, our culture, our history, and our inheritance. . . . The divide and conquer of Aboriginal peoples,

of rural and remote compared to urban, of islanders to mainlanders, and of people to their elected politicians needs to be put right! Democracy needs to be restored! We stand in solidarity with others in the nation to say "NO MORE"; our resistance will continue to grow and we are gaining strength with other First Nations, environmentalists, free thinkers, land protectors, river keepers, democracy fighters, and those who know the destruction of our most precious lands is wrong![14]

At the opposite end of the country to the west, in front of the office of Ryan Leef, the Conservative MP for the Yukon, about two dozen people showed up, waving signs, declaring, "protect the land & water," "#idlenomore," "Our Home and Native Land," and "For our Children's Children!!!!!!"[15] Here, too, the national event provided a platform for local concerns in addition to concerns about the omnibus bill. Cherish Clarke wanted the MP to take action:

Ryan Leef is our Member of Parliament and he needs to know that we want him to vote against the legislation. We do have First Nations here in the Yukon that are still under the Indian Act and this is just the beginning of the Conservative agenda, this is just the beginning of the changes that are coming and if it's frightening now, like we should just wait until 2013, 2014, 2015, it's just going to go on and on and on unless we stand up as a grassroots movement and get it to stop.[16]

Leef responded, arguing that the Government of Canada had consulted with First Nations and that the Idle No More message about unilateral government action was inaccurate.[17] First Nations were not convinced and remained to protest.

Similarly, on the same day, at a Winnipeg gathering, an unidentified man reminded everyone, "This is our land and we are not going anywhere."[18] The National Day of Action in this part of Canada drew close to three hundred people to rally at the Manitoba Legislature. They carried signs, waved flags, and listened to speeches lambasting Bill C-45. The informality of the politics stood out: "We don't need people with headdresses, we need the common, the common Aboriginal, the common Indigenous person to lead this charge," the same participant said.[19] Event coordinator Jerry Kim-Daniels connected the rally to the government's actions, and at the same time underscored the multifaceted approach individuals across the country were taking to Idle No More events: "There's a whole slew of issues that we can rifle off here. The impetus of why we're here today is Bill C-45."[20] Manitoba Grand Chief Derek Nepinak urged the people gathered to "continue to question everything," and noted, "It's been a long time in the making and it's really coming together." He also importantly called attention to the utility of social media, calling it "a powerful weapon and powerful tool when we need it to be."[21]

And so it also went in northern Ontario. Around fifty First Nations people gathered outside the Federal Aboriginal Affairs Office in Thunder Bay on the same day. They flew the Canadian flag upside down, drummed, sang, and chanted "Idle No More" over the course of an hour-long event. Erin Bonnell, a passionate woman protesting at the event, declared:

> We have to do something here in Thunder Bay. We have to stand in solidarity with our brothers and sisters across the island. But most importantly, I wanted to honour the call, summoning of all the pipes, all traditional people together. With what Stephen Harper is doing, with the legislative assaults on our people, it is an act of war. . . . All territorial people, all tribal people, by the laws of the creator, by the tools that [we] carry, the drums that we carry, we have a duty, a sacred duty to answer that call. As warrior men and women across the continent, these boundary lines mean nothing when it comes to the unity of our red nation. We will defend our territories. We are serious. We will stop any movement if it means bringing Canadians to the attention of their sacred duty which is to peacefully co-exist and to share the lands. First Nations people do not benefit from the extraction of the wealth of resources from our territories. We get scraps.[22]

The participants were eventually asked to leave the area, moving a woman to declare that they deserved "[f]reedom to express ourselves." She added, "It's peaceful."[23] Another was angrier: "We're gonna take action. If you try and kick us out of here we're going to take action. We're going to take over this place and we'll sit in just like people did in the 70s when they sat in at Indian Affairs. We'll sit in. Don't kick us out of here like the government kicked out our leaders at [the] department building. Don't you dare do that to us!"[24]

The intense commentary at this event was mostly directed at Prime Minister Harper and the Conservative government. As Bonnell commented, "If it means we have to wake up our brothers and our sisters because there is only one race, the human race stands to be annihilated with what Prime Minister Stephen Harper is doing. Prime Minister Stephen Harper must not be given that power to pass and make laws without consulting."[25]

Up until this point, and during the day of action on December 10, 2012, Idle No More generated public interest and support pretty much on its own; local and national press coverage from mainstream media was limited. Derrick O'Keefe, a reporter and editor with the progressive online news magazine, *Rabble.ca*, complained that even CBC's usually reliable program, *The National*, which is generally supportive of Aboriginal causes, skipped over Idle No More's National Day of Action. He declared himself "still shocked by the silence from the mainstream media on the 'Idle No More' Indigenous rights protests this week."[26] Another commented: "Waubgeshig Rice @waub. It was exciting to follow #idlenomore on twitter today, but disappointing not to see coverage on national news broadcasts."[27] Some supporters of the movement, however, viewed this lack of attention as an asset and an opportunity. As one observer tweeted: "RIIC News @riicnews RT @arnelltf: We can't rely on mainstream media, we have to do it ourselves. Spread the word/photos/videos on yr social networks #IdleNoMore."[28] And Ryan McMahon observed, "Comedy @RMComedy. No mainstream national coverage of today's #Idle-NoMore action speaks to the need for our own independent media. #IndigenousAlJazeeraTV."[29]

If the conventional media were not paying attention, Twitter, Facebook, and other social media sites were instantly on the ball. Photographs of activists gathering and YouTube videos of full rallies, including drummers and dancers, circulated; videos of speakers and events, of placard-bearing protestors making their case against the government were uploaded and shared. The Aboriginal groundswell attracted international attention almost immediately. The hacker collective Anonymous—a pain in the backside of governments and special interests around the world—shouted out: "Anonymous @YourAnonNews Be sure to keep up with & support #IdleNoMore, indigenous peoples in Canada are rising up en masse against centuries of colonial oppression!"[30] Others piped up, too, not only voicing support but offering it: "Dakota J Lightning @dakotalightning. Who can put me in touch with the creator of the #IdleNoMore website? This native geek would like to help out!"[31]

The mainstream media now had something to report, and yet they still moved slowly at first. Their stories were perfunctory, describing the actions and capturing some of the key messages. A *Huffington Post* article by Lauren Strapagiel, for example, identified the multiple events and recounted the tenor of the complaints through one of the protestors: "'The treaties were set by our forefathers,' Clarence Whitstone of Onion Lake, Saskatchewan, told Global News. 'They lit the path for us, and if the legislation is passed down to us, like Bill C-45, then we'll be losing our lands . . . there will be nothing left for future generations. That's what we're protecting here, that's what we're here for.' Other attendees said that for too long, bills with such far-reaching implications as C-45 have been debated behind closed doors and this day of action is a way for aboriginal people to demand a spot at the table."[32]

On several levels, the first National Day of Action marked the end of the attempt to coordinate or orchestrate the Idle No More protests. There is no evidence of a deliberate decision to take a new direction. Instead, it appears as though the people simply took over, just as the organizers of the first gatherings in Saskatchewan must have hoped would happen. Groups picked up on the Idle No More message and format, which was inexpensive, easily reproduced, and readily adapted to local conditions. As events started to pop up all across Canada, the movement grew enormously, seemingly overnight. Flash mob Round Dances, rallies, and blockades started to appear spontaneously, it seemed, throughout mid-December and on; in some cases, hundreds and thousands of people were in attendance. So, despite the lack of national news coverage of the initial events, the movement grew rapidly, and by late December 2012, what had only a month earlier been a local protest against a remarkably complex and little-understood piece of federal legislation had evolved and attracted both national and global attention.

A rally in Halifax, for example, organized for December 14, 2012, was the handiwork of two Mi'kmaq single mothers, Molly Jean Peters (Paq'tnkek) and Shelley A. Young (Eskasoni), supported by other young women. Marchers, led by drummers and singers, ended at the Parade Square, where speakers encouraged the crowd, and dancers and drummers performed a Round Dance. It was the first time participants performed a Round Dance at an Idle No More event.

The Mi'kmaq, said Young, picked up on the national momentum: "[W]e saw that people in the rest of the country were standing up for it, and we were, like, how come we're not doing anything for it? We have to do something." The commitment to traditional culture at the Halifax event was evident: "One of the things we made sure that we were doing was infusing culture," said Peters. "We wanted to make sure our Elders were here; we wanted to make sure we had our songs here, our dance here, our medicines. It was most important that those were here. That helps to set the tone that this is a peaceful, positive rally. Our children are here, our Elders are here, and we are here to send a message, and we don't want that message to be overtaken by anything negative. We wanted to keep it positive."[33]

Aboriginal women, key players from the earliest stages of the movement, figured prominently in the Halifax event. Peters declared, "Women are having conversations in communities, and one of the conversations is we need to raise strong leaders, and I think as mothers, that really stuck with us. We need to raise a generation of strong leaders, and the benefit that we have on our side right now is that we're the largest, fastest-growing demographic in Canada, our youth. So, we have volume. We have volume in numbers, volume in spirit, volume in heart. We're there, and the people are ready. All they needed was for somebody to just light the spark, and say okay, it's time to do this, we're going to do this."[34]

That day in Halifax, Jaime Battiste, the citizenship coordinator for the Kwilmu'kw Maw-klusuaqn Mi'kmaq Rights Initiative, spoke about the multiple concerns Aboriginal people had, which Idle No

More was helping make public. He made it clear that the adults were rallying for the children who would follow them: "We're here for our communities so that we don't lead in every negative statistical category that makes life sometimes unbearable in our First Nation communities. We're here for our nation, united, saying that we're going to put aside all of our differences and stand together in solidarity."[35] The First Nations gathered in the Nova Scotia capital wanted much more: "We are also here to talk about what isn't in Bill C-45. There isn't a thing about the illegal confiscation of our lands and resources in that bill. There isn't a thing for reconciliation for the history of colonization and assimilation they've put on us. There isn't a peep about equalized education funding, safe drinking water, or an inquiry into missing and murdered women in our communities."[36]

On the same day that this rally in Halifax occurred—December 14, 2012—the Canadian Senate passed Bill C-45. Aboriginal leaders condemned the decision—really a rubberstamping by the Senate of an action taken by the House of Commons—describing it as a betrayal of Indigenous interests. As Ontario Regional Chief Stan Beardy commented, "At no time in the nine months that Bill C-45 was being considered did the Government of Canada discuss any matters related to it with First Nations—this bill breaches Canada's own laws on the fiduciary legal duty to consult and accommodate First Nations. The Canadian government just gave birth to a monster."[37]

Idle No More's primary cause had been passed into law. The rallies, speeches, and singing had not been able to overcome the Conservative majority in the House of Commons and Senate. However, because of the momentum the movement had already created, because of the other regional issues that Aboriginal people were bringing to their events, and because of the personal nature of Idle No More, none of the participants felt that the movement was dead.

When the national media did become involved, they gave their attention unsurprisingly to the large rallies held in the major cities where there was ready access to radio, television, and newspaper reporters. But many of the Idle No More events—and over time, most of them—occurred outside major metropolitan areas. On December 15, 2012, the day after the omnibus bill was passed into law, Tricia Beaulieu of the Sandy Bay First Nation in Manitoba drew close to two hundred people from Sandy Bay, Long Plain, and Swan Lake to the

Trans-Canada Highway near Portage La Prairie. Beaulieu provided a classic explanation of the manner in which the Idle No More message translated into action:

> I heard there was a rally. Where was that? BC, I believe . . . They were getting progress there, and then I thought . . . Why don't we do something? Why isn't anybody coming together and doing something? So I slept on it Wednesday night. I woke up Thursday: "I'm doing it. I'm gonna do this for the people." So I went to work, looked at my employees, asked them first, "You think I should do it?" A few said, "Right, let's do it," they said. Then now here I am. . . . I'm not just doing it for myself, I'm doing it for everybody—giving them a voice. I'm standing here for the people that couldn't be here today, who've passed on. . . . I'm here for the Elders who couldn't get out of bed . . . to be here. So I'm here. I thought, "I'm 25, might as well just take control of it."[38]

Carrying signs marked with "My Home and Native Land," "Oh Canada, Our Home is Sacred Land," "No 2 Bill C-45. Harper Sucks!" and "Idle No More," participants at the rally marched peacefully, under the close but friendly eye of the Royal Canadian Mounted Police.

RCMP Inspector Ron Russell worried about the safety of the marchers, who wanted to block the highway in protest. He tried to convince the protesters to keep off the wintry, busy road, telling them they were breaking the law but indicating that he had no intention of arresting them so long as they followed protocol and moved the assembly off the highway. Emotions ran high. Beaulieu, crying and upset at this point, responded to the RCMP and to the protestors gathered around her: "I'm willing to go this far, for you all. I do this for your treaty. I went this far, now I'm breaking the law for you all to get your treaty back. I'm doing this for all you people. Look deep in your heart, understand."[39] Others thought they had a reasonable point to make by slowing the traffic on the highway. As one male demonstrator put it:

> First Nations people have been inconvenienced for decades and maybe even centuries . . . so it's a small price

to pay today for a little bit of inconvenience on behalf of Canada . . . to highlight some of, all of the wrongs, injustice that we are facing day in and day out. So this bill that was passed is very, very detrimental to First Nations people. From this point on, it's going to have a negative impact and the government doesn't seem to be listening. . . . There doesn't seem to be any partnership with First Nations people through the treaties. It's been disregarded, disrespected and trampled on. That is the issue. So to take about an hour, two hours, away from Canadians but still allowing them to go through doesn't seem to be a big inconvenience. I think Canadians should understand, and I think the majority of Canadians understand how this looks.[40]

Tricia Beaulieu summarized the rally thus: "We will not be quiet no more. I speak for our ancestors, our Elders, our children, our future."[41]

Idle No More's Saskatchewan founders, who had no desire to control the rapidly spreading movement, encouraged the growing multitudes interested in airing grievances and celebrating Aboriginal cultures. They also kept the spirit of the movement alive and in the public's mind, using Twitter, the Idle No More website (launched on December 4, 2012), and Facebook to spread the word about the movement. And so, activity proceeded, without strong organization or centralized control but also without the anarchy and socio-intellectual diversity of the previous year's chaotic Occupy movement. Occupy had drawn large crowds, produced prolonged sit-ins, and garnered global media attention, largely related to the central critique of the growing wealth securely held by one per cent of the population and the inequality of the modern economy. But the Occupy movement generated an often critical response, particularly from the middle class and the business community. Both condemned participants for over-simplifying financial realities and ridiculed them for impossible utopian governance models and dirty campsites. [42] That the Occupy events attracted all manner of critics, protestors, and special-cause activists diluted the core message and created conceptual disarray. In the months to come, Idle No More would be regularly compared to the Occupy movement, largely as a way of suggesting that the absence of a formal organization would undercut its viability and impact.

Yet from its earliest days, Idle No More was different. Like Occupy, it allowed for individual sentiment, but because it was local, personal, and sprang from common experiences and values, the movement was strengthened by each individual and each unique event. It eschewed central control or coordination, and it did not fall apart for the lack of it. The message was extremely simple: stand up, be heard, and let the country know that Aboriginal peoples, communities, and cultures are alive. Certainly, there were common threads holding the movement together in some way: critiques of Bill C-45, environmental concerns, and anger at the Government of Canada. But these unifying elements, often and powerfully expressed, represented only the surface of Idle No More. As the country soon discovered, rally by rally, gathering by gathering, something much deeper and more meaningful was under way.

Rumblings of the movement's acceleration came, appropriately, from Saskatchewan, this time in the form of a Round Dance at the Cornwall Centre mall in Regina on December 17, 2012.[43] The flash mob—generated by a digital shout-out to local residents to head to the site—grew to over one hundred people who for fifteen minutes drummed, sang, and danced around the large Christmas tree in the mall. There were no speeches, but dozens of people stood and watched the peaceful event. The Regina gathering drew many families and children; it was more celebration than angry outburst, marked by happy cheering at the end. To a casual, outside observer, it may have seemed meaningless and unfocused. In a video of the event, a woman can be heard asking about the purpose of the event. In response, another woman identified the Idle No More connection and made a brief reference to the political protest. Another flash mob swarmed into the same mall two days after Christmas.

The flash mob idea—spontaneous, joyous, and celebratory—spread quickly across the country. Twitter commentators and contributing writers to *The Winter We Danced*, a valuable compendium of commentaries on and responses to Idle No More, deemed this iteration of Idle No More as "The Round Dance Revolution." West Edmonton Mall, one of North America's largest shopping complexes, also hosted one of Idle No More's signature events. Hundreds of people jammed into the mall. Hundreds more, including many non-Aboriginal people, watched on. Thirteen drummers played and sang; women, men, and children joined in the Round Dance. The huge hall echoed with the beat of the drums and the strident cadence of Plains singing. An older Aboriginal man, standing on the edge of the gathering, declared himself happy with the turnout and called on other Canadians—some 37,000 people watched the video in the two days immediately after the event—to join the movement, protect the land, and respect First Nations. He was pleased, too, that non-Aboriginal people showed up and stayed: "I think having this here today, it's a support that our people need to get from both sides. As we can see, our people coming together and other people are here supporting us. This is a good thing. You know, I think that the government officials should see this . . . I think that it is finally happening, but we need to be heard so things can move on the way they were meant to be—to be in balance."[44]

Flash mob Round Dances popped up all over the country, with Saskatoon following in the footsteps of Regina and Edmonton on December 20: "neeshy @neeshy 19 Dec 2012 Wuts this I hear about a Flash Mob Rounddance at Midtown Mall today in Saskatoon? 7pm if I'm not mistaken! SEE YU THERE! :) #IdleNoMore #RT"[45]

Between 1,400 and 2,000 people, including approximately 400 to 500 Idle No More supporters and 1,000 or more onlookers, flooded into Saskatoon's Midtown Mall. More would have come had mall security not blocked a sizable number from joining in. There were a few signs and a Mohawk Warriors flag in evidence, loud cheering, and an air of celebration. In addition to many spectators recording the event on cellphones, the media showed up, clearly curious about the movement that was picking up speed and creating drama across Canada. The dancers had fun. When the drumming stopped, members clapped and cheered, chanting "Idle No More," and then asking for more. The drummers started up again, and the largely youthful crowd did not need speeches to fire them up.[46] They clearly knew why they were there: to celebrate being Aboriginal.

As the Round Dance rallies proved, the power in the Idle No More movement truly rested with the people, who determined the when, where, what, and how of events. The flash mobs were quirky, purposefully aimless, filled with meaning, but lacking the standard organizational elements of a well-oiled protest meeting. There was youthful energy, loud singing, and spontaneity. Idle No More's goal of empowering and representing the Aboriginal people of Canada was being met at each of the events. Other flash mobs and Round Dances followed, including ones held at the Rideau Centre in Ottawa; at the Mall of America in Minnesota; in North Bay, Ontario; and at the Polo Park Mall in Winnipeg.

And there were others still to come.

A SIMPLE DANCE WITH A PROFOUND MEANING

The Round Dance emerged as the most prominent symbol of the Idle No More movement. It is an uncomplicated dance, typically involving a group organized in a circle, singing and moving slowly to the beat of a drum. The dance is inclusive and welcoming, its deep rhythms inviting all comers into the act of celebration.

· The Round Dance is a well-established cultural element among prairie First Nations, typically serving as a high point in powwows. It lacks the drama and flair of many Aboriginal dances, such as the elaborate and costumed performances of West Coast First Nations. As David Courcheme, Jr., an Anishinaabe cultural leader, commented, "Our people had this great faith that there was great power in the Round Dance. The dancing itself was calling the spirit to help in healing whatever the community was in need of healing."[47]

The Round Dance serves many purposes; it helps a community deal with grief and sorrow, celebrates cultural strength, and provides a means for sharing joy and happiness. The dance is dominated by the simple beat of the drum and the accompanying singing; the shuffling steps ensure that no one is intimidated by performance requirements.

Like many Aboriginal cultural traditions, the Round Dance became less common over the years, a victim of efforts at assimilation and the suppression of Indigenous cultures. As Aboriginal peoples have gained confidence and gathered strength, public events, including the Round Dance, have become more commonplace.

Idle No More, which itself represented an assertion of Indigenous self-confidence and determination, resurrected the Round Dance on a national scale. The rhythm of the dance was a simple, clear, and welcoming affirmation of Aboriginal resilience and determination. Combined with Idle No More events, the Round Dance returned to prominence throughout Canada.

To maintain the momentum, Idle No More founders announced a second National Day of Action and Solidarity for December 21, 2012, urging Aboriginal peoples across the country to take to the streets once more, in peace and with determination. They wanted the government and non-Aboriginal people to notice and to understand that the collective silence was over. In the first half of December, Canada took notice and was, to put it plainly, puzzled. By this time, the contentious omnibus bill, Bill C-45, had made its way through most of the parliamentary process. By the middle of December, it seemed there was no longer a great deal to be gained politically. But still the people came. They danced and sang and drummed. They spoke of their hurt and frustrations, of their dreams and their resilience. But mostly, they danced and sang and drummed. To most non-Aboriginal people, this growing Round Dance Revolution did not make a great deal of sense.

Just as non-Aboriginal Canadians were adjusting to this strange mobilization, this passionately peaceful set of rallies, it got bigger. Starting with the December 21 events, Idle No More became something much greater, a movement unlike any other in Canadian history, with rumblings sweeping across the reserves, through Canadian towns and cities, and, surprisingly, reaching out beyond Canada's borders.

Idle No More found new allies among protestors and activists across Canada and around the world. The Occupy movement, the loose coalition of anti-establishment forces that had launched earlier, joined with the First Nations protestors. Occupy Canada announced a series of rallies connected with the Idle No More National Day of Action, and they would begin these supportive rallies in Egypt, the symbolic heart of the Arab Spring movement. Other events followed, in a curious mélange ranging from small First Nations reserves to major international metropolitan centres: Sioux Lookout; Denendeh; Owen Sound; Peace River; Prince Albert; Saskatoon; Winnipeg; Hamilton; Sudbury; Ottawa; Montreal; Toronto; Vancouver; San Francisco; Los Angeles; and London, England.

Idle No More had suddenly gone global, with Indigenous peoples and their supporters standing up worldwide in support of Aboriginal rights and Aboriginal peoples in Canada. The events were not centrally coordinated and certainly not orchestrated, but they shared certain elements: prayers and ceremony, singing and dancing, drumming, flags and placards, more than a few condemnations of Prime Minister Stephen Harper and his government, angry speeches (but fewer in number, and less angry than one would think), and affirmations of Indigenous determination and persistence. The Montreal event, for example, featured guest speakers Viviane Michel, president of Femmes Autochtones of Quebec; Karine Gentelet of Amnesty International; Chelsea Vowel, activist/blogger @apihtawikosisan; and a Round Dance led by Marie-Ceine Charron, hoop dancer. In Edmonton, the December 21 event started with an assembly at Kinsmen Park and a march of several hundred protestors to Churchill Square.[48] The two hundred people who marched in Yellowknife were welcomed by Dene National Chief Bill Erasmus.[49] The group assembled indoors, where there was a presentation of gifts to the youth organizers and the Elders, who showed up in significant numbers, and a welcoming and thank you to the Royal Canadian Mounted Police. Although Occupy was involved, this was not an Occupy event; it was not, like Occupy, an anti-establishment movement with a rather uneasy relationship with authorities. Idle No More had the strength to join with Occupy while maintaining its unique identity.

The public paid more and more attention to the events—their size, scale, crowd behaviour, political statements—and the media picked up on the trend. In a country where a gathering of a half dozen people is sufficient to attract television cameras and reporters, it is hardly surprising that the sight of hundreds of Aboriginal people, often with made-for-TV posters, colourful Indigenous flags, and more than a few people wearing traditional clothing, drew the attention of journalists. The events were also tailor-made for grandiose headlines: "Idle No More Protests Hit Calgary and Southern Alberta,"[50] "Idle No More Sweeps Canada and Beyond: Aboriginals Say Enough is Enough,"[51] "First Nations and Idle No More Push for Reckoning."[52]

Participants and organizers recognized that what they were doing was important; they began to see that their events could be "a spark that will ignite a thousand people," as Métis artist and writer Aaron Paquette, a participant in the Edmonton rally, said passionately to those gathered:

> You are a spark that is starting a fire that will spread across this land, and it will be a fire that doesn't burn, but a fire that cleanses; a fire that ignites in our hearts and creates light. No more living in darkness. Our time now is to be light in the world. Everyone who is here today, you are a spark that will ignite a thousand more people. We will be one million strong. We are here together, no matter your background, no matter your colour, no matter your history. You are here, we are here, one heartbeat. The road ahead will not be easy. They will try to stop you. They are becoming afraid of your power. We are here. We are still alive. This is our time![53]

In the same vein, Nocokwis Greyeyes, one of the December 21 event organizers in Peace River, Alberta, said, "Today was amazing. *Hai hai* for all who came. Everyone was needed and I am so grateful that you were all here. Our communities are filled with amazing . . . people and I'm glad to live in the same territory as you all."[54] And Melaw Nakehk'o, a youth organizer of the Denendeh Gathering, active from the earliest days of the movement, spoke to the crowd in Yellowknife:

> To me, Idle No More, it's also about a cultural revitalization. As a movement, it's an Indigenous resurgence. We have to maintain our land connectedness; we have to be strong in our culture; we have to be on the land and asserting our treaty rights because they can't do anything if we're on the land. Myself as a moose-hide

tanner, I think about the work that I want to do. I want to tan moose hide for the rest of my life, but if the water is poisoned and if the land is dying, then I can't do that and I can't teach my kids that when they grow up.[55]

Of course, the rallies, while celebratory, were also nearly always political. Prime Minister Harper and his government were called out thousands of times across the country. Speaking in Dease Lake, British Columbia, a tiny community on the Stewart-Cassiar Highway, Hu Wani Dene (Sonia Denis) was blunt: "Stephen Harper, this is wrong . . . what you are doing to our people, to all people, to all nations. We are going to stand up to you and we are going to stay in charge because this is our land. You are just a visitor here and there is no reason why the government should have so much right over this. These youth that I brought here are standing up and they're going to stand with thousands of other people."[56]

Another theme present at the rallies continued to be concern for the future and for Aboriginal youth. In fact, this concern was even more dominant than the anger expressed regarding the prime minister and toward Bill C-45. At one rally in Sarnia, Ontario, on December 24, 2012, Janelle Nahmabin, a mother protesting with her daughter next to her, declared:

> I stand in front of everybody because I'm here to fight for my daughter . . . if Harper needs a face, this is a face: my daughter! I'm worried about our future. If you have children, you'll stand, too! We want a future for our children and our children's children. I am so scared of what this bill is going to do to them and I am here. . . . [My daughter] is going to have to grow up into this. She has no say, so this is our job. Every one of us here, all over Canada, all over the world. We have a voice and we're going to say it. "Idle No More!"[57]

The crowd echoed her chant; "Idle No More" rang out over the assembly.

Ta'Kaiya Blaney, an eleven-year-old singer, songwriter, and activist from Sliammon First Nation, addressed the crowd at Simms Park in Courtney, British Columbia, on December 29, 2012. In this instance,

Bill C-45 was front and centre. The young girl celebrated the gathering of so many First Nations people: "we are standing on unceded territory and we have that right and that's what Idle No More is all about. It's about us standing up and speaking up. We've never really been asleep, and now more than ever we're awake and we're standing up." She continued, "I think it's so important that . . . we're standing here today because . . . we're not waiting for our governments to change things; we're not waiting for the authorities to change things anymore, because we know now . . . that if we keep waiting for change, it's never going to come."[58]

Ta'Kaiya Blaney was not alone, as hundreds of other Aboriginal Canadians expressed their deeply felt views about the country. The Idle No More gatherings of December 21 and the ones spinning out from them had a common purpose and a shared language, and they continued to be powerfully peaceful. During the Winnipeg event on December 21, for example, the Manitoba Keewatinowi Okimakanak (MKO), an organization of northern chiefs, circled the airport terminal road in vehicles, cheering and proudly displaying their flags. While they slowed traffic considerably, they sought primarily to draw attention to their cause and not to disrupt travel plans. The group later regrouped for a ceremony at the Oodena Celebration Circle at the Forks in downtown Winnipeg, and then thousands marched to the Manitoba Legislature where they performed a Round Dance around the building.[59]

When more than a thousand people formed a flash mob in downtown Toronto that same day, at one of the busiest intersections in the city (Yonge and Dundas Square), the city streets became snarled with traffic, much to the chagrin and anger of motorists. However, the mob moved on quickly without causing excessive delays and ended its actions with the first of a series of Toronto-based teach-ins, with Tantoo Cardinal, Hayden King, and Rebeka Tabobondung as featured speakers.[60]

Others took more disruptive—but still peaceful—action. Again, on December 21, the Aamjiwnaang First Nation, protesting the movement of chemicals across their land along the St. Clair River in southern Ontario, blocked a railway track that crossed their reserve, walked through Sarnia, Ontario, and then, for several hours, shut down Highway 402, a busy Ontario thoroughfare.[61] The Aamjiwnaang railway blockade lasted for almost two weeks, ending peacefully with the

First Nation having made their point about their concerns over the shipment of chemicals.[62]

First Nations across Canada followed the emerging national and global developments with interest, fascinated and empowered by the fact that their rallies had garnered worldwide attention. Non-Aboriginal people from outside of Canada clearly connected with their cause and understood the need for solidarity and action. A series of tweets sent out in support of Idle No More captured the international sentiment that was growing rapidly.

> **Norlaine Thomas** @Norlaine
> Idle No More protest in Egypt. EGYPT. They are protesting our government in EGYPT. Doesn't that say something? #cdnpoli[63]

> **Diana Day** @DianaDaydream
> Idle No More from Ukraine: http://youtube/9aevM1G9ddQvia @youtube #idlenomore
> – brought a tear to my eyes to see the love and support from afar!![64]

Non-Aboriginal Canadians reached out in support:

> **Scott McF** @ScottMcFad
> As Cdns we pride ourselves in being progressive & open-minded which is ironic given our abysmal record on human rights. Props to #idlenomore[65]

> **Arün Smith** @arun_smith
> For those of us who are settlers on this land, we must take responsibility to ensure that we are no longer idle. #idlenomore #solidarity[66]

> **Luke Bradley** @Lukeafbradley
> Aboriginal communities must reach out and educate Canadians. We simply do not understand what is going on. #idlenomore is a great step.[67]

As Luke Bradley's tweet suggests, there was support, but there continued to be confusion also in non-Aboriginal quarters. Perhaps most perplexing to onlookers were the rallies that on the surface seemed to have no political message or purpose. At such events, people gathered in large numbers, many young adults and children and often a significant number of non-Aboriginal people, simply to declare their presence. Two rallies in Moncton, New Brunswick, for example— one at Regent Mall[68] on December 24, 2012, and another at Champlain Place[69] the following year on December 27, 2013—consisted of drumming, singing, and a ten-minute Round Dance. There were no speeches recorded at either of these events. But there were indications of the broad intent that surrounded the rallies. The Moncton events attracted individuals, Aboriginal and non-Aboriginal, demonstrating against the natural gas fracking and exploration activity that was beginning in the province, one of many issues that intersected with Idle No More agendas.

And yet, the Canadian media and the people of Canada generally found it hard to locate a key message or demand in the scattered, complex, and varied rallies of Idle No More. They looked to key spokespeople and found some remarkable individuals who came forward, typically to explain the movement rather than to draw attention to themselves. The four women who founded Idle No More made a deliberate point of making sure that the story was not about them. While they modestly took some credit for getting things going, Jessica Gordon, Sylvia McAdam, Sheelah McLean, and Nina Wilson emphasized the grassroots nature of the movement. Speaking to David Gray of CBC Radio's *Calgary Eyeopener* in Calgary on December 21, McAdam said of the movement, "When I started reading [Bill C-45], I have a law degree, I had a hard time understanding it and I couldn't fathom how ordinary grassroots people could even begin to read this, not that I'm questioning their intelligence at all, but there is a lot of 'legalese' utilized in these documents, and it's a massive document. It's well over four hundred pages. So, I told Nina and Jessica, 'We have to do something.' There's a thing called acquiescence, which means your compliance is consent. We can't be silent; silence is consent."[70]

More than a few critics mocked the name of the movement, declaring that they thought the idea was that First Nations would be looking for jobs.[71] Quoting âpihtawikosisân, a Métis woman from the

Plains Cree–speaking community of Lac Ste. Anne, Alberta, Jessica Gordon fired back: "'Idle No More' is not a chastisement or accusation of laziness on the part of Native peoples, many of whom have been labouring for years for their communities. It is a rallying cry that can be taken up by all of us living in these lands. It says, 'time to be active, time to put in the effort, time to learn, time to grow, time to make change.' For those who have been doing this work all along, it also means, 'you are supported, we will stand with you, you will not be alone in this.'"[72]

In the midst of the first round of Idle No More gatherings, Sylvia McAdam spoke to Anna Maria Tremonti on CBC Radio's *The Current*. This interview marked the first national introduction to one of the founders and the cause they had triggered. McAdam started by commenting on Bill C-45: "We wanted to let people know that this is what's happening, and barely anybody knew about it, and it wasn't right. So, we started doing teach-ins." She specifically noted the changes to the Navigable Waters Protection Act as an example of their concern with the omnibus bill. The women had been upset with the scale and breadth of the bill, the lack of consultation, and the need to defend "ourselves against these bills that are going through because it does feel like we're being attacked."[73]

As always, even as they articulated the logic and passion behind the protests, McAdam and others were quick to divert attention from themselves: "This is a grassroots movement. If they choose to voice their protest peacefully in whatever way they can, through music, dance . . . you're witnessing the grassroots people telling the Conservative government, 'you do not have our consent,' and if there were consultations done, they were obviously not done properly."[74] Even though the grassroots people were the actors in the movement, the founders were in contact with many of them: "We're getting contacted from the Yukon, from Whitehorse, from Vancouver. I know that Vancouver is having a rally or teach-in on December 23, and there's major rallies happening on December 21, as well as other events calling forth all the drums. Not just Indigenous drums, all of the drums, to join us on December 21 to make a statement saying that, through our music, 'you do not have our consent.'"[75]

Idle No More had provided a pathway to a kind of public voice that was very different from the ones Aboriginal peoples were accustomed to. Indeed, the presence of the movement spoke to Indigenous frustration not only with the Conservative government, but also with Aboriginal political representation, including the First Nations chiefs and the Assembly of First Nations (AFN) representatives. The Aboriginal political leadership did throw their support, somewhat unevenly, behind Idle No More, although a few realized that the critique of leadership extended from the Prime Minister's Office to their very own Aboriginal governments. The relationship was an uneasy one, as is shown by one comment Saddle Lake Cree Nation teacher Shannon Houle made about the Aboriginal "Leadership" and Idle No More:

> The Founders and many of the organizers of Idle No More from across Canada have been given word that the Leadership is calling for action in the name of Idle No More. They have also stated in a press release that they have met with Idle No More representatives that support this call. We would like to state that this is FALSE. The Chiefs have called for action and anyone who chooses can join with them, however, this is not part of the Idle No More movement as the vision of this grassroots movement does not coincide with the visions of the Leadership. While we appreciate the individual support we have received from Chiefs and councillors, we have been given a clear mandate by the grassroots to work outside of the systems of government and that is what we will continue to do. We are not trying to have division amongst this movement![76]

The frustration people had with the elected leadership was real. National leaders within the Assembly of First Nations, regional representatives, and band-level politicians were all criticized. One blogger, Ray McCallum, was direct and remarkably candid in his analysis of the situation:

> Our First Nations Women founded the grassroots movement "Idle No More." The First Nations men stole the microphones. I was absolutely incensed that both [Federation of Saskatchewan Indian Nations Chief]

Perry [Bellegarde] and [National Chief Shawn] Atleo and some of the other chiefs [were] grandstanding in the media and many of them totally missing the point. . . . When the Assembly of First Nations was busy just over a week ago in Ottawa nothing was mentioned regarding Idle No More. They were busy pontificating with gusto that is sometimes associated with self-serving rhetoric of keystone chiefs who know naught what they do. It was actually a woman chief who suggested to Chief Wallace Fox, "What are we doing here, shouldn't we be on Parliament Hill demonstrating against the bills that are being fast tracked?", not exactly in those words, but close enough. Chief Wallace Fox brought to it the floor of the Assembly and a few chiefs got up and they started the march towards parliament.

I applaud those chiefs who chose to march to Parliament Hill to state their demands and their right to be heard. This should have been foremost on the agenda at the AFN assembly two weeks ago. Instead they chose to proceed methodically on a set of priorities written months and weeks before. I know that executive bodies behave like bureaucrats and follow steadfastly their agenda items and fluster if there is a slight deviation in their ordered little lives. Some chiefs like to come looking "chiefly" and postulate with puffs of grandeur and play a little politics on the side. In this case, the AFN was not flexible enough to lay aside the agenda items and deal with the current crisis that is hitting First Nations communities.

These self-styled Homies who would play Chief totally missed the boat or the opportunity to challenge Minister Duncan's statement when he said, "Oh, we meet with First Nations over 5000 times a year." By my calculation that would make it 13.6 consultations per day and that is including weekends and holidays. Why, oh, why did not one of our little curmudgeons ask the minister to fess up and show us the details about these so-called consultations? Our leaders are about as slow as molasses in January when it comes to responding to bald-face lies of the Harperites. Instead, if ifs and buts were candy and nuts, every day would be Christmas— just like our chiefs with too many excuses who opt to wait for the proverbial wooden nickel. Now we see them after the fact, with bluster and whistle farts, panning for the media and any fans who care to have them. You may want to ask them what their endgame really is about if they are just now getting on the band wagon.[77]

Idle No More provided a forum and drew attention to Aboriginal issues and causes that had hitherto been given only passing mention in the mainstream media. It also allowed the grassroots a voice that could speak directly to the nation without going first through the traditional leadership. At the same time, the movement required interpreters, seasoned speakers, who could go on radio and television and who could speak to print journalists in response to the now-daily events taking place across the country. Pamela Palmater stepped forward to respond to media requests. *Democracynow.org*, identifying Palmater as a spokesperson for the movement, quoted her as saying, "We, First Nations people, have been subsidizing the wealth and prosperity and programs and services of Canadians from our lands and resources. . . . And that's the reality here that most people don't understand."[78] Palmater would remain prominent in the national commentary about Idle No More, but she was not the movement. Wab Kinew, from the Onigaming First Nation in Ontario, a CBC reporter and broadcaster, and director now of Indigenous Inclusion at the University of Winnipeg, also emerged as an articulate commentator on the Idle No More movement. His regular appearances in the media were marked by a calmness and Aboriginal pride that closely matched the spirit of Idle No More. But Kinew was not the movement, either. And neither was another figure who became prominent in the early days of the movement: Chief Theresa Spence of Attawapiskat, Ontario.

Around Idle No More's first National Day of Action, Chief Spence had started a hunger strike. She chose Victoria Island in the Ottawa River, a short distance from Parliament Hill, to carry it out. For a while, it looked as though this chief, using Idle No More as a scaffold for her own cause, was going to become the face, if not the entire voice, of Idle No More. The national media turned its attention to Chief Spence because her protest was much simpler and easier to convey to the country at large than the myriad voices that had come to represent Idle No More as a whole. But as the nation soon discovered, Chief Spence did not equal Idle No More. In fact, in some ways, she detracted from it, becoming a distraction. The movement of Idle No More was much larger than one person, one community, and one protest, a point with which Chief Spence would later agree.

A succinct message—less than 140 characters as required by Twitter—captured the real essence of the movement up until this point. It was tweeted by JoyArc on December 1, 2012:

> @pmharper The new generation of Educated First Nations people r knocking on your door and they won't walk away #IdleNoMore.[79]

Attawapiskat Chief Theresa Spence
speaking to media, Victoria Island,
Ottawa, January 11, 2013.
Photo: THE CANADIAN PRESS/Adrian Wyld

FOUR

THE OTTAWA DISTRACTION AND THE COMPLICATED EVOLUTION OF IDLE NO MORE

"You can say we're all in the same canoe today; we're all going the same direction. Stephen Harper better watch out. I only got one thing to say to Stephen Harper. I want to say thank you to him. Thanking you for waking up all our people. Waking up all our people!" —Unidentified speaker at an Idle No More event, Ladysmith, British Columbia, December 31, 2012[1]

"This process of marginalizing our political leadership, along with the enforced segregation of our people, is part of a deliberate [attempt] to isolate our people, marginalize our people and ultimately assimilate our people so that our rich heritage can be wiped out and the great bounty contained in our traditional lands be made available for exploitation by large multi-national companies." —Chief Theresa Spence, December 10, 2012[2]

Wh* hen Chief Theresa Spence formally announced her intention to go on a hunger strike on Idle No More's National Day of Action, December 10, 2012, she was no newcomer to the national media. Spence was chief of the Cree community of Attawapiskat, a Treaty 9 First Nation located on the Attawapiskat River near the west coast of James Bay. Her community, trapped in a desperate cycle of poverty and living on flood-prone land, came to the nation's attention in 2011, over a housing crisis. Many community members were jammed into sub-standard housing; others lived in tents. Materials for new, government-built houses sat unused. With high unemployment rates in Attawapiskat and few substantial jobs or business opportunities from a lucrative Impact and Benefit Agreement (IBA) with the nearby De Beers' Victor Mine, prospects for rapid improvement seemed dim. Chief Spence took her cause to the Government of Canada. When Ottawa's response was not fast enough, the chief tapped into concern in southern Canada about the realities of life in poor, northern, Aboriginal communities, and delivered her story to the national press. Accusations flew back and forth, with the chief demanding urgent action and the Government of Canada attributing responsibility for the problems to administrative challenges at the community level. In fact, the government placed Attawapiskat in third-party management as a result of the problems.

During meetings with the Assembly of First Nations in Ottawa in 2012, Chief Spence learned of other communities in similar conditions, hearing reports from another chief about his people recovering from a serious flood and fighting with Ottawa about solutions. She had had enough and wanted to do something. Idle No More provided the call to action. As she said on December 18, 2012, in an exclusive interview with CBC's Chris Rands, "It is the grassroots people that tell the chiefs what they are going through and what to do, and it's important. It's the chiefs' duty to stand behind their grassroots people, and this is what these people are doing. They're [going to] make a lot of noise and they're not going to stop. They are demanding that it's time for peace and a good relationship. That was the intent of the treaty. It's about, you know, honour, respect and to build the peace together."[3]

On December 4, 2012, at the Special Chiefs Assembly, Chief Spence had already announced that she would go on a hunger strike, protesting conditions on reserves and demanding an audience with the government and Crown. Then, on December 10, Chief Spence drew a small crowd to the steps of the Peace Tower on Parliament Hill to make her announcement formal. She joined in the criticism of Prime Minister Stephen Harper and offered support for Idle No More. She criticized the government for ignoring the treaties, imposing the Indian Act, and responding slowly to real crises: "I want the Crown, the prime minister, and all the leaders to sit down and rebuild that relationship and honour and protect the treaty."[4] As she wrote in a letter that she distributed at the gathering, "This process of marginalizing our political leadership, along with the enforced segregation of our people, is part of a deliberate [attempt] to isolate our people, marginalize our people and ultimately assimilate our people so that our rich heritage can be wiped out and the great bounty contained in our traditional lands be made available for exploitation by large multi-national companies."[5] That Aboriginal Affairs Minister John Duncan had responded, in her view, to the Attawapiskat crisis by blaming the community administration only demonstrated how little Ottawa officials understood the desperate conditions.

Spence launched her protest on December 11. She moved into a tent, borrowed from the Assembly of First Nations, on Victoria Island, in the Ottawa River, near Parliament Hill. She did this, she declared, in the spirit of Idle No More. Her frustration with the Government of Canada was clearly matched by her despair over conditions at Attawapiskat. She was determined: "I am willing to die for my people, the pain is too much. Somebody asked me if I was afraid to die. No, I am not afraid to die. It's a journey we have to go on, and I will go and I am looking forward to it."[6] Her action emerged from her daily experiences:

> It's not about anger, it's the pain. The pain is too much. Sometimes you can't describe how it is when you live in this kind of system with the government. It's just too much to see your children, you know, by the time they are six years old, they're in a different world. They're already losing their language. It's important for the

government to recognize and honour the way we used to live. We want that kind of life again. Not for them to control it and say how to live and how to raise our kids, how to teach our kids, how to have our law in our own community because their way, their laws, it's crippling our people, especially the youth.[7]

In the spirit of Idle No More, word about her plans spread quickly:

Krystalline Kraus @krystalline_k 9 Dec 2012
@nothinglin: @waub Hunger Strike by Chief Theresa Spence on Parliament Hill tomorrow #IdleNoMore #cdnpoli #Ottawa[8]

Andrea Landry @AndreaLandry1 11 Dec 2012
Our women are the true leaders of #IdleNoMore - prayers for Chief Theresa Spence as she goes through the hunger strike for her people.[9]

The chief's political statements, crafted in frustration and informed by deeply held beliefs, lacked pragmatism and, from the outset, centred on politically impractical demands. She wanted the Government of Canada to meet with her, insisting that Prime Minister Harper show up, and she also demanded that the Crown be represented, either by Queen Elizabeth II or Governor General David Johnston. As she noted:

I am very disappointed. At the beginning I asked the national chief to write the Crown. . . . It is very discouraging that they are taking a shortcut. . . . All parties need to meet together, not separate. . . . The Crown has been covering their eyes on these violations of the treaties. Johnston needs to tell the prime minister that he has to work with the treaty and the leaders as partners and not go separate ways. The Crown made a promise to First Nations that if anyone violated the treaties they would be punished.[10]

Unfortunately, her insistence on Crown participation reflected a misunderstanding of contemporary Canadian politics, particularly the separation of the Governor General from the daily operations of government, and, unexpectedly, put the Government of Canada in a position where Chief Spence's call to action could be ignored because it did not accord with the realities of decision-making and power in Ottawa. The passion of the Attawapiskat leader was not matched with political astuteness, creating a situation that made it difficult for the Assembly of First Nations and other Aboriginal leaders to throw their full support behind her cause.

However, Chief Spence's action grabbed national attention from the outset. The traditional media, struggling to get a handle on Idle No More, finally had a linear narrative to follow, all of the standard elements of a "real" protest. Here was a leader standing up for her people. Here was a clear set of demands. And here, on Victoria Island, was easily understood and readily described political theatre.

Advocates and activists lined up to announce their support for Chief Spence. Pamela Palmater declared, "Everyone knows where Chief Spence is, everybody does. People from all over the country have gone to see her. I've gone to see her . . . we all know it's the status quo that's killing our people. [Prime Minister Harper] is really offering nothing."[11] New Democratic Party MP Charlie Angus echoed Palmater's concerns and support, calling on the prime minister to intercede to stop the chief's hunger strike: "This is certainly an unprecedented move, the hunger strike, the kind of response that we've seen with these rallies and marches and demonstrations across the country. It needs a higher level of leadership. It needs the prime minister."[12] Angus, who had worked closely with Spence on Attawapiskat issues, made it clear that the chief had been driven to protest: "I know Chief Theresa Spence very well. She's not, you know, in anybody's world view, any kind of so-called radical leader; she's very concerned about the poverty in her community and she told me how heartbroken she was after meeting leaders from across the country who feel that they're going in a dead end and that they feel the government is really putting the screws to the communities and undermining them."[13]

Like many other observers, Angus connected the hunger strike with Idle No More, stating that "people don't just rise up and start doing these flash mobs and protests at Christmas time because they're bored. There is something that's been brewing for a long time. . . . I think Canadians across political spectrums, people I've talked to, say, 'Where's the willingness to fix this? Where's the willingness to do something right?' This is a moment I think that is going to define Stephen Harper as a prime minister."[14]

A group of First Nations women in Toronto went further in their support of Spence, the Attawapiskat community, and other suffering communities by fasting for a day themselves: "She has offered herself as an *ogichidaa-kwe* for her people and in solidarity with other First Nations communities of resistance across Canada until her demands are met or she meets her 'ancestors.' . . . The Idle No More campaign has set fire to Canada's dangerous complacency in the face of First Nations poverty, lack of education, clean water, control of resources and self-autonomy."[15]

Action picked up behind the scenes, with representatives from the Assembly of First Nations, Charlie Angus, and many others asking Chief Spence to take care of her health and to move her protest into a hotel. Many observers across the country urged her to keep up the protest, but to call off the hunger strike, arguing that severe illness or death would not help her community.

The Assembly of First Nations helped with logistics and provided some funding for her supporters, but Chief Spence felt that they were not doing enough to help out. The national organization wanted to be supportive of activism but was careful not to undermine its connections with the Government of Canada. The complexities of the Attawapiskat situation—of the challenges facing any specific First Nation, in fact—made it difficult for the Assembly of First Nations to support the protest wholeheartedly. What is more, the national chief and his staff hoped to play a brokerage role with the Government of Canada and to help solve or resolve the crisis.[16]

While the Assembly of First Nations positioned itself relative to Spence's protest and the Government of Canada remained silent about it, Idle No More participants began to pick up on Chief Spence's cause. During a December 19 march on Six Nations territory, leaders chanted encouragement, "Theresa Spence, we send you our strength. We hear your voice."[17]

At a roadside gathering near Fredericton, New Brunswick, two days later, protestors carried signs criticizing Prime Minister Harper and demanding greater consultation. But present now were also placards declaring "We Support Chief Spence."[18] At a Cree rally in Eastmain, Quebec, on the same day, an elderly man, speaking in Cree, offered supportive words for Chief Spence and for those who had come "to stand together in the fight for our rights." He continued: "Even if we are few in numbers at the moment, our brothers and sisters across the world are with us. I don't know how many are all together across Canada, overseas, too. It's to show our support to Chief Spence. We have to stand together for us to be strong."[19] And a few days after this gathering, on December 24, a video was posted of a flash mob in Fredericton with the following description: "Awesome drumming and completely moving . . . the spirits were with us today as we gathered in the Regent Mall in Fredericton NB in support of Chief Spence and for the Idle No More movement!!! Took place Christmas Eve @ 12 noon."[20] When protestors from Aamjiwnaang First Nation blockaded the CN train track near Sarnia on December 21, 2012, they, too, declared their support for Chief Spence's protest, while trying to handle complaints from government officials, CN Rail representatives, and other Idle No More activists, who did not want disruptions caused during the Idle No More protests.

A New Year's Eve walk from Spruce Grove to Stony Plain, Alberta, also linked support for Chief Spence with regional protests associated with Idle No More. At the end of the event, an RCMP officer addressed the gathering, illuminating one of the most interesting aspects of the movement—namely the respectful relationships between Aboriginal activists and the police: "I'm glad to be here and I'm glad to see that the First Nations are coming together. It's a lawful and a peaceful assembly, so you have a right like any other Canadian to demonstrate in a peaceful manner, and I think it's great, so I'm glad the RCMP can support your initiative here and we wish you guys well."[21] This was not the only time that RCMP officers either supported Idle No More activities or demonstrated partnership with the Aboriginal activists. At rally after rally, the RCMP showed up to oversee the activity and to ensure a peaceful assembly. In many instances, they walked alongside the Aboriginal people, talking to them and even offering words of encouragement. Perhaps events like that at Caledonia, as well as the Oldman River and Oka standoffs during the 1990s—events where heavy-handed intervention had not worked—had led to this different approach by the police to these Aboriginal protests. Whatever the case, the police genuinely seemed to respect and appreciate the peaceful nature of the gatherings.

ABORIGINAL PROTEST IN CANADA

Idle No More attracted national attention almost as much for the unique character of the Aboriginal political activity as for the messages of the movement. Over the past forty years, Aboriginal protests have generated a great deal of national and international debate, often because of the violence or threatened violence associated with the protest events. These protests demonstrated the extreme frustration of Indigenous peoples with regional and local situations, but they also drew worldwide attention to system-wide challenges facing Aboriginal communities in Canada. When Idle No More commenced, many Canadians expected a reprise of the more extensive and highly publicized protests of the past.

Places like Burnt Church, New Brunswick; Caledonia, Ontario; Gustafsen Lake, British Columbia; Ipperwash, Ontario; Oka, Quebec; the Oldman River, Alberta; Rexton, New Brunswick; and Sun Peaks, British Columbia figure prominently in Canadian political history as benchmarks of Aboriginal frustration. In each of these cases, Aboriginal peoples took to the barricades or the equivalent to protest government actions or development activity. The sources of frustration varied widely, from housing and urban developments (Oka and Caledonia) to Aboriginal fishing rights (Burnt Church), from rural development (Sun Peaks and Ipperwash) to interference with Indigenous sacred sites (Gustafsen Lake), from dam building (the Oldman River) to natural resource extraction (Rexton).

In each of these cases, the conflicts were intense, often involving well-defended barriers, prolonged sit-ins, substantial non-Aboriginal frustration, and regional, national, and international Indigenous support. Violence occasionally erupted. Both Oka and Ipperwash involved deaths. The shooting of Dudley George, at the Aboriginal defence line in the provincial park at Ipperwash, led to an important inquiry, as did the situation at Oka, which led to the establishment of the Royal Commission on Aboriginal Peoples. The Caledonia land-claim dispute, which started in 2006 and continues to this day, is the longest running stand-off in Canadian history, generating a great deal of public commentary, much of it hostile to Aboriginal interests.

When the Idle No More activities started, people across the country had in mind these high-profile, long-standing, and occasionally aggressive stand-offs between Aboriginal people, government officials, and the non-Aboriginal public. These uprisings had revealed the determination of Aboriginal protestors and their ability to sustain their anger and frustration over weeks, months, and sometimes years. Non-Aboriginal Canadians, watching large Idle No More groups assemble in shopping malls, on downtown streets, and in many other venues, worried that the gatherings would morph into the more aggressive and confrontational stand-offs that have served as trail markers of Aboriginal protest in recent years. But this did not happen.

Following the start of Chief Spence's fast, Ottawa became, for much of the month, a focal point for national protest. While Idle No More events continued and gained momentum across the nation, reaching into all corners of the country, the national media was watching Victoria Island closely and so Indigenous protestors and their supporters also came to the nation's capital. On December 21, a blustery, snowy day that left Ottawa streets covered in treacherous slush, over a thousand people gathered on Parliament Hill to share the message of Idle No More and to support Chief Spence. Sylvia McAdam, addressing the crowd, reminded everyone of the unique nature of the movement: "I also wanted to let you know that all of this was done by volunteers. We had no financial help from anyone. This was all done by the power and the love from the grassroots people. This is the reason why you are here today, to tell the Conservatives they do not have your consent.

And if the Conservative government does not get the message today, then I don't know what will. We are telling the Conservative government they don't have our consent, and we're not idle about it."[22]

The passion of the movement would have surprised the many Canadian observers who thought Idle No More was a disconnected and disaffected group of protestors. For example, in the heightened action during Chief Spence's fast, Clayton Thomas-Muller, an Aboriginal environmental activist, offered an angry critique of neo-liberalism and Canadian resource policies, laying the problem at the prime minister's feet:

> Stephen Harper may be angry. Stephen Harper may be smart. But there's one thing he doesn't understand. We're not going to give it up, ever. We have survived over 250 [years] of these colonial policies and we are going to be here another 250 years. . . . We will build power for the establishment of the biggest Native and social movement in the history of Canada; we will break down colonial barriers that divide the common people of Canada, a movement that is deeply rooted in an unbreakable foundation of anti-racism, anti-oppression, and anti-colonialism. This sacred day, this winter solstice, send our voices in solidarity to the world that Harper represents, a system of oppression against not only our First Nations, Indigenous peoples, but all people, and against Mother Earth. United we will win a more beautiful world for our children and future generations . . . This is prophecy . . . you are prophecy. . . . We will never stop, not for one second. . . . Mr. Harper you'd better be ready.[23]

As the Idle No More events continued throughout December, Chief Spence continued her hunger strike, with mounting concern about her health in some quarters and, simultaneously, rising cynicism about her protest among non-Aboriginal Canadians. As the days passed, she looked increasingly tired and declared that the liquid-only diet was draining her energy. Supporters showed up at rallies across the country, demanding that the government respond to her protests. Others fasted in support. Sympathizers were as far flung as Egypt, the United Kingdom, the United States, and all across Canada. As one supporter in England said, "The idea that people in this modern world are still willing to do that for something they believe in very deeply is something that just really moves me and it's something I find extremely noble beyond words, and so for me a one-day fast is really the least I can do when you consider the fact Chief Spence is risking her life."[24] Groups as big as the several hundred that gathered in Vancouver, and other events in locations as diverse as Toronto's Eaton Centre and on the rail line near Belleville, Ontario, voiced support for the chief.

Political support increased; by the end of the month, twenty-one opposition MPs and senators had visited Chief Spence on Victoria Island, as much from a desire to create a personal platform for themselves to critique the Conservative government as from any deep interest in Spence's cause. High-profile visits to Victoria Island, particularly from former Prime Ministers Paul Martin and Joe Clark, and Liberal leadership hopeful Justin Trudeau, drew large media crowds. Charlie Angus, whose support for his northern Aboriginal constituency was consistent, said, "Our constituents are saying, 'what is going on in this country that a woman is starving herself a yard away from Parliament Hill and the Prime Minister has walked away?'"[25]

A group called Academics in Solidarity with Chief Theresa Spence and Idle No More launched a website in support of the protest:

> We, as academics teaching in universities, witness the courageous and honourable actions of Attawapiskat First Nation Chief Theresa Spence to defend the land and Indigenous peoples of Canada. . . . We call on our government to meet immediately with Chief Spence and to initiate a comprehensive plan to address the urgent situation in Aboriginal communities across this country. . . .
>
> We stand in solidarity with Chief Theresa Spence's attempts to change the abusive manner in which the Canadian Government has ignored, threatened, and bullied Indigenous peoples. . . . [W]e recognize that Canada's history is one of exploitation, dispossession

and marginalization of Indigenous peoples, denial of their rights and sovereignty, indifference to their suffering, and in many cases the destruction of their land. We also recognize the strength, resilience, and profound respect for Mother Earth that exist in Indigenous communities and welcome this current mobilization against the government-sponsored destruction of the environment.

We urge all people of Canada to enter into respectful dialogues about Aboriginal rights and treaties, and to take meaningful action in your communities to ensure the honouring of our treaties, respect for self-determination, and the protection of our environment for the generations to come.[26]

Over 1,600 people signed the academic group's open letter.

###

E ven with all the support she was receiving, Chief Spence's protest and fast rested uneasily with many Idle No More participants and followers, and with the Canadian public at large. People stopped calling Spence's protest a hunger strike when news emerged that the chief was on a fish-soup diet[27]—this caused considerable derision among sections of the non-Aboriginal population, whose sympathy for the protest started to decline rapidly by the end of 2012. The Aboriginal response was different. Many Idle No More activists continued to declare their support for the chief's fast or indicated that they had been inspired by her courageous stand. Still, for others, Chief Spence's situation was ambiguous and confusing, and it created serious difficulties for people who supported the broader Idle No More cause, but had questions about the chief.

On December 30, 2012, the chief issued a declaration to mark the twentieth day of her protest:

Today is the twentieth day of my hunger strike, and I give thanks to the Creator for allowing me to see this day. I acknowledge all prayers and support I have received by both Indigenous and non-Indigenous peoples, both in Canada and worldwide. . . . I would also like to acknowledge all the helpers here who continue to do their best to look after me. . . . In reflection, we are the original inhabitants and stewards of our land. When European explorers came to our land, they were seeking economic advantages or escaping conditions of poverty in Europe. Our ancestors welcomed them and the bounty entrusted to us by Mother Earth. In exchange for the graciousness of our forefathers, when we entered into treaties we were relegated to living in small, desolate tracts of land called reserves, and we were also made wards of the state through the statutes contained in the Indian Act. Modern governments have encouraged the process of segregation by introducing numerous legislative statutes to restrict and remove any say from our communities over our traditional lands that were used by our forefathers. Modern governments have actively engaged in a process to isolate our political leadership by introducing mechanisms that do not recognize our government structures and actively introduce and seek a means of controlling what is said by our leadership, and [any] further means to remove our access to our traditional lands. This will not happen without a fight from our people, and now is the appropriate time to call for unity. This is a call to arms, and a call to action in the most peaceful and respectful way that reflects our natural laws as Indigenous nations. First Nations leadership needs to take charge and control of the situation on behalf of the grassroots movement. We need to re-ignite that nation-to-nation relationship based on our inherent and constitutionally protected rights as a sovereign nation. We are demanding our rightful place back, here in our homelands that we call Canada. I reiterate that simple message that I am asking for: I call upon Her Majesty the Queen to fulfill her fiduciary responsibilities that they undertook when they signed the original treaties with our people, and for the Crown to come to the table along with the prime minister of Canada to have a meaningful dialogue about restoring the respect of the political and economic relationship with our people. The Creator put us here for a reason. The Creator wants us to love and respect each other. The Creator wants us to work together here on Mother Earth. I know that some non-Aboriginal citizens may not understand this statement, but through education and in the spirit of love, hope, and prosperity for all, we can achieve this. Thank you, all, for the love and support you have shown, and thank you for your continued prayers. *Meegwetch*.[28]

It was at this point that the Conservative government finally acknowledged Spence's protest, but it was in a way that did nothing to bring the two sides closer together. To counter any support for the chief's actions, and perhaps to draw attention away from the Idle No More movement as well, the Government of Canada released an unflattering audit of Chief Spence's Attawapiskat office, sullying her reputation, raising the stakes, and muddying the waters. Most commentators were much less caustic than Ezra Levant, the outspoken critic who routinely attacked Spence's fast from the Sun TV News platform, although talk-radio programs also blistered with rage and condemnation focused on Chief Spence.

While some of the revelations were old hat and others exaggerated or misrepresented, the audit and resulting criticism chipped away at the chief's credibility and damaged her protest. Relations between Chief Spence, her handlers, and the media became testy; supporters kept journalists at bay. One of her supporters from Attawapiskat, Danny Metatawabin, said, "Because of that leaked document with the audit report, we just don't want any negative vibes inside that fence. Inside that teepee, in that sacred fire, it's all sacred to us. . . . We don't want to allow any media inside the boundaries of the sacredness of that fire, and we need to protect the chief. She needs to be at peace, focused on what she needs to do, and that's all we're asking for."[29]

Support for the chief came and went in waves. Grand Elder Raymond Robinson of Cross Lake, Manitoba, fasted in sympathy with her. And by the New Year, while many non-Aboriginal people continued to mock and criticize Chief Spence, more non-Aboriginal Canadians stepped up to support her, with individuals visiting her to offer encouragement. Lara Purvis, identifying herself as a settler ally from Ottawa, responded to a tweeted request for supplies: "I think that a lot of people who are settler allies such as ourselves feel a sense of helplessness in this situation in that we don't know how we can support and how to contribute in a way that would be appropriate."[30] Cultural Survival, a major Indigenous rights organization, criticized Canada for continuing "the most shameful practices of racism, imperialism, and renewed conquest."[31] The globally recognized human rights agency, Amnesty International, connected Chief Spence's protest and Idle No More: "It is tragic that a hunger strike and Canada-wide protests are necessary, in order for Indigenous peoples to bring attention to violations of their dignity, treaties and human rights. Our organization strongly supports human rights education. We urge all Canadians to engage with Indigenous peoples, to help educate others, and to support the current movement of awareness raising and ensuring vital reforms."[32]

Because of the released audit, Chief Spence and her First Nations government found themselves grilled relentlessly in the media, led by the intensely hostile Ezra Levant. The Sun-TV commentator investigated financial challenges at Attawapiskat, describing payments to Chief Spence's partner and to the chief, cataloguing government spending on the reserve, and alleging malfeasance on the part of the chief. Levant also attacked Chief Spence personally, wondering aloud how she seemed to have lost little weight despite the fast and mocking the discovery that she was retreating to a hotel room each night instead of remaining in the teepee on Victoria Island.[33] Critical evidence against Chief Spence mounted. Medical specialists compared her apparent medical condition with the symptoms of those enduring lengthy hunger strikes and concluded that she was not suffering as expected.

National Chief Shawn Atleo, driven to near exhaustion by the intense political pressures brought on by in-fighting with the Assembly of First Nations, the unrelenting media coverage, and difficult discussions with the Government of Canada, sought a resolution to the impasse. Several Chief Spence supporters—including interim Liberal leader Bob Rae; Romeo Saganash, the New Democratic Party

Aboriginal Affairs critic; and Deputy Grand Chief for northern Ontario, Alvin Fiddler—worked to get the chief to end her fast. Prime
Minister Stephen Harper, pushed by many Canadians to accede to
Chief Spence's demand for a meeting—but also supported by many
others for rejecting the request—held out. Feverish, behind-the-
scenes negotiations finally led to the prime minister's offer to meet
with National Chief Atleo and First Nations leaders, including Chief
Theresa Spence, if she wished to come. Atleo welcomed her participation. Separating the political from the ceremonial, it was agreed that
following the political meeting with the prime minister and his officials, the group would attend a ceremonial meeting with the Governor General. It was an elegant solution, allowing all sides to save face.

So on January 4, 2013, the prime minister officially announced that
he would meet with First Nations leaders: "It is in this spirit of ongoing dialogue that, together with Minister Duncan, I will be participating in a working meeting with a delegation of First Nations leaders
coordinated by the Assembly of First Nations on January 11, 2013. This
working meeting will focus on two areas flowing from the Gathering:
the treaty relationship and aboriginal rights, and economic development."[34] Harper did not acknowledge Chief Spence's demands in the
context of his announcement, but instead harkened back to a January
2012 meeting—the Gathering—with National Chief Atleo and other
leaders, and the commitment he made at the time to hold further sessions. As concessions go, his was carefully worded and unremarkable.
Still, in the context of Chief Spence's protest and the national anxiety
raised by Idle No More, the agreement to meet with Atleo and other
Aboriginal leaders was a significant step.

During this time, First Nations across the country continued to
express their support for Chief Spence, whose actions had now largely
pushed Idle No More off the front pages. A Parliament Hill rally on
January 10, 2013, in support of Spence attracted some four thousand
people. Some chiefs, particularly in western Canada and Ontario, declared that they could bring the economy to its knees through the
protests. Lynda Kitchikeesic Juden, coordinator of an Idle No More
event in Ottawa, distanced herself from the aggressive plans: "My aim
is not to anger the people of Ottawa. We don't want conflict with Canadians because they'll miss the point if they're angry."[35]

The Assembly of First Nations was more equivocal and struggled to figure how best to respond to Chief Spence and, more broadly, the Idle No More movement. As the Aboriginal People's Television Network suggested, "Idle No More as a movement is not clear about what they want from the chiefs. Statements have been made that the chiefs are not communicating with grassroots. Chiefs are clear they are not here to take over the movement, but support the activities. . . . Chiefs agree with [Idle No More] statements in principle, but at issue is how do we carry this out and continue to co-exist peacefully in this country?"[36]

Indeed, intense debates about Chief Spence caused tensions among Aboriginal leaders. As one reporter observed, "While Spence's protest may be forging a bond among First Nations women leaders, her refusal to budge over the past few weeks has divided the Assembly of First Nations and prompted questions about the leadership of Atleo."[37] And yet, former National Chief Phil Fontaine observed, "[though] there will be some that now question Chief Spence [, the] fact is her action, the Idle No More movement, the Assembly of First Nations, in all pursuing a common cause, all of those actions have resulted in a meeting with the prime minister. There's some real opportunities there and we shouldn't lose sight of that fact."[38]

Chief Spence greeted the prime minister's announcement by declaring that she was "really overjoyed" and that she would continue the fast until the meeting took place.[39]

Within a few days, however, Chief Spence managed to complicate what seemed to be a clear victory. After initially indicating that she would attend the meeting with Prime Minister Harper, Chief Spence changed her mind. She declared that Governor General Johnston should also attend the meeting and wrote to the Queen to demand that Johnston be ordered to participate. For his part, Prime Minister Harper indicated that he would only attend a portion of the meeting, a seemingly gratuitous rebuke of First Nations leaders. Governor General Johnston, when asked, declared that he would not participate in working meetings between Aboriginal leaders and the prime minister and his officials. What had promised to be a symbolic and high-profile meeting had devolved into something of a farce.

The days passed, criticism mounted, and so did concern about the chief's health. Many urged Chief Spence to give up her fast. Murray

Sinclair, head of the Truth and Reconciliation Commission and a respected Aboriginal jurist from Manitoba, commented on January 11, 2013: "I would [...] also ask that those who can, ask Chief Theresa Spence and the other hunger strikers to bring their hunger strikes to a halt. Their stance has achieved far more than they may have dreamed or sought. Any damage to them, or their loss, would hurt us in ways we cannot calculate."[40]

#

When the Assembly of First Nations did finally meet with the prime minister and other officials on January 11, 2013, Idle No More reached out, attracting attention and producing over 260 events around the world, from a Solidarity Drum Circle in Nelson, New Zealand, to a march on the Canadian Consulate in Sydney, Australia. In Temuco, Chile, organizers staged a Solidarity with Idle No More event—*Acción de arte por la Paz, contra el racismo y la violencia*—while a flash mob was called for in Inari, Finland. German supporters carried out a Round Dance in Berlin, and others in Venice, Italy, held a demonstration in support of Idle No More. Mayan supporters in Mexico hosted a sacred gathering on Isla Mujeres, and Nigerians joined a solidarity walk in Benin City. In Colombo, Sri Lanka, a solitary protestor showed up at the Canadian embassy. Supporters gathered across the United States: in Honolulu and Las Vegas; Milwaukee and Las Cruces; Devil's Lake, North Dakota and Cahokia Mounds, Illinois; Montpelier, Vermont and Naples, Florida; New York City and Santa Fe; Pueblo, Colorado and San Carlos Apache Tribal Nation in Arizona—as well as in dozens of other locations across the country.[41] Never before had a domestic Canadian movement attracted such global attention. Most of the events were small, many were on university campuses or in Indigenous communities, but the number and magnitude of international Idle No More sympathy events on January 11 was simply remarkable.

So, too, was the Canadian response. Among the many events, there was a St'wxwtews information roadblock at Cache Creek, British Columbia, and a rally in Antigonish, Nova Scotia. The Stó:lō gathered at the Coqualeetza Grounds for a prayer circle, and there was a mini powwow in Dryden, Ontario. Fort Qu'Appelle, Saskatchewan, hosted an "Honour Our Treaties Unity" walk and a "Peaceful Slow-Down" barricade. There was a sunrise ceremony at Point Pleasant Park in Halifax and a "Standing-As-One" rally on Highway 37 near Iskut, British Columbia. Kelowna hosted a Round Dance and Kitchener-Waterloo a solidarity rally. Organizers called a flash mob Round Dance in Mashteuiatsh, Quebec, and a Global Day of Action in Moberly Lake, British Columbia. A large rally in support of Chief Theresa Spence was held in the Montreal Convention Centre, and the Okanagan Nation held the "Solidarity Swim." Ottawa's event was called "10,000 Voices Can't Be Ignored" and it promised to be the "[m]ost powerful powwow Ottawa has ever seen. Bring your regalia and your drums!" Quebec City hosted *manifestation en soliderité*. Rainy River, Ontario, held a candlelight vigil and bonfire, while St. John's, Newfoundland, called for a rally and peaceful protest. The Sturgeon Lake Cree in Alberta held a solidarity walk, and the Tr'ondëk Hwëch'in held an Idle No More Worldwide event in Dawson City. In Tuktoyaktuk, on the shores of the Arctic Ocean, organizers held the "Youth Information, Solidarity Assembly and Drum Dance" at the local school. Among the many events in Vancouver was a flash mob at the CTV offices. And at Whitefish Bay, Ontario, protestors slowed down traffic and sang.[42]

These were dramatic events. Some one thousand people joined the rally at the Palais des congrès in Montreal, a convention centre downtown: "Young people, union representatives and provincial politicians were in the group. Some waved Mohawk and Quebec flags and danced to the beat of native drums."[43] Chief Allan Adam of the Athabasca Chipewyan First Nation from northern Alberta addressed a gathering of several hundred people during an Idle No More protest in Edmonton, declaring that the Government of Canada had to back down on Bill C-45 or face the consequences: namely, blocking the highway to the oil sands. "Highway 63 to the oil sands will be shut down. That will happen and I guarantee this. . . . I fear for the worst if the prime minister doesn't retract some of the bills that were passed."[44] There were rail blockages in Nova Scotia and small roadside protests across the country. Manitoba Grand Chief Derek Nepinak from the Assembly of Manitoba Chiefs declared the events to be a "great victory": "There is a great power that's emerging once again. . . . The warrior spirit of our people is once again across the land. It's very strong."[45]

The Idle No More event in Ottawa on January 11, 2013, made clear that Idle No More was not a chief-led movement. Firmly separating the movement and chiefs and yet bringing them together as partners—at least in this particular instance—the call to action for this day declared, "We stand united. Chiefs and Idle No More coming together."[46]

When Chief Spence addressed the gathering, she reiterated her call for a meeting that included all leaders—chiefs, prime minister, and Governor General: "I hear it's a working group meeting but it's not; it's nation to nation. I want the chiefs to have this meeting with the prime minister and the Governor General because, you know, it's been so many years that have been given away with the violation of the treaty, and we're giving them this opportunity for them to, you know, resolve the broken promises from the treaty."[47] She declared that she was not attending the meeting because the Governor General would not be in attendance.

Other First Nations leaders also chose not to attend the meeting, and they were angry with National Chief Atleo for proceeding; many argued that he had no mandate to speak to the Government of Canada. As Serpent River Chief Isadore Day commented, "The talk is that a lot of people aren't happy, obviously, you know people are shocked, folks are saying that the best thing for people to do is take a bit of a step back and go home and do some thinking. . . . How could, in one day, the national chief say we are united and that we are all standing behind Chief Spence and in the next day, take this entourage to a meeting? That is not sitting well with the majority of the chiefs in assembly."[48] Atleo's decision to meet with Harper was made in full understanding of the criticism and refusals of other chiefs. He made it clear that proceeding with the meeting was, in his view, in the best interests of First Nations across Canada.

Evidently, many Aboriginal people agreed with National Chief Atleo. On the day of the meeting, a group of people, gathered in support of the chiefs' meeting with the prime minister,[49] met on Victoria Island and began an event with opening prayers and songs, including an honour song for Chief Spence. The group then marched to Parliament Hill, led by drums, dancers, and eagle staffs (long poles adorned with eagle feathers, sacred symbols of nationhood). They were met by the chiefs as they continued to a rally on Parliament Hill. Loud "Idle

No More" chants reverberated across the city. Elder Raymond Robinson, who had joined Chief Spence's fast, addressed the crowd: "I have waited for this day, for a long time. It's one of the proudest moments to see our people, a nation, rise together and tell the Harper government, 'You will never divide us.' . . . We are all brothers and sisters no matter where you come from, where you've been, what colour you are. We are one nation! All of us. A moment I will remember. I always aspired to see this day. All of us, as nations, have suffered. Every one of us."[50]

They also heard from two Algonquian grandmothers. As one of them said, "We make these demands on behalf of all those who cannot speak. The land, the water, the animals, and the future generation, their very survival depends on our success. This is our responsibility as grandmothers." Danny Metatawabin (spokesperson for Chief Spence), Mohawk activist Ellen Gabriel, youth representatives, Inuit Throat Singers, and women drummers were also present at the rally.[51]

For the participants, the Ottawa event was life-changing. A journalist captured the feeling of the day, and the First Nations' commitment:

> A massive Round Dance also framed the lawn of Parliament Hill at one point and the drums shook the air. "I am blown away, I am filled with pride, I am just standing here trying to take this in," said Molly Peters, a Mi'kmaq Idle No More organizer from Nova Scotia, who was standing on the steps of Parliament Hill watching the Round Dance slowly turn on the lawn below. "I came for unity," said Stacie Landon, from Neyaashiinigmiing First Nation in Ontario. "I am here for my children's future." Janice Trudeau, from unceded Wikwemikong First Nation, said she took to the streets in Ottawa in solidarity with other Indigenous people. "I came in solidarity with other Anishinaabe people to form a united front against Harper," she said.[52]

The rally then moved on to the Langevin Block, where the chiefs would meet with the prime minister. Chiefs who had refused to meet with the prime minister joined the marchers: even though they did not agree with the meeting, they still wished to add their voices to the grassroots gathering. Grand Chief Derek Nepinak of Manitoba, who stayed out of the meeting, commented that he was "ecstatic about our drums and about our people today."[53] *Indian Time* reporter, Kaniethonkie, described the next steps: "The Chiefs walked toward the front line of protestors in a show of support that proved to be a very emotional and powerful union. The front line of protestors consisted of those carrying ceremonial staffs, Chiefs, and flag holders with singers and drummers following closely behind. There were many groups of singers who weaved throughout the march lending spiritual support by their songs and drumming."[54]

The meeting went ahead, surrounded by controversy and internal protest. Regional leaders struggled with whether or not to join National Chief Atleo and the prime minister. A large and determined group of Aboriginal women blocked the entrance to the meeting room, convincing several of the leaders to turn back. In the end, chiefs from Ontario, Manitoba, and the Northwest Territories joined Atleo in the meeting. Saskatchewan's delegation was divided and several, including Grand Chief Perry Bellegarde of the Federation of Saskatchewan Indian Nations, boycotted the meeting.[55] Those who stayed away declared that the meeting had no standing and Atleo had no mandate to negotiate with the prime minister. The meeting—which could not possibly match the pressure that led up to it—drew a crowd.

It was an impressive group, even with the absentees. The government's side included: Prime Minister Stephen Harper; Aboriginal Affairs Minister John Duncan; Treasury Board President Tony Clement; Health Minister Leona Aglukkaq; Parliamentary Secretary Greg Rickford; Aboriginal Affairs and Northern Development Canada officials, including Deputy Minister Michael Wernick; and senior assistants and senior officials from the Privy Council, Natural Resources, and Human Resources and Skills Development Canada. The Assembly of First Nations delegation included: National Chief Shawn Atleo, Terry Paul, Debora Robinson, Regional Chief Roger Augustine, George Ginnish, Regional Chief Ghislain Picard, Grand Chief Matthew Coon Come, Leo Omani, Norma Johnstone, Marcel Head, Regional Chief Jody Wilson-Raybould, Grand Chief Ed John, Doug White, Regional Chief Mike Smith, Eric Fairclough, Grand

Chief Charles Weaselhead, Grand Chief Roland Twinn, Sasha Maracle (Youth Council), and Bertha Commanda (Elders Council).[56]

After the more than month-long lead up, the events with the prime minister and Governor General were almost predestined to disappoint, largely because the Government of Canada did not wish to appear to be bending to Chief Spence's protest. The national chief carried a list of topics into the meeting, including a long-standing request for a national investigation into murdered and missing Aboriginal women, revisions to Bill C-38[57] and C-45, improvements to schooling, and a Cabinet-level commitment to elevate the discussions of First Nations–Crown relations. They came out with much less than they'd hoped for, no more than a prime ministerial assurance that there would be "high-level" meetings on treaty implementation and outstanding land claims, and further discussions of remaining issues.

The subsequent meeting with the Governor General went off with appropriate pomp and circumstance, hosted by the gracious David Johnston and attended by Chief Spence. The Governor General had no ability to address Chief Spence's lofty aspirations for the meeting, which ended without formal discussions. The Rideau Hall gathering was a ceremonial event and included a greeting from the Governor General and Aboriginal ceremonies, including an Elder's prayer and a smudging ceremony.[58] With that, Chief Spence's odyssey was over.

The events of January 11, 2013, did not solve the specific grievances brought forward by Chief Spence—the crisis in Attawapiskat was being addressed by Aboriginal Affairs. Nor did the meeting reassure supporters of the Idle No More movement that the government had turned the corner on Aboriginal issues. After the meeting, National Chief Atleo stepped aside for two weeks to recover his health. Indeed, no one really emerged unscathed from the crisis inspired by Chief Spence. The chief had her personal affairs dragged before the public, often unfairly, and her muddled demands, inconsistent behaviour at the end of the protest, confusion about the hunger strike/fast, and revelations about management issues at Attawapiskat made her a less sympathetic figure than she was before her protest began. The Government of Canada, including the prime minister, came off as heavy-handed and callous, offering neither Chief Spence nor National Chief Atleo any significant concessions. The Assembly of First Nations came out of the process badly divided—partly between those who attended the meeting with the government officials and those who stayed away—and isolated from the increasingly influential Idle No More movement.

National Chief Atleo had produced the meeting with the Government of Canada but the process exacerbated cracks within the Assembly of First Nations and created a platform for his critics, particularly former AFN national chief candidate Pamela Palmater, who demanded more assertive approaches to government. Taiaiake Alfred, the influential Mohawk activist and academic from the University of Victoria, declared, "I think it's a major crisis for Shawn Atleo, and it's a crisis as well for the AFN as an organization because if they can't deliver something meaningful in the minds of the people involved with Idle No More, they're in serious danger of being seen as an irrelevant force or, even worse, as part of a collaborating mechanism with the Government of Canada on their agenda."[59] Prime Minister Stephen Harper, already seen by many Canadians as cold, solidified his hard-hearted image in his unwavering refusal to speak to Chief Spence, although the same behaviour earned him accolades with many in the non-Aboriginal community. At the end of the fast, over half of the respondents to a survey on Chief Spence indicated that they felt her protests would not advance Aboriginal interests.[60]

Nonetheless, after the fact, Chief Theresa Spence was lauded by thousands, but not by as many as had shown their support for her at the beginning of her fast. At a celebration held to acknowledge her contributions, First Nations leaders, largely from northern Ontario and Manitoba, issued a statement demanding that the Government of Canada adopt a new approach to Aboriginal affairs. The event was not well-attended, though, with far fewer people than one might have expected given the scale, length, and intensity of Chief Spence's protests. As *The Globe and Mail* observed:

> The sparse crowd greeted Ms. Spence as if she were a rock star—or a saint. At least one chief has referred to her as "our Mother Theresa." Ms. Spence's decision in early December to embark on a hunger strike has made her a beloved figure for many First Nations people. And, although her fast was separate from the protests of the Idle No More movement, she has become an icon

for those who are dancing in malls and rallying in the streets to draw attention to native issues. But Ms. Spence is also a polarizing entity. Those Canadians who are fed up with complaints that native people have been marginalized and their lands unfairly exploited readily point to her flaws.[61]

Chief Spence's protest was not a specific part of Idle No More. Her actions were, as she observed from the outset, *inspired by* the Idle No More rallies. The chief's protest and the Idle No More movement, however, were connected in the public's mind, to the detriment of Idle No More. The intense focus on Chief Spence's fast during the month of December and into January drew attention away from the other rallies going on across the country. Moreover, as Chief Spence attracted criticism, the mud splashed equally onto Idle No More. The media often got it wrong, too. When commenting on Spence's impact, one reporter reversed the relationship between the movement and the fast:

> Theresa Spence has put Native issues clearly in the public eye. She helped inspire those Idle No More protests but she became a bit of a distraction when she missed her first best chance to get off centre stage back when the prime minister met some chiefs two weeks ago. Now that she's fading out of the picture, the Assembly of First Nations will try to push forward using this new declaration as a blue print for negotiations, but the government's resisted many of those demands and there's no sign that's going to change.[62]

Ernie Crey of the Stó:lō Tribal Council in British Columbia said of Chief Spence, "While she was a sympathetic figure in the early going and a bit of a rallying point for some Aboriginal peoples and even non-Aboriginals peoples, I don't know what contribution her effort really made."[63]

Chief Spence's protest muddied the line between Idle No More and the First Nations political organizations in the country. While the chiefs had previously been in the background of Idle No More—in part because people were frustrated with them, too—the high politics of meetings with the prime minister and Governor General raised the profile of the events. Discussions amongst the chiefs began to focus on announcing a national day of protest, complete with the very roadblocks, blockades, and economic disruptions that most Idle No More organizers sought to avoid. The chiefs wanted to pressure the Government of Canada into action. A December 28 memorandum circulated through the Assembly of First Nations captured the chiefs' confused relationship with the movement:

> Idle No More as a movement is not clear about what they want from the chiefs. Statements have been made that the chiefs are not communicating with grassroots. Chiefs are clear they are not here to take over the movement, but support the activities. Self-determination, indigenous sovereignty and protection of land and water are primary objectives of Idle No More. They are adamant that our treaties are not made with the Canadian state. Chiefs agree with statements in principle, but at issue is how do we carry this out and continue to co-exist peacefully in this country. . . . It was clear that a lot of the activities under the banner of Idle No More are outside the control of chiefs. Chiefs can and should support "direct action" activities and these will be up to individual bands however.[64]

The national Aboriginal organization was clearly struggling to find a way to fit Idle No More into its broader political activities.

In his extended commentary on the conflation of Idle No More and Chief Spence, writer and University of Manitoba Ph.D. candidate Matt Sheedy observed that Spence's fast drew national and international attention—including a seven-hundred-person blockade of the Brooklyn Bridge—but it also shifted the focus from general grievances to specific ones:

> [T]he media's penchant for fixating on symbolic figureheads like Chief Spence has presented a significant barrier to connecting the dots between this movement and

the ongoing legacy of colonialism and racism, along with the broader issue of neoliberal capitalism. . . . But the disproportionate focus on this confrontation between Canada's First Nations chiefs and the federal government has had the effect of placing undue emphasis on the traditional channels of power, when in fact the true source of the movement's vitality is in the thousands of ordinary citizens who are being mobilized and energized, both online and in the streets.[65]

But here, Chief Spence's protest was seen by Sheedy and others as important to the broader movement, up to a point:

Changing the narrative does not, of course, mean dismissing Chief Spence's hunger strike altogether, but rather seeing it as a conduit for the voices of those who have been long suppressed. Chief Spence has helped to galvanize tens of thousands of First Nations people and their supporters to take to the streets like never before, performing Round Dances and drum circles, marching on government offices and businesses, hosting teach-ins, building communities' ties and engaging in slow-downs and road blockades. . . . In a social movement's lifespan, this early phase of spectacle is a chance to help change the narrative, to organize alternatives and to turn away from past mistakes. But after the spectacle dies down, the real work begins.[66]

It is impossible to disentangle fully the early days of Idle No More from Chief Spence's fast. The chief's protest clearly arose out of the gathering social movement; it seems unlikely that the fast would have started without it. It is also clear that Idle No More had considerable momentum on its own, including the lead-up to the December 10 National Day of Action, which marked the start of Chief Spence's fast. At this point, the two merged in the public's mind: her protest was microcosmic, symbolic, and representative of the demands and expressions of the broader scope of Aboriginal frustrations. But if Chief Spence's actions drew attention to the movement over the month and a half that followed, it also meant that Idle No More became trapped in the rhetoric, demands, and tactics of the Victoria Island protest. As Spence became the focal point, as non-Aboriginal support for her action dissipated, as ridicule replaced sympathy, and as her supporters on the Opposition benches in Parliament and in other quarters urged her to end a protest that had become counterproductive, attention shifted from the streets to the Assembly of First Nations, from the rallies still going on across the country to negotiations between the national chief and the prime minister. This, ironically, was the opposite of what the founders of Idle No More had meant to do. As Sylvia McAdam said, "I know the media has said that she is a part of Idle No More, but with all due respect to Chief Spence, Idle No More began before she decided to do her hunger strike against the Conservative government."[67] But McAdam's comments were not a rejection of the chief's position: "Chief Spence has since ended her hunger strike and she has thirteen declarations of commitment that are going to be pushed forward. And they are similar to the goals of Idle No More."[68]

The commitment mentioned by McAdam came out of the meeting with Aboriginal and federal politicians at Rideau Hall in Ottawa on January 11. On January 23, the Assembly of First Nations, the Liberal caucus, and the New Democrat caucus addressed protestors with the following declaration, which provided support for Chief Spence's fast and added political legitimacy and heft to her effort, if after the fact:

> [W]e solemnly commit to undertake political, spiritual and all other advocacy efforts to implement a renewed First Nations–Crown relationship where inherent Treaty and non-Treaty Rights are recognized, honoured and fully implemented as they should be, within the next five years.
>
> This Declaration includes, but is not limited to, ensuring commitments made by the Prime Minister of Canada on January 11th, 2013 are followed through and implemented as quickly as possible as led by First Nations on a high-level priority with open transparency and trust. Furthermore, immediate steps are taken working together to achieve the below priorities:

1. An immediate meeting to be arranged between the Crown, Federal Governments, Provincial Governments and all First Nations to discuss outstanding issues regarding the Treaty Relationship, as well as for non-Treaty area relationships.

2. Clear work-plans that shall include deliverables and timelines that outline how commitments will be achieved, including immediate action for short, medium and long-term goals. Addressing the housing crisis within our First Nation communities shall be considered as a short-term immediate action.

3. Frameworks and mandates for the implementation and enforcement of Treaties between Treaty parties on a Nation-to-Nation basis.

4. Reforming and modifying the comprehensive claims policy based on inherent rights of First Nations.

5. A commitment towards resource revenue sharing, requiring the participation and involvement of provinces and territories currently benefiting from resource development from traditional lands.

6. Commitment towards ensuring a greater collective oversight and action towards ensuring the sustainability of the land through a sustained environmental oversight.

7. A comprehensive review and meaningful consultation in regards to Bill C-38 and C-45 to ensure it is consistent with Section 35 of the Constitution Act (1982).

8. Ensure that all federal legislation has the free, prior and informed consent of First Nations where inherent and Treaty rights are affected or impacted.

9. A revised fiscal relationship between First Nations and Canada that is equitable, sustainable and includes indexing and the removal of arbitrary funding caps.

10. A National Public Commission of Inquiry on Violence against Indigenous Women of all ages.

11. Equity in capital construction of First Nation schools, including funding parity with Provincial funding formulas with additional funding support for First Nation languages.
12. A change in how government operates that would include direct oversight, a dedicated Cabinet Committee and Secretariat within the Privy Council Office with specific responsibility for the First Nation–Crown relationship to ensure implementation.
13. The full implementation of the United Nations Declaration on the Rights of Indigenous Peoples – UNDRIP.[69]

The declaration, which was comprehensive in nature and more dramatic than the country had seen in some time, garnered surprisingly little media attention. By this point, the Canadian public clearly preferred to see the fast over and the protests moved out of the news.

The postmortem on Chief Spence's protest began almost immediately after she ended her fast. The declaration didn't figure in a January 24, 2013, article in the *Toronto Star*'s online arm, *TheStar.com*, which, editorially, is generally supportive of Aboriginal rights, but in this case, was quite critical of Spence and, by association, Idle No More:

> That is the raw message of the youth-driven Idle No More movement as well. It is a demand for justice that political leaders should take to heart. Spence's fast was controversial. Skeptics questioned how much she really accomplished, apart from a hurried, firefighting meeting on Jan. 11 between Harper, Assembly of First Nations Chief Shawn Atleo and other chiefs. Many Canadians take a dim view of Idle No More, and doubt that her fast will have lasting impact. A critical audit of Attawapiskat's books didn't help. Moreover the AFN very nearly split as Spence and younger voices defiantly challenged traditional negotiating methods. But divisive or not, this was a cry of anguish that cannot be ignored.[70]

Keith Beardsley of the *National Post* also offered a harsh assessment of Spence and a telling assessment of the relationship between her and Idle No More:

> To her credit, when Spence began her "hunger strike," she did succeed in creating a spike in interest in some broader aboriginal issues. However, her stubbornness and overplayed hand will have nullified much of the good will she initially gained for First Nations issues with the general population. . . . National Chief Shawn Atleo has been weakened, perhaps fatally, and no amount of phony rhetoric about going forward united can cover that up. . . . Some would argue that Spence has instilled a sense of pride in members of the First Nations, especially the younger generation. I would argue that with a rich history, culture and traditions, pride has always been there and any renewed interest is more likely due to the founders of the Idle No More Movement, not Chief Spence. It is this grassroots movement that deserves the credit for getting the government's attention. Yes, Spence was and still is an inspiration to some of the participants in this movement, but she was never a spokesperson for it. . . . In other words, not much has changed.[71]

Unfortunately, much of the critical commentary about Spence's action was personal, criticizing her for not showing any real side effects from her hunger strike / fast. She was accused of using up a lot of the good will Idle No More had generated, and of drawing attention away from the broader movement for Aboriginal rights.

An Ipsos Reid poll generated in mid-January 2013 found evidence of wide-ranging Canadian concern about conditions on reserves. But the same poll showed two-thirds of Canadians felt the Government of Canada paid too much for Aboriginal support programs. Only one-third thought the First Nations protestors were justified in blocking roads and railways. A full 60 per cent believed that Aboriginal peoples brought their problems on themselves, and a full 81 per cent said

Canada should require more accountability from Aboriginal govern-
ments. Put differently, Idle No More and particularly Chief Theresa
Spence had not brought about a major shift in Canadian attitudes.
Indeed, fewer than 30 per cent of Canadians gave a positive rating for
Chief Spence. Idle No More, at only 38 per cent, did not fare all that
much better. Prime Minister Stephen Harper had a 46 per cent approval rating, five points lower than the Assembly of First Nations.[72]
That Idle No More managed to maintain some distance from Chief
Spence proved to be a smart decision. As one political columnist noted, "It was a wise move because Spence, along with some of the more
militant chiefs, pose a serious public relations problem for the whole
First Nations population: Spence has lost much of her credibility because of her unclear demands and because of the damning Deloitte
and Touche audit, which suggested a lack of financial checks and bal-
ances in her community of Attawapiskat."[73]

In the end, Chief Spence's protest both expanded public awareness of Idle No More and narrowed the public perception of what the
movement was about. The chief's fast and Idle No More were tangen-
tially connected. On balance, the attention focused on Chief Spence,
including her convoluted demands, troubled past, and inconsistent
behaviour, detracted substantially from Idle No More. The movement
was on a roll before December 11 and the start of the Victoria Island
protest. Although rallies continued, the movement's tenuous connection to Chief Spence confused many participants and observers. For
Canadians as a whole, Chief Spence was easier to understand than
Idle No More, her demands more consistent with earlier Aboriginal
statements, her tactics easier to confront. A fast combined with outra-
geous demands ironically proved much easier to deal with and comprehend than dozens of rallies of drummers, dancers, and singers.
For two months, at a crucial time in the evolution of Idle No More,
Chief Theresa Spence unwittingly and unintentionally drew attention
away from the spontaneous and wide-ranging rallies. Individuals
within Idle No More, including the founders on several occasions,
stood apart from Chief Spence. It remained to be seen if Idle No More
could rediscover its independence and distinctive voice.

The Twittersphere struggled to find the right epitaph for Chief
Spence's protest:

Clinton Bishop @ClintonBishop 21 Jan 2013
Chief Theresa Spence's 15 minutes of fame has hit
the 20 minute mark. I'm growing extremely tired.
#idlenomore[74]

wišqii @robdennisjr 23 Jan 2013
#J24 #ChiefSpence will end her hunger strike. Her
sacrifice has nurtured my soul in the biggest way. She
#Inspires & I Am #IdleNoMore[75]

Kateri Sa'n @KateriSan25 23 Jan 2013
Chief Spence is an Aboriginal woman national leader!
She will always be remembered and respected by our fn
peoples #IdleNoMore #ChiefSpence[76]

The Nishiyuu Walkers arriving at Victoria
Island in Ottawa, March 25, 2013.
Photo: Ben Powless

FIVE

THE WINTER
OF THE DISCONTENTED

I dle No More had a life beyond Chief Theresa Spence. The Victoria Island protest was a distraction from the main movement, although the overlap of language, values, and aspirations made it difficult for Idle No More to disassociate itself from her and her protest. At event after event, participants lauded Chief Spence and called her an inspiration. But the movement was about far more than the specific issues that convinced the chief to launch her fast.

It is impossible to separate Idle No More from Chief Spence or to determine what would have happened to the movement if her protest had not occurred. The media spotlight shifted to Chief Spence immediately after she entered the teepee on Victoria Island and did not swing back to the broader movement until after the meeting on January 11, 2013, and the rallies associated with it. The Ottawa protests made for great theatre, particularly when questions whirled around Chief Spence's management of Attawapiskat and the financial problems in the community.

Even though Idle No More's reputation through association with Spence may have suffered some blows, the movement scarcely lost a step through January 2013 and into the rest of the winter. To the surprise of many observers, Idle No More did not peak after the events of the first weeks of December or lose momentum because of the Ottawa protests. Its ability to persevere through the Spence distraction marks Idle No More as a movement that was quite different from other social movements of our time. The Arab Spring uprisings had obvious targets—corrupt and despotic governments—and clear ambitions to tear down the old regimes. The Occupy movement lost public sympathy remarkably fast when it could not build beyond an incredibly effective positioning as "We are the 99 per cent," into anything more than an inchoate, anti-"lots-of-things" movement. Idle No More had a confusing name, no clear objective (beyond protesting Bill C-45 that nonetheless passed Parliament in December 2012), and no formal structure or organization, but somehow it continued to gather strength as the winter progressed.

Indeed, in the first month of the movement (November to December 2012), it appeared as though Idle No More might construct a long-absent bridge between Aboriginal and non-Aboriginal people. Many non-Indigenous Canadians shared portions of the Aboriginal agenda. Some, including church groups, supported Aboriginal political and legal aspirations. Environmentalists, who have often had uneasy relationships with Indigenous communities,[1] seemed to have an obvious common cause with Aboriginal opposition to Bill C-45. Trade unions, anti-poverty activists, slow-growth advocates, and Canadians worried about the cultural challenges facing Indigenous communities all had reasons to band together with First Nations, Métis, and Inuit peoples. Idle No More offered a political spark, a loose framework, and an inspiration. At rally after rally, non-Aboriginal people attended and often participated in the speeches, singing, and dancing. And so, as the movement held, a side benefit to the initiative designed to inspire and motivate Aboriginal people in Canada arose: the potential to build stronger ties between Indigenous and non-Indigenous peoples.

The contretemps in Ottawa did not help the bridge-building. While Idle No More was given higher profile because of Chief Spence's protest, it was also threatened by the protest's collapse and by the failure of the Government of Canada to make any meaningful concessions on any Aboriginal issues and demands. By the middle of January 2013, Idle No More seemed destined to come to nothing.

Yet, the movement gained strength and purpose. Rallies continued, new groups joined, and peace and cultural celebrations dominated. Instead of dragging the movement down, the end of Spence's protest and the associated criticism stripped Idle No More of political baggage. That Chief Spence herself did not claim leadership of Idle No More, that Idle No More did not claim ownership of Chief Spence's protest, made it clear to those watching that Idle No More was not a standard political protest, tied to typical issues and prevailing political structures. Neither the conciliatory National Chief Atleo nor the more outspoken critics of the Assembly of First Nations, like Pamela Palmater, spoke for Idle No More. And Idle No More did not need them to mobilize people and get messages out to the nation. Its persistence after the fizzling out of the Ottawa protest was at once the most puzzling and the most meaningful aspect of Idle No More: Idle No More was unlike any previous Aboriginal movement, protest, mobilization, or set of activities.

Indeed, as Chief Spence's time in the spotlight came to an end, Idle No More rallies continued across the country, and around the world. Consider the following short list of events and activities, all carried out in the spirit of Idle No More.

January 16, 2013—Uashat, Quebec: This marathon five-hour event, presented in Innu and French, included a Round Dance, drumming, many speeches, and a small protest rally that grew from around thirty to approximately sixty people.[2]

January 17, 2013—Iqaluit, Nunavut: Even a bitterly cold day could not keep people away from the small rally at Four Corners, called to support Idle No More. As Courtney White, the event organizer, commented: "We're here to support Idle No More. We need to become allies with other First Nations and Aboriginals across Canada so we are here to show our support. . . . We're not here to anger people, we're here to make people stop and look and see what's going on. And we don't want to have people angry with us for blocking their day, ruining their day—taking long to get home after work. . . . I don't think a lot of people understand how it [the removal of environmental protections] affects us up here as well. But . . . through Facebook and social media, we're educating everybody to let them know that it does affect everybody in Canada."[3]

February 11, 2013—Prince Rupert, British Columbia: At least sixty marchers gathered near Highway 16, close to Prince Rupert on British Columbia's Northwest Coast, and participated in a smudging cere-mony. This is the western end of the "Trail of Tears," the Yellowhead Highway along which many Aboriginal women have gone missing. It was an impressive gathering of Tsimshian, Gitxsan, Haida, Nis-ga'a, Tahltan, Tlingit, Haisla, and Wet'suwet'en people. They sang and drummed, oblivious to the wind and cold, before marching, some in traditional dress, to the Lester Performing Arts Centre, where, for four hours, they heard speakers, sang songs, and listened to stories.[4] As Ta'Kaiya Blaney, the youthful Aboriginal activist, said at the end: "What I've been taught, what my dad tells me, what my *koopa*, my *chi-chia* tell me, is that we've been given a voice. The Creator gave us a voice to speak out, to be those stewards and those caretakers and be responsible [for] that land. That's our responsibility. We've been given that voice for a reason. . . . Don't be afraid to speak up."[5]

Not all of the events went well. Mashteuiatsh First Nation in the Saguenay–Lac-Saint-Jean area of Quebec, for example, organized an event for March 21, 2013, but no one showed up. The next day, a small group of about two dozen rallied in Roberval, Quebec. Some took the small turn-out as a sign that the movement was running out of steam. One woman at the event responded to the suggestion, saying: "It's possible it is slowing down but there are also people who are scared. We are being recognized as mean protestors. Some are also asking if this is a good way to act because the government is not reacting."[6]

But Idle No More was not running out of steam. And even if it looked like the government was not responding—and it was true that no official changes in policy had been made—politicians and civil servants were taking active note of the transformation taking place across the nation. Dealing with the Assembly of First Nations, tribal councils, and individual chiefs was difficult enough. The passion, dis-satisfaction, and energy unleashed by Idle No More was diffuse, com-plicated, and difficult to contain, and close observers knew that the political environment for Aboriginal affairs in Canada had changed because of it. The movement had regained its strengths, deepened its hold on its supporters, and maintained the attention of the public at large. Among Aboriginal people, particularly the young, Idle No More had awakened deep spiritual and cultural feelings. Young people were prepared to take action and were increasingly determined to step forward.

For many Aboriginal youth, the Idle No More rallies and speeches were not quite enough. Drawing on Aboriginal traditions of journeying and storytelling, these young people opted to launch long-distance marches, counting on drawing supporters along the way and attracting media attention as they approached their destinations. A group of marchers from Bloodvein and Hollow Water First Nation started a four-day walk beginning in their communities and ending at the Manitoba Legislature in Winnipeg.[7] About thirty people participated in the march that stretched over two hundred kilometres along Highway 59 on the east side of Lake Winnipeg—a lake that has been deemed the world's most threatened lake by the Global Nature Fund in 2013. The young walkers reached the Legislature on January 28, 2013. They were joined en route by people from Black River and Brokenhead First Nations. Upon arriving, Ninoondawah Richard, a young man from Sandy Bay First Nation, commented: "I'm so emotional right now because I did a two-hundred-kilometre walk from Bloodvein and everything, helping youth to stand up for what they have to believe in, their future."[8] Over eight hundred Idle No More protestors gathered at the Legislature, and Buffy Sainte-Marie sang from the front steps. A large Round Dance took place at 5 pm.

Another group of young marchers followed two weeks later: fifty youth walked 250 kilometres over four days from Jackhead First Nation, located on the shore of Lake Winnipeg, to Winnipeg. Aboriginal youth from Fisher River and Peguis First Nations joined them as they passed by. As Ben Raven, one of the organizers, said on the steps of the Manitoba Legislature at the end of the march on February 11, 2013, "without these youth, there is no future."[9] The march sparked a larger youth gathering in Winnipeg—the Indigenous Nations Movement Youth Forum—which drew together First Nations, Inuit, and Métis young people to fight for a different future. Tyler Duncan, a sixteen-year-old from Norway House Cree Nation, captured the spirit of the event perfectly: "Most of the time when you see us in the media, it's how poor, it's how absolutely deplorable we've been treated and the living conditions we live in. . . . For the first time basically in history First Nations people look empowered, look strong, and they look like they mean something."[10] The circles of Idle No More influence continued to grow larger and larger.

One long march, the Journey of Nishiyuu, stood out among all the others. This march saw a small group of Aboriginal youth conduct a two-month-long, 1600-kilometre walk from the James Bay community of Whapmagoostui in northern Quebec to Ottawa. This epic walk, organized and led by David Kawapit, Jr., and inspired by Chief Spence's fast, was the first of the long walks. It started on January 16, 2013. Seven young Aboriginal people—Jordon Masty, Stanley George, Jr., Travis George, Johnny Abraham, David Kawapit, Jr., Raymond Kawapit, and Geordie Rupert—accompanied by forty-nine-year-old Isaac Kawapit, set out. Jordan Masty, a twenty-year-old, was assigned the honour of carrying the ceremonial staff, which had been given to the Cree by the Algonquins. As he noted, "I had to take care of it like a human being."[11] David Kawapit, Jr. is a vision walker, and Chief Spence's actions sparked in him a vision of a wolf (representing the First Nations people) and a bear (representing the Government of Canada). As Kawapit, Jr. said, "A wolf alone can be easily killed by [a bear], but with its brothers and sisters everywhere, it can call upon them and it can take down the bear with ease. . . . That is what became the unity part of this. We all need to stand together."[12] The journey was truly impressive, a massive test of commitment and determination, as Isaac Kawapit made clear:

> The 1,500-kilometre trek began as the first walkers set out from Whapmagoostui. The weather that day was −50 C. Over snow and ice, with mukluks and wooden snowshoes, the young people and their 49-year-old guide headed south toward Ottawa, relying on the support of people they met along the way. As they travelled, others joined them. They slept huddled together in tents. When it was cold, their tuques froze like helmets. Sometimes they were up to their knees in slush.[13]

They passed through Chisasibi, Wemindji, Eastmain—where almost forty additional young people joined in—and Waskaganish. As they continued south, they were joined by another 150 youth in Mani-waki. Another hundred or so linked up with them as others dropped off along the way. This was no easy journey. Two dozen walkers received medical treatment for foot ailments when they reached the Kitigan Zibi Anishinabeg First Nation territory. Three other marchers were hospitalized in Maniwaki, Quebec. Nevertheless, having followed traditional Aboriginal trade routes, the marchers—between 250 and 300 of them—walked into Ottawa together on March 25, 2013, a triumphant and remarkable end to one of the most difficult and sustained youth protests of our time.

The journey ended dramatically. The marchers stopped at Victoria Island, the site of Chief Spence's protest, where they were joined by a crowd of close to 3,000 supporters. They then moved on to address an even larger gathering under the Peace Tower on Parliament Hill. Speaking for the youth, exhausted but pleased, David Kawapit, Jr. said, "This is to show the youth have a voice. It's time for them to be shown the way to lead. Let them lead the way."[14] They met with Bernard Valcourt, the new Aboriginal Affairs minister, and secured a promise from him to visit northern Quebec. As an e-mail from the minister's office commented, "The minister acknowledged their determination and commitment and he expressed a desire to engage youth in the key issues facing communities across the country."[15]

The walkers, introduced by Green Party leader Elizabeth May, received a standing ovation in the House of Commons. May used the opportunity to criticize the prime minister, who was in Toronto welcoming a pair of pandas coming from China that were to take up temporary residence in the Toronto Zoo. Outside Parliament, National Chief Shawn Atleo lauded the walkers, "We're in an incredible moment where young people are pushing for change. . . . My optimism and hope particularly springs from the energy of the young people who are leading the way forward."[16]

The Aboriginal Peoples Television Network provided a powerful description of the event:

> Then, with the pounding of the drum reverberating off concrete and pavement, the crowd spilled out and across the Portage Bridge before flowing onto Wellington Street, engulfing it from curb to curb. Chanting

"Harper, Harper" and "Nishiyuu, Nishiyuu," they reached Parliament Hill where they were met by a sea of people that parted before them, forming a narrow path up to the steps of the Peace Tower. Many in the crowd gestured skyward after spotting what appeared to be an eagle soaring through the clouds. . . . The walk was also a healing journey for the walkers. One of them, Raymond Kawapit, 20, lost his 17-year-old brother to suicide. A photo of his brother in a hockey uniform was pinned to his pull-over coat. "I went to see my grand-mother," said an emotional Kawapit, his words trans-lated from Cree into English by an interpreter. "[She said] when a person makes this journey, when they take that journey, that is where they find healing and that is why, for myself, I took this journey." Kawapit said he discovered along the journey that others also shared a similar grief. "I thought I was alone in my grief when I first started out," he said. "I found that they were griev-ing for their own family, for the brother that they lost." There was also Abby Masty, 11, who joined with the original walkers in honour of murdered and missing Indigenous women after she had a dream about walk-ing down a trail on a sunny day out on the land. "My mom asked me why I wanted to walk. I said, 'I want to help people because of all the women that are suffering and Elders'" . . . "Women need to heal and as a nation we can heal together."[17]

When the speeches were over, the drumming started. The marchers and their supporters joined in a large and enthusiastic Round Dance, covering much of the lawn in front of the Canadian Parliament. The symbolism, the courage, and the determination were powerful.

Several things stand out about the Journey of Nishiyuu. Sustained media coverage—and a well-developed social media campaign—fol-lowed the walkers as they made their way south. The national news programs provided regular updates on the group. It was, after all, a great story: soft-spoken but determined young people from isolated northern communities few Canadians had even heard about were braving intense winter conditions to make a peaceful march to Ottawa to bring their concerns and dreams to the attention of the government. For a country that constantly bemoans the apathy of youth and the unwillingness of young Canadians to engage with public affairs and politics, this was the kind of positive, uplifting story that should have grabbed the attention of non-Aboriginal Canada.

But news stories did not create a groundswell of sympathy. Rather than becoming the iconic journey of Idle No More, Nishiyuu became, instead, just another long and sporadic story line, largely lost in the cacophony of political noise surrounding Idle No More. Canadians like long-distance journeying—from the epic journeys of the voyageurs through to the determined marathon of Terry Fox, from the somber disappointment of Steve Fonyo to the globe-circling drama of Rick Hansen. But in the end, as the walkers got closer and closer to Ottawa, a lack of interest on the part of Canadian citizens stood out. Even Peter Mansbridge's accounts on *The National* were more along the lines of documenting a singular, remarkable act of fortitude by determined young Aboriginal people rather than covering the event as one of national significance. As well, Idle No More groups did not rally to the Nishiyuu walk in a particularly strong manner, largely because their events focused on local issues and not national campaigns. Non-Aboriginal Canadians mostly ignored the event, and only a handful of supporters paid more than passing attention to the march. And so, this admirable walk by a small group of Aboriginal youth inexplicably failed to capture the national imagination.

It was, however, perfectly conceivable, in the context of dozens of Idle No More events collectively drawing thousands of participants, combined with the widespread unhappiness with the Harper government among Canadians as a whole, that the entrance of the young walkers into Ottawa could have been truly triumphant. Their determination was impressive, their peaceful cause worthy, and their commitment to the future praiseworthy. It is difficult and wrong to criticize a march that drew hundreds of media references and that ended with thousands of people celebrating on Parliament Hill, or to suggest that the young people did not achieve their goals when they had walked for two months, across the sub-arctic, in bitterly cold winter weather to deliver a message to the (absent) prime minister and the country.

LONG MARCHES

Long marches, often including dozens if not hundreds of participants, all of them walking together to create a highly visible demand for social justice and change, can be very compelling. Marginalized and often ignored people take to the rails, streets, or highways, looking to draw attention to their cause and support for their movement. The long march is a time-honoured and generally peaceful way of promoting social change.

Indian social activist Mahatma Gandhi led one of the most famous journeys for social change, the Salt March of 1930. This march was held to oppose a new salt tax and, more generally, the oppressive hand of British colonialism in India. Many Indians joined him en route, sparking widespread civil disobedience against British authorities and launching India on a path to independence.

In the early twentieth century in Canada, a series of protest marches were enacted by the Doukhobors, a religious sect with several colonies in the western provinces, demonstrating their frustrations with the Canadian political and legal system. Their protests, which continued into the post–Second World War period, coalesced around a demand for religious freedom and recognition of their communal property rights, and often ended with some of the protestors stripping naked, an act that gained the attention and disapproval of the authorities and the public.

In 1935, in one of the most important protests ever held in Canada, hundreds of unemployed men from western Canada, ignored and seemingly without political support, decided to take their complaints to Ottawa. They jumped on trains heading out from Vancouver, and the movement gathered strength and protestors as it moved eastward. The Government of Canada, unsure of how to deal with the protest, tolerated the On To Ottawa Trek for a short time before deciding to end the journey in violence, with a police attack in Regina, Saskatchewan.

Protest marches have also been undertaken in the United States. The Civil Rights movement, for example, gained great momentum through a series of marches between Selma and Montgomery, Alabama, a distance of more than eighty kilometres. And the 1963 March for Jobs and Freedom, which drew thousands of African Americans and their supporters from across the country, culminated in a mass meeting in Washington, DC—an event highlighted by Martin Luther King's "I Have a Dream" speech.

Two of the most iconic events in Canadian history—Terry Fox's Marathon of Hope (from St. John's, Newfoundland, to its unplanned and tragic end at Thunder Bay, Ontario) and Rick Hansen's Man in Motion around-the-world journey that ended in Vancouver—demonstrated the power of prolonged, physically difficult, and socially motivated undertakings to capture the nation's attention. Fox and Hansen conducted non-political journeys designed to raise public awareness of humanitarian causes rather than to spark political protest.

Others have adopted the long-march concept for political or economic reasons. Farmers in Canada, France, and England, angry with government policies, have organized "marches" of tractors and other farm equipment to deliver stern messages about their frustrations. The tractor protests often draw dozens, if not hundreds, of farmers to the cause, snarling local traffic and making for dramatic television. Truck drivers in Canada, the United States, and other countries have used similar tactics, typically regarding gas prices and regulatory matters.

HISTORICAL ABORIGINAL WALKS: Other long marches have been utterly tragic. The Trail of Tears, as it has come to be known, was the forced removal march in the 1830s of American Indian tribes of the southeastern United States; using military force, the American government relocated these tribal nations by foot to "Indian Territory" in Oklahoma. Thousands of Aboriginal people died along the way. A most sorrowful event, it reminds one of how Aboriginal walks have a historical resonance and weight, entering the collective memory of the continent long ago. But this collective memory of the long walks and marches that have been recorded in North America also include powerful ones that have empowered Aboriginal peoples. In 1972, beginning on the west coast of the United States and ending in Washington, D.C., the Trail of Broken Treaties captured international attention and resulted in some concessions on the part of the United States government.

Done carefully, a prolonged march holds media attention, brings new supporters on board, and forces governments to consider changing course.

Indeed, the marchers did not fail, but the country did. This was a heroic and dramatic walk, a brilliant illustration of the peaceful and constructive approach that Idle No More brought to the challenges facing Aboriginal people in Canada. The march seemed an ideal bridge from the early weeks of the movement, across the chasm created by the national debate about Chief Theresa Spence, to the young Aboriginal people determined to make a difference in the country. The presence of the prime minister could have sent a powerful message to the country that the government was watching and listening to Aboriginal youth. What happened, instead, was depressingly predictable: the Government of Canada maintained a deliberate distance, and while Opposition politicians supported the walkers, their impulse to use the walk to criticize the government at the final rally seemed more partisan than unifying. The warm reception given to the marchers within Parliament recognized their personal and physical achievement but did not culminate in a national acceptance of their cause or endorsement of their dreams for recognition and Canadian attention to the challenges of northern Indigenous peoples. The Journey of Nishiyuu was an opportunity to draw the country together around a remarkable attempt at reconciliation and outreach. The country did not rise to the occasion.

It is tempting to imagine what could have happened. It could have unfolded like this: As the marchers got within a day's walk of the nation's capital, several thousand Aboriginal youth would have joined the march, a coming together of impressive proportions. As they neared the city, thousands of non-Aboriginal supporters would have been waiting, producing one of the largest peaceful marches in the city's history. The coming together of Aboriginal and non-Aboriginal people, united behind the grit, courage, and commitment of a small group of Aboriginal youth, could have brought the Idle No More movement to a glorious moment, giving the nation and the world a glimpse of what the future might hold for the meeting of peoples and cultures in common cause. The rally could have been of such a scale that the country as a whole could not have helped but take notice and taken part: in hundreds of communities across Canada, Aboriginal youth could have derived inspiration from the final stage of the Journey of Nishiyuu and held peaceful celebrations of their own. The sight of hundreds of thousands of Canadians—Aboriginal and non-Aboriginal—united in song, dance, and commitment to a new future could have then signalled a new era in Canadian public life, one that extended, and even perhaps completed, the founding hopes and aspirations of Idle No More.

It is equally tempting to go on with this imagining—envisioning a very different but also potentially constructive response to the arrival of the walkers in Ottawa. Perhaps it could have unfolded in this way: media attention to the Journey of Nishiyuu would have built systematically, demonstrating to Prime Minister Harper and his government that Canadians understood the core message of Idle No More. Worry would have spread throughout the government and amongst the politicians about an Aboriginal movement that had grown beyond the boundaries of electoral politics. Realizing the need to understand and respond to Idle No More and to contain the mounting furor surrounding the journey, Prime Minister Harper would make quiet arrangements to meet with the marchers well before they reached Ottawa. He would drive a couple of hundred kilometres north of the city and, without media coverage or public attention, walk for most of the day with the young Aboriginal activists. The walk would provide him with an opportunity to connect with the marchers and to discuss government plans and priorities. Prime Minister Harper would then return to Ottawa and, in an important press conference, express his admiration for the Aboriginal youth and for the aspirations of Indigenous Canadians. No promises would be made, largely because (and unlike with Chief Spence) the activists pressed no particular cause except for a desire for greater understanding and more openness. It would not be dramatic, and there would be no grand, transformative political statement, but the tenor of the Canadian conversation about Aboriginal issues would have changed perceptibly. A new future would thus become possible.

Unfortunately, neither of these scenarios occurred, as we well know.

What instead became clear, from the lack of response from Prime Minister Harper and the Government of Canada generally, was that the march generated no groundswell of public support or Canada-wide insistence that the government react. It is hard to imagine quite the same convergence of event and non-response: brave and determined young people, engaging in a dramatic and impressively peaceful demonstration that tested their determination and physical abilities, are shunned by the very government they were trying to impress. The Journey of Nishiyuu showed how deep and how far the spirit of Idle No More reached into the hearts and souls of Aboriginal peoples across country. The journey also revealed, no doubt to the dismay of the walkers and those who supported their expedition, that Idle No More had made no comparable penetration into the general Canadian psyche and, perhaps as a consequence, had neither pushed the public nor the Government of Canada into action.

When the Journey of Nishiyuu started, it seemed tailor-made to elevate Idle No More to the next level, to be the single event that pulled the movement above the confusion created by Chief Theresa Spence's fast in Ottawa. How could a country not be moved by such a remarkable and meaningful statement, such an extended demonstration of youthful and Aboriginal determination? It seemed the very embodiment of Indigenous spirit and tradition, a long, challenging march through the Arctic winter undertaken with the sole purpose of alerting the country to the determination of Aboriginal Canadians. The rallies, the speeches, the temporary blockades, the dances, and the singing all seemed to be prelude to what might have been the perfect antidote to the person-centred media event that surrounded Chief Spence.

The Journey of Nishiyuu, in retrospect, marked the symbolic end of Idle No More as a truly national movement, to the extent that it sought to bring together Aboriginal and non-Aboriginal people in common cause to address the root causes of Indigenous marginalization. In the heady early days of Idle No More, exemplified by the

Indigenous and non-Indigenous members of the founding group, the aspiration was to bring Aboriginal and non-Aboriginal Canadians together and to seek collective solutions to both the immediate political challenges of Bill C-45 and the structural barriers that prevented Aboriginal peoples from sharing in national opportunities. Chief Spence's distraction in Ottawa turned the attention toward the intricacies and shortcomings of Aboriginal governance. Of all of the Idle No More activities, the Journey of Nishiyuu provided precisely the high-profile, unthreatening activity that could have drawn all Canadians together.

The journey might have been a symbolic end of one facet of the movement, yet it was not the last of the marches and not the last of Idle No More. The Nishiyuu marchers inspired many people across the country. On March 19, 2013, another march, called "A Sacred Journey for Future Generations," began at Stanley Mission, in north-central Saskatchewan, the walkers heading to Ottawa, a journey of over 3,300 kilometres.[18] It ended on June 21, 2013, in Ottawa. It started with four walkers from Stanley Mission ranging from fourteen to forty-nine years old: Kara Charles, Bruce McKenzie, Joyce McKenzie, and Marge McKenzie. Three others—James Martell, Brad McKenzie, and Charissa Tootoosis—joined in Prince Albert and one more, Nancy Greyeyes, joined in Saskatoon. Three more—Bryan Waciston of Onion Lake, Rueben Roy of Beauval, and Geron Paul of English River—connected with the group in Winnipeg. Sharron Belay from Nipissing First Nation joined in at Thunder Bay. The walkers even outfitted themselves with panda hats, a clear message to Prime Minister Harper who had opted to welcome the Chinese pandas to the zoo rather than meet with the Nishiyuu marchers when they arrived weeks before. Nancy Greyeyes warned Canadian officials that they were out of step with the environment. She warned them of *mistikwân*. "It means big head," she says. "You get too big a head and, you know, it's in history . . . any time humans think they are smarter than god and can out-think god's plan, they're wrong; it's going to come to catastrophic consequences because of it."[19]

Vice-chief Brian Hardlotte of the Prince Albert Grand Council addressed the group during a rally in Winnipeg:

We the leadership are here today to support the walkers from Saskatchewan. . . .[A]s we all know the government of the day has passed legislation . . . that would damage our environment, and our First Nations people all across Canada have opposed this legislation. So, the purpose of this walk, these brave warriors are doing, is that walk to Ottawa. . . . I'd like to thank the Idle No More movement for waking up the leadership, for waking up the grassroots people. . . . But I like to leave with this important message: . . . You possess great determination and you have shown that. You possess great perseverance. You have faced great difficulty already in your walk. You even faced discouragement in your walk. So, as the leadership, leadership across Canada, in Saskatchewan, Manitoba, we encourage you, we encourage you to continue your walk.[20]

Bruce McKenzie, speaking on behalf of the walkers, highlighted their concern for the environment: "As you can see there's a lot at stake. The animals, they don't have a voice. . . . And most importantly our future generations are at stake. Those are the ones that are going to be born into this environmental impact if everything goes through, so we need to bring awareness and bring a voice to our ancestors that did for us in the past."[21]

These walkers, like the ones before them, made it to Ottawa. The journey took a long time. A few opted out, one broke an ankle in northern Ontario, and others joined for parts of the walk. On National Aboriginal Day, June 22, 2013, the walkers from the Prairies covered the final short steps from Victoria Island to Parliament Hill. Other First Nations supporters—including drummers, singers, and dancers—joined them for the triumphant final leg of the journey. They stayed a short time before heading back, planning to meet up with supporters en route. Like the previous long marches, their journey was remarkable, a truly impressive demonstration of commitment. Their undertaking speaks volumes about the determination of Idle No More supporters and the lengths to which they were prepared to go to protest government policy and assert Aboriginal priorities. The participants marvelled at the support and encouragement they received along the walk; they took strength from people who cheered them on.

Equally important, however, was that the majority of people in Canada did not rise to the celebration of "A Sacred Journey for Future Generations," any more than they did for the Nishiyuu marchers. These were remarkable expeditions, launched spontaneously, drawing on the support and encouragement of First Nations along the route. The country has rallied around less impressive and less articulate demonstrations over the years, from the Occupy gatherings to pro-marijuana events to massive demonstrations in Quebec organized to protest tuition-fee hikes for university students. By the spring of 2013, Canadians had started to show Idle No More fatigue. With so many events, so many speeches, so many ideas, and no coordinated effort to build national interest, attention and support faded through the winter, a process aided by the drawn-out Chief Spence fast and the January debacle over the meeting with the prime minister. That the marches did continue demonstrates continued Aboriginal resolve and, more importantly, shows that many young Aboriginal people in Canada remained inspired by Idle No More and the call to peaceful, culturally based, and assertive action.

As I have noted already, the meaning and sustainability of Idle No More remains unclear to many. Because the movement is continuously framed as a protest by the media—kill Bill C-45 (a failure), support Chief Theresa Spence (another flawed and unsuccessful attempt), and force a major change in the policies of the Government of Canada (strike three)—it is easy to write off Idle No More as an impressive, noisy uprising of little lasting significance or consequence.

However, even in January and February of 2013, it was possible to see the lasting impact of Idle No More, which started by changing the perspectives of Aboriginal people and challenging them, individually and collectively, to take greater responsibility for their future and their relationships with non-Aboriginal people. The success of Idle No More should not be measured by the size, number, and continuation of rallies. Idle No More did not initially aspire to be a permanent protest movement. Its genius is that it defies standard conventions and yet is ideally suited for the state, condition, and aspirations of Aboriginal Canadians at this time. What the general public appears to miss is that there is a depth and breadth to Idle No More that is far greater than a handful of rallies, a few passionate speeches, and the occasional traffic disruption.

Idle No More rose from Aboriginal unhappiness with the status quo in Aboriginal and non-Aboriginal politics. People are coming together to express their profound frustration with the long-standing stain of racism, discrimination, poverty, and marginalization that characterizes Aboriginal life in Canada. At the same time, the people behind the movement knew that things are changing. More Aboriginal students are in colleges and universities. Aboriginal businesses are growing in number and success. Aboriginal development corporations have emerged as major players in the national economy. And by this time in Canadian history, there have been significant court victories, including the Haida Nation and Taku River Tlingit decisions (2004) that established the "duty to consult and accommodate" Aboriginal communities.[22] The passage of the United Nations Declaration on the Rights of Indigenous Peoples in 2007, and Canada's belated signature on the document in 2010, have given international credibility to Aboriginal aspirations. An emerging Indigenous middle and professional class has been supporting ever more Indigenous engagement with the mainstream economy, government, and political system.

But the empowerment of Aboriginal individuals had made the pain and suffering of Indigenous communities even more egregious and frustrating. Idle No More sought, therefore, not simply to protest but more so to galvanize Aboriginal people, and not just the new professional and business elites, but all of the people and all of the communities. It was a call to take control of the future and reject poverty and marginalization as an inevitable aspect of Aboriginal life. To this end, in mid-February 2013, students and community representatives gathered at the Idle No More Education Teach-In at the Kenjgewin Teg Educational Institute on Manitoulin Island. As part of the activity, participants wrote their thoughts about Idle No More on cue cards, which were then captured on a video. The statements, representing Aboriginal and non-Aboriginal thoughts and aspirations, spoke directly to the broader values of the movement, focusing more on process and long-term change than short-term politics and protests. The cue cards included a wide variety of comments:

"You are the change. Believe you're the change. Be the change."

"Idle No More is about <u>human</u> rights & democracy! Interested yet?"

"My heart, my children, my future. I am IDLE NO MORE!"

"Stop Genocide through Legislation."

"No Corporate Nation."

"Our rights, our children, our land, our water, our community!"

"Bill C-45. Look, learn, protect our waters."

"Honour our treaties."

"We teach our children we're all the same colour inside."

"Let us all open our minds to each other's stories."

"Stop Harper from destroying our land."

"Free Mother Earth. Show love, show respect."

"Grassroots leadership in its purest form."[23]

While non-Aboriginal observers focused on the direct political consequences of Idle No More, the movement itself sought long-term change. At another deliberately introspective event at a meeting of the Songhees and Esquimalt First Nations near Victoria, British Columbia, people gathered to strategize, draw strength, and support one another in the belief that they could change the future. Participants were asked to address a single question: "What does Idle No More mean to you?" As with the teach-in on Manitoulin Island, the answers given on Vancouver Island speak to the sense of Indigenous empowerment, pride, and gritty determination that had swept across the country:

> PERSON 1: "Idle No More is an opportunity for people to come and meet with us, talk with us and understand our issues. A lot of people don't understand that we as Native people are governed by the Indian Act. The Indian Act was written in 1857, something like that, and it still, it still rules us. It still governs what it is we can and cannot do. People think that we're just kind of free-spirited Native people but we're not. We live on reserves and reserves are restricted. We don't even own the land. The land is actually owned by the government."

> PERSON 2: "First of all, I think a chance to follow the leadership of Indigenous people who are standing up for our water and our air and our environment and work with them. I think it's a tremendous opportunity. But beyond that selfish perspective, that starting point, I think it's also, it's an opportunity for restorative justice because we've had a lot of apologies to Indigenous people, but apologies don't mean a lot. And I think that starts with affirming the treaty rights of Indigenous people, affirming the constitutional rights of Indigenous people in Section 35 of the Constitution. That's what this movement is about."

> PERSON 3: "I'm glad to see that so many people are passionate and that we're coming together in that way of the eighth fire, as children of the eighth fire. As the Hopis call us, the rainbow race of people, the rainbow warriors.[24] And we're really fighting for clean water for those grandkids that haven't come and the great-grandkids of those great-grandkids that haven't come. Idle No More—never be idle. Never be idle. I'm homeland security. How can I be idle?"

PERSON 4: "So, Idle No More is an international rising of all peoples, all colours, all races. We invite you
to walk with us for a better day, a better life for everyone and to start treating the earth with respect because
she is our mother, she is who sustains all life. [Someone
asks, "What does it mean for us to walk together?"] To
me, it means that it's part of the prophecy that all people rise. The earth would be so sick that we need to all
stand together as one people. We're from the human
race. What it means is we're walking towards a better
world. We have got to stop the crooked politicians and
corporations that are destroying the earth. And we
need to get started. It's very important work."[25]

The comments emphasized the importance of community, coming together, standing up for the environment, and finding common
causes between Indigenous and non-Indigenous peoples. To the extent that these commentators captured the response of the broader meeting and those Canadians who were watching Idle No More
closely, the movement was pulling people in the right directions.

Idle No More founders Jessica Gordon (along with her "little activist," ten-month-old daughter Robinson Gracie Watson) and Sheelah
McLean spoke at the People's Social Forum in Ottawa on January 26,
2013. There were speeches and a question-and-answer period at the
end. As Gordon observed, "Anything that we have done from the very
beginning has been from the heart. It's for our people. Not only Indigenous people but all of Canada, all of Turtle Island as well. Speaking from the heart that we are in this together. . . . I will never say that
I speak for the people. I listen. I pass along any kind of information
I have to them, as well. And I seek assistance for people. In a humble
way, I know that we do not have answers and we do need help. And I
look forward to moving ahead."[26]

McLean offered important insights into the movement when she
commented that she was interested in:

[b]uilding consciousness in Canadians about Indigenous sovereignty and Indigenous rights and that this
is Indigenous land and consciousness about what's

happening to our environment. You can see none of us are experts in social movements, this is a grassroots movement. . . . You can see how leadership activated across Canada. And, I mean, we started in Saskatoon knowing that we wanted to take the petitions . . . and take the ideas and get as many Canadians to understand these bills as we possibly could. But we also recognize that these bills are symbolic of something much bigger and a long history of this happening across this continent.[27]

Gordon clearly believed that Idle No More was a very different kind of movement:

Maybe Idle No More has grown so globally . . . because there are the grassroots people that never had that chance to go on board with any of these other activist movements and social movements. . . . They didn't know how to . . . become active. Now because of Idle No More, they say, "Oh, okay, it's just the regular Joe that's able to, you know, to coordinate an event, coordinate a rally." So, I believe that, too, is the reason why it's gotten so big. . . . It's everybody that is able to contribute, and I think that's the beauty of it. . . . And it doesn't just have to be the seasoned activists. . . . We're a living testament to that, too, because I've never stood in front of . . . this type of forum before, and this is an amazing feeling.[28]

The forum provided two of the founders with an opportunity to reflect on what had been a remarkable few months. The women did not push themselves forward as traditional leaders; they maintained the pattern of highlighting the movement rather than their roles. They understood—and appreciated—that they had tapped into a deep vein of frustration and pride, determination and anxiety about the future. Their observations make it clear that they were surprised by the scale of the Idle No More movement but not by the intensity of the Aboriginal support. Rarely in the past have movements continued without charismatic and managerial leaders; Idle No More founders, however, trusted in the passion of local organizers and the people's commitment to cultural resilience and Indigenous rights.

In many respects, the first two months of 2013 represented the high point of the Idle No More movement. By this time, Chief Spence and her protest were no longer a distraction. Many more meetings, national and international dialogue, continued media attention, and nervous concern among governments across the country kept the movement's core message alive and demonstrated that Aboriginal people were far from content with the status quo. The passage of Bill C-45 in December 2012 had already diffused the movement's focus so that it had taken on a long list of political and cultural grievances. This, in turn, shifted the emphasis from immediate political action to broader social and cultural mobilization, a fundamental strength of Idle No More. That the people came to the rallies, Round Dances, and other events demonstrated the staying power of a movement that most commentators thought would last but a few weeks. At the same time, the movement's founders and key organizers maintained the values of Idle No More, refusing national efforts to turn them into politicians and focusing their efforts on collective education and long-term capacity building.

Idle No More was focused on three things: ensuring that Indigenous peoples understood the root causes of Aboriginal marginalization, mobilizing Aboriginal people to defend their interests, and maintaining a commitment to peaceful and culturally focused demonstrations of Aboriginal determination. The other elements—building common cause with non-Aboriginals, defeating Bill C-45, criticizing Prime Minister Harper, disrupting non-Aboriginal communities, or supporting specific Aboriginal political processes—were not as fundamentally important. Even though the movement's focus was not widely recognized and the public was largely nonplussed and losing interest, at this point in early 2013 Idle No More remained remarkably on course.

This is why: even as Idle No More was starting to lose public attention, it was becoming ingrained in the lives and minds of Aboriginal peoples in Canada. By March 2013, Idle No More was not so much a political protest as it was the largest and most sustained affirmation of Aboriginal determination and culture in Canadian history. For the people behind the movement, including the founders and the many hundreds of young and not-so-young community leaders across the country inspired by each other's words and actions, Idle No More was more about changing the confidence and commitment of Aboriginal people rather than achieving any particular short-term, political agenda. Idle No More was not about leading an uprising but about empowering Indigenous people to determine their own futures, rediscover their own voices, and find strength in knowing that Aboriginal peoples and communities across the country shared in their vision of the future.

Those who saw the waning national interest in Idle No More as a sign of the failure or collapse of the movement had it wrong. Idle No More had, by February and March 2013, already started to change the mindsets and actions of Aboriginal peoples and the country as a whole. Far from failing, Idle No More had done far more than anyone would have imagined just months before at the end of 2012. Just as the movement was becoming more routine in the minds of outsiders, it became more complex, weaving itself into the political and social fabric of the nation with a speed and reach far greater that anyone would have thought possible. As the winter drew to a close—always slowly and unevenly across the country—expectations were high for the expansion and strengthening of Idle No More. After all, if the movement could mobilize thousands of people in hundreds of events through the winter months, surely the warm, summer weather would lend itself to even greater activism.

SIX
WHAT HAPPENED TO SOVEREIGNTY SUMMER?

A s the winter of 2012–2013 wound down, authorities braced for the further radicalization of Aboriginal peoples and acceleration of Idle No More protests. All the signs were there: successful rallies, long marches, and a growing number of outspoken critics of the country—particularly Pamela Palmater—presenting themselves as spokespeople for Idle No More or as inheritors of the movement's spirit and values. The Government of Canada had stared down Chief Theresa Spence, and even the intervention of National Chief Shawn Atleo had wrung only the smallest concessions from Prime Minister Harper. It hardly seemed possible. Mass protests, well-behaved rallies, clearly articulated anger with the country as a whole, and still no major changes in policy, no new funding commitments, and no olive branches extended to the Indigenous peoples of Canada. Just wait, the quiet rumble had it, for the coming Sovereignty Summer, a phrase coined by the founders to describe the months to come.[1]

Yet the founders of Idle No More made no threats for the spring and summer of 2013. As before, and in a manner that defied easy political explanation, the four founders remained remarkably low-key, participating in many events but staying out of the spotlight, focusing more on supporting and educating individual coordinators than playing the traditional leadership roles that many people wanted them to assume. The national media continued to have difficulty coping with the "oddity" that was Idle No More, even though the founders and regional coordinators now continued to be clear about the movement's intent: Aboriginal empowerment and a renewed national commitment to Aboriginal legal and treaty rights.

The open arms of Idle No More invited Aboriginal peoples to organize their own events, make their own statements, and pursue distinctive agendas and priorities—which made the movement seem complicated and confusing to the media and general public. Still, the attention given to Idle No More ensured larger and more attentive audiences than ever before for Aboriginal people speaking out against the government or general patterns of discrimination. Many Aboriginal Canadians found their voices, and others, whose voices were already strong, took the opportunity to speak, too: from outspoken Manitoban Chief Terry Nelson to Professor Pamela Palmater, from the Anishinaabe musician and broadcaster Wab Kinew to lesser-known regional figures. The speakers ranged from conciliatory to radical, from the cautious to the explosive. The media, acting incautiously, freely associated speakers with the core of the movement, even though (as with Chief Theresa Spence) the connection was, at best, tenuous.

But the voices did seem to be building to a crescendo. The frustrations were clear. The continued lack of government response gave more credence to the Aboriginal protests and seemed to confirm the Indigenous assertion that politicians and civil servants were uncaring and unbending. The progression was auspicious: from teach-ins to rallies, fasts to marches on Parliament Hill, political speeches to education sessions. It seemed that participants in the movement were gathering the strength necessary for a sustained effort. With anger building, with more and more dramatic statements about future actions, the more extreme statements rang only too true. The Government of Canada was not listening. Change was not happening. Bill C-45 had not been stopped. The United Nations Declaration on the Rights of Indigenous Peoples was not being applied in Canada. More action was needed—urgently.

Observers preferred to view the movement as First Nations versus Government of Canada, a view that missed much of what was going on across the country. For example, on April 1, 2013, a small rally took place on the roadside in Sagkeeng, Manitoba. The placards and signs highlighted a different set of priorities: "Big Projects, Big Dollars – Accountability"; "If people are afraid to speak out on issues in Sagkeeng, then something is wrong"; "Chief chooses Jets game over people's interests"; "The Indian Act chiefs are part of the problem, NOT part of the SOLUTION"; and, of course, "Idle No More." This event focused on demands for a new local chief and council, with speakers asking, "Where is our money?" One person's sign read, "A vote for our chief is a vote for Harper :("; and another, "Poverty – vs – Chief." A speaker argued, "Indian Act chiefs are the problem, not part of the solution. Remember that, people. We want change! We need accountability not backdoor deals! . . . [O]ur people have nothing. Our youth have nowhere to play but the roads and the ditch. Something is not right. We need change in this community. We want our leaders to fight for our people, not to fight against us." In this instance, the chant that rang out over the crowd—"Silence no more"—was directed at local First Nations politicians and not just the Government of Canada.[2]

Outside observers also often missed Idle No More's commitment to peaceful and non-aggressive action. From the outset, the movement had warned against violence, disavowed direct action, asked participants to avoid disrupting non-Aboriginal communities and people, and avoided interfering with economic activity. The kinds of protests that garnered attention and generated severe anti-Aboriginal backlash at Caledonia, Oka, and other Indigenous uprisings were, in the spirit of Idle No More, to be avoided at all times. Groups that blocked roads or railways were encouraged by local authorities and Idle No More representatives to pull them down. Round Dances in malls were short and non-disruptive. Reading through thousands of pages of newspaper articles and viewing videos of hundreds of Idle No More events, one finds there is little evidence of angry outbursts and threatening language on the part of participants. When it was present, it was most often on the part of observers, who directed anger and threats against the Idle No More participants. This was an impressive aspect of Idle No More: the remarkable peacefulness and gentleness of the thousands of participants. Peace is quiet, however, and Canadians chose not to hear the silence. They listened, instead, for the noise of the radical few within the movement, the critics who assailed the government for ignoring them and the public for racism, those who cajoled, threatened, and spoke ominously of the protests destined to come in the spring and summer of 2013.

In June 2013, Idle No More launched the ideas behind the Sovereignty Summer campaign, which, despite the threats mentioned above, promised continued peace, but did encourage "bolder" and more "direct" actions:

> Officially launched on June 21 by Idle No More and Defenders of the Land, a network of Indigenous communities in land struggle, Sovereignty Summer is a campaign of coordinated non-violent direct actions to promote Indigenous rights and environmental protection in alliance with non-Indigenous supporters.
>
> Sovereignty Summer actions aim to bring attention to the Harper government agenda, which undermines the rights of Indigenous Peoples, Canadian citizens, and the ongoing policies disrupting Indigenous people's lives—such as land claims, third party management, and no free and prior consent to development on Indigenous lands. We are in a critical time where lives, lands, waters and Creation are at-risk and they must be protected.
>
> The Harper government is moving quickly to pass the suite of legislation (C-45, C-428, S-2, S-6, S-8, S-212, C-27, and the First Nation Education Act) that undermines the treaties, our nation-to-nation relationship and Indigenous sovereignty, which is the last stand to protect our lands. Idle No More calls on non-Indigenous people to join Indigenous communities in coordinated non-violent direct actions in the summer. Alternatives will only come to life if we escalate our actions, taking bold non-violent direct action that challenges the illegitimate power of corporations who dictate government policy.[3]

The statement included a comprehensive list of expectations for government action, a collection of aspirations that reflected the growing complexity of the movement:

> Our demands are clear and in accordance with the principles of coexistence and mutual respect between Indigenous and non-Indigenous Peoples. We demand that Canada, the provinces, and the territories:
>
> Repeal provisions of Bill C-45 (including changes to the Indian Act and Navigable Waters Act, which infringe on environmental protections, Aboriginal and Treaty rights) and abandon all pending legislation which does the same.
>
> Deepen democracy in Canada through practices such as proportional representation and consultation on all legislation concerning collective rights and environmental protections, and include legislation which restricts corporate interests.
>
> In accordance with the United Nations Declaration on the Rights of Indigenous Peoples' principle of free, prior, and informed consent, respect the right of Indigenous peoples to say no to development on their territory.
>
> Cease its policy of extinguishment of Aboriginal Title and recognize and affirm Aboriginal Title and Rights, as set out in Section 35 of Canada's constitution and recommended by the Royal Commission on Aboriginal Peoples.
>
> Honour the spirit and intent of the historic Treaties. Officially repudiate the racist Doctrine of Discovery and the Doctrine of Terra Nullius, and abandon their use to justify the seizure of Indigenous Nations' lands and wealth.
>
> Actively resist violence against women and hold a national inquiry into missing and murdered Indigenous women and girls, and involve Indigenous women in the design, decision-making process and implementation of

this inquiry, as a step toward initiating a comprehensive and coordinated national action plan.

Indigenous communities have the right to determine the development on their traditional and treaty territories. In defending their right to say "No" to unwanted development, First Nations like Barriere Lake, KI [Quebec], and many others are advancing alternatives that help us re-imagine our relationship to the environment. Across the country, people are increasingly supporting First Nations who are trying to protect lands, waters and air for everyone, and to win recognition of marine protections, of sustainable forestry, of local, just economies, and of the principle that we must respect the environment that we are a part of.

We are calling on non-Indigenous people to join Indigenous communities in coordinated non-violent direct actions in the summer. Alternatives will only come to life if we escalate our actions, taking bold non-violent direct action that challenges the illegitimate power of corporations who dictate government policy.[4]

A new image of Aboriginal engagement was emerging, in part through the participation of Indigenous communities in resource development and also through the growing expression of Indigenous intent included in Idle No More. The message, while not completely consistent, was that Aboriginal people wanted to protect the environment. Many Indigenous communities were prepared to participate in resource development, provided Aboriginal rights were recognized, Indigenous peoples played a major role in project approval and environmental oversight, and if there were appropriate returns in terms of jobs and business opportunities. This more conciliatory approach was largely missed because of the assertiveness of Idle No More and the tendency of many non-Aboriginal people to hear only those parts of the Indigenous comments that they expected.

The idea of a Sovereignty Summer worried the general public in Canada. Those with long memories recalled the 1990 Oka stand-off in Quebec and the ongoing land dispute in Caledonia, Ontario, which started in 2006 and was still active in 2014. Some simple mathematics: large-scale Aboriginal protests over land and governance rights multiplied by the reach and intensity of Idle No More rallies equaled one heck of a summer of disruption. There was substance to the concerns. After all, in asserting their Aboriginal and treaty rights, Indigenous Canadians had for almost half a year been laying the foundation for a more expansive demand for government action. Aboriginal people had mounted a sustained campaign through the harshest of Canadian seasons, demonstrated by hundreds of separate events and hundreds of thousands of tweets, e-mails, and Facebook entries. Indigenous youth, adults, and Elders gathered under often-frigid winter conditions, sustaining their energy and commitment through difficult circumstances. Logic suggested that the spring and summer months would bring even more activity.

Non-Aboriginal people continued to be active and welcome participants in Idle No More, though they were not dominant or even always prominent. One example of an event in the spring of 2013 was a rally held on April 5 at Simon Fraser University's Convocation Mall in Burnaby, British Columbia—the "Idle No More Rally at sfu." The rally was co-organized by Lindsay Wainwright and Loryn Blower (White Turtle Warrior) and sponsored by the First Nations Student Association and supported by Simon Fraser Public Interest Research Group, as well as the Simon Fraser University's Women's Centre and the Indigenous Student Centre. The event's coordinators and campus organizations invited the university community, Aboriginal and non-Aboriginal people alike, to the rally, to show solidarity with Aboriginal Canadians. The call to the rally spoke to the declining public attention to the Aboriginal cause: "The Idle No More movement may not be front-and-centre in national media coverage right now, but that doesn't mean Aboriginal students, staff and alumni at Simon Fraser University have forgotten about it."[5] As Lindsay Wainwright commented, "We want to educate the general sfu population about Aboriginal peoples today, our histories, and also to raise awareness about the many common misconceptions that are prevalent in our society about them. . . . We believe that decolonization in Canada needs to be a group process that involves both Indigenous people and settlers. We want to help the sfu community to understand what decolonization means and why it's important. Our hope is that people who attend the rally will be inspired to take action and learn more."[6]

The SFU rally included the standard appeals to historical understanding and recognition of the cultural depredations of First Nations people. Blower, a Métis woman known by her traditional name White Turtle Warrior, and a student at Simon Fraser University, said:

> In order to teach about the cultural assimilation and subjugation of First Nations individuals in Canada, we're Idle No More and we want to know more. We also want others to know more. . . . Are we all living under a rock, sheltered by our own denial? Did this system of colonial assimilation work so well? It must! People are still disgustingly racist. It may not be apparent in day-to-day life, or maybe it occurs as the norm, and we take it for granted. Take a look at the comments section of online news articles today—it is quite revealing of people's true thoughts and intent where harsh words are felt with 'ordinary' Canadians saying things such as, "all natives should be shot."[7]

Lisa Yellow-Quill, an Anishinaabe woman and a noted anti-colonial, non-violent community activist who works to end violence against Aboriginal women and girls, agreed. Yellow-Quill, whose traditional name is Blue Thunderbird Woman / Strong Medicine Woman Standing, added to White Turtle Warrior's comments, saying, "The policy was to eradicate us from this territory like we were fauna, like we were in the way of progression. Like we did not, we were not a necessity. The treaties that are in place today, you know, were not a land surrendered. Those were coerced. First Nations people were starved, you know, they were imprisoned, they were hurting when those treaties were signed. They were signed under duress. And today those treaties are still being negotiated under duress. [A man in the crowd yells, "Shame!"] Shame!"[8]

Leading up to the promised Sovereignty Summer, Idle No More became less about government policies—although condemnations of Prime Minister Harper and his government continued—and more focused on collective education and the declaration of cultural determination. The much-hated omnibus bill had been passed into law. Waging a campaign against a bill that was already enacted had little potential for success. So the focus shifted from arguing against the legislation to using the bill as a means of demonstrating the fundamental unfairness of the Canadian system toward Indigenous peoples. Politically, the goal had shifted from a struggle over a piece of legislation to an attempt to revisit the fundamental structures of the country.

At an April 19, 2013, meeting in London, Ontario, event organizer Elizabeth Wemigwans addressed the group: "It's about our life, our future generation." She continued, speaking about the youth standing together in Idle No More: "It is just that time for them where they . . . want to speak up and they don't want to sit behind and not do anything because they see their parents . . . they see their friends and they see everybody else stepping up and standing up for what's right."[9] At a comparable rally in Edmonton on May 1, which drew between eighty and one hundred people, Shannon Houle, a Grade 4 teacher from Saddle Lake Cree Nation, offered similar views: "As you all know, Canada is not a very . . . kind environment, therefore we have to work together. We have to unite. We have to respect each other and honour each other. . . . As we stand here united, we need to remember we are borrowing all of this from our children. It's our responsibility to educate our children, others, and ourselves, and how we're going to save all that is familiar. We need to rethink our relationship with Mother Earth."[10] Houle included a critique of government policy in her speech, but she clearly prioritized maintaining solidarity and continued engagement within the Aboriginal movement.

Through the spring, the Canadian public seemed curiously unmoved by some of the most remarkable and peaceful public displays of sustained discontent in decades, if not generations. Some of the most affecting and sustained demonstrations were those conducted by youth—the long marches, which began in the cold months of January and extended into the spring and summer of 2013. The Journey of the Nishiyuu is one example, but consider another walk launched in Winnipeg in late March by fifteen First Nations young people who arrived in Ottawa on May 13. This group was inspired by the youth who walked from Bloodvein and Hollow Water to Winnipeg in January, and the other Manitoba group that marched from Jackhead First

Nation to Winnipeg in February. The group had conducted three previous marches before deciding to walk through wintry conditions over two thousand kilometres in forty-five days, from Winnipeg to Ottawa. They were united under the Youth for Lakes (Y4L) banner. They hoped to maintain pressure on the Government of Canada regarding treaty rights and the protection of waterways, seeking as well to demonstrate that young Aboriginal people shared adult concerns about the environment and the status of Indigenous peoples in Canada.

One of the marchers, Victor Thomas, had been part of a week-long February march from Skownan First Nation. On March 28, Skownan First Nation Chief Cameron Catcheway sent off the fifteen young walkers with strong words: "These young people, showing great leadership and bravery, should be commended for doing their part in protecting Mother Earth."[11] Followers on Facebook and Twitter kept track, offering words of encouragement as they went. Caelah Hardisty spoke out: "I ask kindly that my friends and their friends light a quick smudge every morning at 8:45 am or [offer] a nice prayer for our brother and sisters walking to Ottawa for Youth for Lakes, to ensure them safe travels and protection against negative minds. They're walking for every individual in Canada."[12] Idle No More founder Jessica Gordon noted that the marches powerfully represented "our culture and our connection to the land."[13]

When they arrived in Ottawa, they walked to the now-symbolic Victoria Island and were welcomed by drumming, prayers, and speeches by Claudette Commanda of the Algonquin Nation and Grand Chief Derek Nepinak of Manitoba. When the youth walkers arrived at Parliament Hill, they found a Bangladeshi protest under way. The Youth for Lakes walkers encouraged the Bangladeshi crowd to join them, but they left.

The Parliament Hill event included greetings from Grand Elder Raymond Robinson; David Kawapit, one of the Journey of the Nishiyuu walkers; and Kluane Adamek and Jeff Copenace of the Assembly of First Nations. After a round of speeches to a disappointingly small crowd of a few dozen people, and an open microphone, they left for a wrap-up dinner at a friendship centre. Grand Chief Ray Robinson welcomed the marchers:

These youth have realized where they belong in this order of life. That [they] are the youngest, and [they] need
to preserve the waters, the lands, the resources. And
they are doing it, and I cannot be prouder as an Elder
that our youth, as the prophecy was foretold, that the
seventh generation are going to light the fire, and the
youth are leading with the igniting of the fire, and this
is just another example. . . . This is a proud moment for
all Canada, and all Canada should extend their grati-
tude . . . to all of these young people who have risen to
take leadership and to take charge and to be part of the
entirety as a nation.[14]

Ben Raven (Running Buffalo), one of the marchers, spoke to the
absence of Prime Minister Harper: "You continue to do this to our
people, not just our people, your own. This is not for Indigenous people: we're doing this for you; we're walking for you because you won't.
We're talking for you 'cause you won't. That's what we're here to do.
We're here to bring that awareness across this country. It's going to
happen. Your time is coming."[15] He continued, speaking to the deep
sense of loss and determination that animated Idle No More: "Me, being an urban Native, born and raised in Winnipeg, Manitoba, I lost
my culture. . . . I didn't understand the culture, but I slowly started
to pick it up, and I heard my calling. What Idle No More did for a lot
of our people, it shook us to the core; it allowed us to really feel and
understand who we are. Because when you understand your culture,
you understand yourself, and I got to learn that. When I walked this
journey, it taught me so many different aspects of life and about our
Mother [Earth]."[16]

The speeches at the friendship centre were long, passionate, and
articulate. The sense of accomplishment was palpable, as was the
pride and sense of community the marchers had created and shared
during their long journey. The walkers spoke for themselves and for
future generations. They celebrated Aboriginal cultures and mourn-
ed the lingering impact of colonial policies, residential schools, and
marginalization. They knew, from conversations across half the country, that other First Nations shared their frustrations and dreams for
autonomy and greater partnership with non-Aboriginal Canadians.

There were strong words for the prime minister and the Government of Canada, but the participants were as hopeful as they were angry.

If there was sadness during this day of celebration, it was because so few participated. Like the Nishiyuu walkers, Youth for Lakes attracted only a small gathering on Parliament Hill. Indeed, protest inertia had set in. And yet the rally, distributed via live-streaming video, attracted more than two thousand online hits from around the world:

Y4L RALLY, PARLIAMENT HILL, 13 MAY 2013 – 15 MAY
GLOBAL AUDIENCE

01. Canada—1465	15. Australia—3
02. USA—324	16. Hong Kong—2
03. Netherlands—66	17. India—2
04. Dominican Republic—31	18. Italy—2
05. Spain—29	19. Turkey—2
06. Germany—15	20. Switzerland—1
07. UK—15	21. Finland—1
08. Czech Republic—13	22. Portugal—1
09. France—13	23. Ukraine—1
10. Romania—9	24. Belgium—1
11. Bosnia & Herzegovina—4	25. Algeria—1
12. Ghana—4	26. Pakistan—1
13. Brazil—4	27. Lithuania—1
14. Sweden—3	28. Poland—1[17]

The survey of data reveals that the live stream attracted 834 unique viewers who, combined, watched almost 45,000 minutes of the Ottawa activities. While the rally's online audience was not as immense as those for the online videos of protests in Egypt during the Arab Spring in early 2011 or Occupy Wall Street—which, by September 26, 2011 (at the height of the movement), had served 231,000 people a total of 14.4 million minutes of live video coverage[18]—the worldwide public engagement of the Youth for Lakes rally was significant, if far from overwhelming. What really stood out, though, were the two parallel responses to this rally and Idle No More. First, there was what appeared to be rally fatigue from Idle No More supporters, who, by this time, had been observing and participating in hundreds of events for more than half a year. Second, non-Aboriginal Canadians were (once again) almost completely unmoved by what was, by any measure, an impressive and heart-warming accomplishment. As time went on—and here I fully recognize that there were hundreds of non-Indigenous peoples who supported individual events—non-Aboriginal interest turned from mild curiosity to tolerance and, by early summer 2013, to what can only be described as boredom. If First Nations peoples needed proof that they were on their own, the steadily declining attention to Idle No More activities in the media and the general public sealed the deal.

However, the low attendance at the Youth for Lakes event in Ottawa did not mark the nadir of Idle No More. Events continued into the summer, but they were less dramatic and less systematic than in the past. The nation paid less attention. Flash mobs no longer surprised people. Round Dances had become commonplace. The passionate words and strong commitments, still empowering to Aboriginal participants, had lost their impact, their capacity to shock, motivate, or inspire most non-Aboriginal Canadians. Still, the continuing activities were not tiny, and Aboriginal interest remained solid. For example, on June 21, 2013, National Aboriginal Day, Idle No More Québec and the Cercle des Premières Nations de l'Université du Québec à Montréal (First Nations Circle of the University of Quebec at Montreal) drew hundreds of people to a large and vocal rally in Montreal. Groups represented at the event included: Quebec Native Women; the Coalition for the Rights of Indigenous Peoples in Quebec; Amnesty International (Canada's francophone branch); Greenpeace Quebec; Quebec Women's Federation; the Association for Student Union Solidarity; the Montreal Central Council of the Confederation of National Trade Unions; the David Suzuki Foundation; the Quebec Public Interest Research Group at the Université du Québec à Montréal ; the Réseau québécois des groupes écologistes; Nature Quebec; the Rivers Foundation; Friends of the Earth Quebec; the Project Accompaniment Quebec-Guatemala (Todos por Guatemala); the Native Youth Sexual Health Network; and S.O.S. Poigan. As a young woman, identified as Megan, said, "I'd like to tell everybody that, no matter what kind of language you speak, whether it's verbal language or visual language or dance, find your language, find your voice, and speak as loud as you can because we're idle no more!"[19]

Although it had become old hat to some in Canada, Idle No More had become the national Aboriginal brand, instantly recognized for organized, peaceful, cultural, and passionate events. Many regional and national reasons for Indigenous assemblies—ranging from National Aboriginal Day to the release of research on nutritional experiments on Indigenous peoples published by Dr. Ian Mosby of Guelph University—operated under the Idle No More umbrella. Dr. Mosby's report, for example, was shared across the country on an online Spreecast. Demands that the Government of Canada "Honour the Apology," and push forward on reconciliation arising out of the residential school settlement, were connected to Idle No More events.[20] Organizers in Whitehorse, as well, connected the movement to residential school issues during July 25, 2013, events. The Facebook page associated with the Whitehorse rally hinted at the declining power of the repeated call to protest.[21] Some 1,500 people were invited to the event. Only fifty-three indicated they planned to attend and another twenty-one suggested that they might participate.

Idle No More banners, along with placards protesting northern resource development, greeted Prime Minister Harper on August 19, 2013, when he visited Hay River, Northwest Territories. As one of the organizers stated about the group's presence:

> [This] is symbolic of some of the goals that Idle No More has, and we have, together, as people in our community here. . . . [We] want to see protection over our waters and rivers like we've had in the past, and for Aboriginal and sovereignty rights that Aboriginal people in Canada have, and what we've said is [that] this is a peaceful event, they've all been peaceful and I'm so thankful for that. . . . I have asked if Mr. Harper would stop and talk to us and so if he does Joanne is going to say a few words to him, and we said, you know, he is our Prime Minister and that is our government so we will be respectful towards him. . . . I know that the grannies will conduct themselves in a respectful manner. That's why they're always here.[22]

The Prime Minister did not stop to talk.

By the time of this event at Hay River, it was clear that Sovereignty Summer had not happened on the scale and with the intensity many had expected. Yes, events happened across the nation during the summer of 2013, but many were small, and public attention had sharply diminished. Still, the concept remained alive, the Aboriginal passions intact, and the determination to change Canadian policy firmly entrenched. In the summer and through the fall, Aboriginal people and their supporters continued to gather, to celebrate, and to announce their determination to change Canada in their favour. The events were different, though, and even more than ever, they took on the character of their local communities, organizers, and specific themes.

At a Saskatoon youth rally, held on September 5, 2013, a small group of drummers and singers gathered in a community park. The presence of police cars raised concerns that they would be shut down, leading one singer to declare, "You know, don't let them intimidate you. This is your country, this is your land and your territory. [Tapping on a drum, cheering.] You are allowed here. Your voice, your drum, your song. We'll wake this community up."[23] At this event, as with others, the police found themselves caught between their need to maintain public order—including responding to complaints about noise, road blockages, and the like—and the desire to avoid inflaming sensitive situations. Throughout the Idle No More movement, the police opted to avoid confrontation and to work instead to ease tensions.

The movement continued into the fall. On October 7, 2013, Idle No More hosted close to fifty events in Canada and internationally to recognize the 250th anniversary of the Royal Proclamation of 1763, one of the most important documents in Canada in terms of defining Indigenous rights. As Clayton Thomas-Muller of the Mathias Colomb Cree Nation in northern Manitoba, and a frequent organizer of Idle No More events, noted: "We are using this founding document of this country and its anniversary to usher in a new era of reconciliation of Canada's shameful colonial history, to turn around centuries of neglect and abuse of our sacred and diverse nations."[24] Edmonton was one of many communities that hosted a gathering that day.[25] In Saskatoon, a flash mob danced across the University of Saskatchewan campus—the intellectual hearth of Idle No More—and ended with handshaking ceremonies designed to celebrate and promote reconciliation.[26]

One of the largest October 7 events was a youth meeting in Victoria that attracted close to 250 participants to the grounds of the British Columbia Legislature, providing dramatic evidence of the staying power of Idle No More. Speakers talked about Aboriginal identity, historical injustices, white oppression, and the negative consequences of resource development. Huge banners criticizing pipeline plans and demanding attention to Aboriginal rights waved over the large and vocal crowd. The speakers challenged the audience members to rise up against oppression. As an unidentified speaker observed:

> The genocide that has faced our people, the waves of oppressions, the systematic matrixes against us, is still going on today. It's going to continue on after today, and we see it. We see in the academic structures, where they miseducate youth, they miseducate people. Even in the post-secondary world, the miseducation still goes on because they deny us our genocide. They deny us that our ancestors were systematically destroyed. We see this within the laws of legislation, the building right behind us.
>
> The laws that they put up there to strip us of our identity. We see within the policing. [Crowd: "Shame!"] We see it in the policing right now [Crowd: "Shame!"], and it doesn't matter if they're, you know, the Victorian police or it doesn't matter if they're RCMP, we still have our murdered and missing women that are going on right now. [A man: "No More!" A drum beats.] And from these policing agencies, do we hear about a rigorous investigation to uncover this mystery? [Crowd: "No!"] Do we hear it from the Victorian police? [Crowd: "Never!" and "No!"] No! They're denying that responsibility that these women, these human beings, are going missing [Crowd: "Right!"] from one side of Turtle Island to the other. [Crowd: "Shame!" A drum beats.][27]

DEMANDING AN INQUIRY

There is not a direct line between the Idle No More movement and the demands, continuing into 2015, for an inquiry into the large number of murdered and missing Aboriginal women in Canada. But the spirit of Idle No More, the emergent power of Indigenous peoples, is clearly alive in the assertiveness and determination of those pushing for an inquiry.

For several years, Aboriginal peoples across Canada have been agitating for greater attention to the large and growing number of murdered and missing Indigenous women. Much of the effort comes from women who are frustrated with the shocking incidences of violence directed at their sisters, aunts, mothers, and daughters, and the lack of official or general attention to the issue.

The inquiry effort, which draws attention to fundamental injustices in Canada, shares a great deal in common with Idle No More; it is peaceful, quietly insistent, informally coordinated, and largely driven by women, and it has a significant number of non-Aboriginal supporters.

Many non-Aboriginal people underestimate the seriousness and complexity of the inquiry movement. Some commentators observe, correctly, that most of the violence directed at Aboriginal women is inflicted by Aboriginal men. The women behind the inquiry demand know this, often only too well. Just as Idle No More participants criticized Aboriginal and non-Aboriginal political leadership equally, so those demanding an inquiry are equally concerned about non-Aboriginal attacks on women, Aboriginal attacks on women, and the lack of systematic government attention to a serious national problem.

The strength of Idle No More rests in the manner in which it challenged Aboriginal people to organize and speak out in defence of their own interests. Since Idle No More changed the national conversation about Aboriginal issues and mobilized Indigenous peoples to push harder and more publicly for attention to their rights, there have been many examples, local or broader, of Aboriginal people stepping forward to demand the attention of government and the public. In all like-lihood, the power, passion, and determination demonstrated during the height of Idle No More will show up in many future protests, demands, and movements such as this one.

###

*I*dle No More was not about a single issue, even one as complicated as the protest against the omnibus bill. Instead, it was a movement focused on leading Aboriginal people to stand up for themselves and to find strength in collective action. In this instance noted above, where the speaker makes reference to the large number of murdered and missing Aboriginal women, individuals were encouraged to share their concerns about the past, present, and future. While this opening up of the movement made it seem unclear at times, the surfacing of the many and complex issues facing Aboriginal peoples ultimately gave Idle No More additional power and community support. Closing in on a year from the start of Idle No More, the Victoria participants made it clear that their passion had not abated at all; from their perspective, the movement was alive and well. Another speaker commented:

> As the First Peoples of this land, we are standing up with our brothers and sisters. All across this land, in unity we stand and we say, "No more!" [Crowd: "No more!" Cheering.] No more will we be deliberately ignored no matter race, colour, or creed. [Cheering. Drums beat.] No more will we say yes to dirty oil, pipelines, tankers, drilling, and poisoned water. [Cheering and drumming.] I'm here as a front-line woman from the tar sands, whose nation is currently involved in one of the country's highest profile litigations against the Canadian/Alberta governments for over 17,000 treaty violations on our land [Crowd: "Shame!"], encroachment of industry, and we say, "No more!" [Crowd: "No more!"] Harper! [Crowd: "Harper!"][28]

154

The themes were familiar, echoing the comments from the first months of Idle No More. Criticisms of the prime minister and other politicians—British Columbia and Alberta premiers Christy Clark and Alison Redford, in this case—featured prominently, as did calls for government action and attempts to mobilize Aboriginal and non-Aboriginal people to challenge their governments. As the speaker continued, "Today we begin our decolonization. Today we take back what was never theirs in the first place [cheering and drumming], and if the governments won't acknowledge our inherent right to the land, then their lease is up."[29]

Powerful speakers continued to address receptive and passionate participants throughout the land. In a growing number of cases across the country, the convergence of political and economic protests and Idle No More methods capitalized on the international reputation of Idle No More, thereby raising the profile of what otherwise would likely have been a localized or single-issue demonstration. On October 18, 2013, for example, a large crowd gathered in Montreal in front of the Westmount RCMP headquarters. This event was being held in solidarity with a blockade in Elsipogtog, New Brunswick; it concluded without conflict between the RCMP and the marchers.[30] The Elsipogtog rallies near Rexton, New Brunswick, were held in solidarity with Mi'kmaq people who were trying to stop natural gas exploration on their traditional territories. It was the Idle No More network that produced these sympathetic gatherings for this one specific blockade, and it did so while maintaining the peaceful nature that had characterized the movement's events over the past year.[31] In this instance, the Montreal rally was followed by comparable protests in Vancouver, Calgary, Saskatoon, Winnipeg, Ottawa, Iqaluit, and Whitehorse, among other communities. In some ways, this linking of the Idle No More movement to specific protests or localized causes diverted attention away from the broader movement and its wider issues.

Indeed, despite this growing network, the one-year anniversary of the first Idle No More gathering at Station 20 West in Saskatoon occurred just a few weeks later and it was surprisingly muted. Some concurrent events were held, including a Main Street Medicine Walk in Winnipeg that focused attention on the urban homeless. Pamela Palmater, who had appeared regularly at Idle No More events throughout the year, declared on the one-year anniversary: "The spirit of Idle

No More is still alive and well." She continued, "You know, we raised awareness all over the world, we inspired people."[32] Another speaker, Jerry Kim-Daniels, commented, "People are more serious about Aboriginal issues, Indigenous issues . . . [T]here's been a lot of successes that we can highlight as a movement."[33] And that same day, a virtual gathering and webinar series, #INM1YR, connected followers to speakers like American Indian activist Winona LaDuke and University of Saskatchewan professor Priscilla Settee.[34] A couple of weeks following the one-year anniversary, a small gathering of about sixty people assembled on the grounds of the Alberta Legislature on November 28, 2013, chanting: "Ain't no power like the power of the people, because the power of the people don't stop! . . . This is what [power] looks like. [Cheering]."[35]

That the rallies continued, even in the absence of extended media coverage, speaks volumes about the determination of Aboriginal people and the growing list of grievances, concerns, and priorities emerging from the communities. A rally on Parliament Hill on December 10, 2013, drew fifty or so participants, and saw speakers add the proposed Government of Canada First Nations Education Act to their list of concerns.[36] The previous year, several thousands of marchers had gathered at the same place in one of the largest expressions of outrage and determination in the first wave of Idle No More protests. The December 2013 gathering was just as determined, just as passionate as its predecessor. The spark was there, but the fuel appeared to be running out.

There was a sense, even among Idle No More supporters, that the movement's best days were behind it. But what really happened was a repurposing of the effort, the focus shifted from organizing a flurry of events under the Idle No More umbrella to upholding Idle No More as an achieved space, a platform from which Aboriginal people could push forward on a variety of fronts. At a December 2013 gathering at Winnipeg's Polo Park Mall, Dennis White-Bird, a former grand chief of the Assembly of Manitoba Chiefs, already speaking about Idle No More in the past tense, said, "I think Idle No More was very much about public education. It has certainly drawn tons of people to take notice of First Nation issues throughout Canada and our relationship with the Crown and the government of Canada. . . . I think that Idle No More has really opened the eyes of the Canadian public. And it's

. . . forced people to really notice Crown–First Nation issues through-out Canada."[37] Another Manitoba protestor, Leah Gazan, captured the significance of the movement to the less politically active:

> Being an Indigenous person in this country, you know, you're born into a political crisis and it really makes me feel hopeful . . . that change is possible, that people are waking up from both within and outside of our com-munity, you know. We've gone through a great time of darkness. And I just feel a hope that I haven't felt ever in my life. . . . I mean, we see movements that are pop-ping up all over this country that have been inspired by some of the actions in Idle No More, including El-sipogtog. . . . We're standing strong on our lands, you know, and in return we're protecting all Canadians. So, I think we've already made change.[38]

By December 2013, while, organizationally, Idle No More appeared to have slowed if not stalled, the movement had created a web of sup-porters, common interests, and shared values across the country and internationally. Even more important, it had elevated the belief with-in the Aboriginal communities that they had the power, determina-tion, and capacity to make a difference in their own lives and in the trajectory of the country as a whole.

And so, the year 2013 ended much as the previous year had done, with flash mobs across the country demonstrating the continued relevance of Aboriginal protest. In addition to the Winnipeg event, Round Dances occurred, for instance, in Fredericton, Lethbridge, Montreal, Toronto, Saskatoon, Sudbury, and Surrey. A series of small-er activities also took place, such as the Treaty Information Check Stop in Delaronde, Saskatchewan, which consisted of a traffic slow-down to provide information about the land and Treaty 6 territory.[39] And hundreds of people gathered on Dundas Street in Toronto on December 21 and then moved inside the Eaton Centre.[40] Participants gathered to dance and sing, with large numbers of curious onlookers watching the events in the atrium from the three levels of the mall.

A similar group formed up in the Metropolis at Metrotown mall in Burnaby, British Columbia. One woman had the crowd chant with her as she spoke: "Those that came before me. This fight is for all of us, and I invite you to come and join us to stand in solidarity, in love, and in spirit with those who are fighting to protect the land, to protect the air, and to protect the water not just for our children but for all of our children."[41] The crowd cheered. Another speaker, Dan Wallace, took a more combative tone when he spoke, noting:

> Resistance is in my family and what I'm suggesting from this point on, because things are going to be getting really heavy this summer and this spring, that we need to start showing serious effect in this country. And Vancouver is a prime example of where we can actually hurt the Canadian economy. We cannot be afraid of doing that because we're in this mall of complacency, consumer complacency right now, and we need to start showing the rest of the world the real reasons why we are stopping them because nobody is really hearing what needs to be said. We're all talking about it amongst ourselves, but there's the masses of you that are out here right now. You need to stand up, you need to wake up, and you need to open your ears because we're not doing it just for ourselves, we're doing this for you! We are protecting your water. We are protecting your food supply because it's ours. And we want you and expect you to stand up with us.[42]

Wallace's sentiments were not uncommon across the country—the Warrior movement of young Aboriginal people ready to take direct action in defence of Indigenous interests is a long-standing testament to this reality—but they were not central to Idle No More. What's more, the Idle No More movement—though no longer the large-scale movement it was in it early days—continues to remain true to its founding principles, as shared on its website:

> Idle No More calls on all people to join in a peaceful revolution, to honour Indigenous sovereignty, and to protect the land and water.

INM has and will continue to help build sovereignty and resurgence of nationhood.

INM will continue to pressure government and industry to protect the environment.

INM will continue to build allies in order to reframe the nation to nation relationship. This will be done by including grassroots perspectives, issues, and concerns.[43]

Saskatoon, the launch site for Idle No More, provided a telling denouement for the movement as it was in 2013. Organizers called for a flash mob at the Midtown Plaza for December 21 to mark the anniversary of the movement. The event, held in the same complex where the rally had startled Canadians and awakened nationwide interest a year ago, ran into difficulty. Mall security blocked some people from attending. Sheelah McLean criticized the action: "The Midtown Plaza is making a critical mistake in blocking people from coming. This is a public space."[44] Mall assistant general manager Della Keen said that the mall had not received advance notice and had taken steps to "ensure the security and safety of our guests." Marlene McKay, a participant from the northern community of Cumberland House, was upset about the efforts to control the event: "Aboriginal people are here. We can't be silenced. We have voices, too. It's time."[45] It was, in the end, a muted celebration, attracting only a few dozen people and lacking the drama and scale of the previous year. Idle No More, in its iteration as a stand-alone movement, seemed to be fading. But as McLean observed about both the Saskatoon rally and the movement as a whole, "Corporate media describe it as dead just because people aren't in the streets, [but] it's as strong as ever."[46] She was right, although most Canadians viewed the petering out of the rallies as the end of Idle No More.

In the end, there was no Sovereignty Summer of mass rallies and protests, no rights revolution, and no sustained activities over the following months. But Idle No More did not disappear. The rallies continued, voices were raised, songs sung, and drums played. The events were smaller and drew less attention. There was plenty of room for new voices, different words, and renewed expressions of cultural confidence and political determination, even if media and public attention had faded.

Though appearing as a spent national force at that time, Idle No More, at the time of this writing in fall 2014, remains active and dynamic, one of the most remarkable, sustained, and culturally rich movements in Canada history. Its website continues to be a resource for people and organizations interested in the movement's values. Idle No More associates show up to help community leaders organize rallies or protests. The founders continue to address Aboriginal and non-Aboriginal gatherings across the country and internationally. Idle No More is not a one-shot or one-year occurrence. Instead, as it gathered momentum and evolved, it changed the vocabulary of a nation and inspired a generation of Aboriginal people and their supporters. This reach and impact continues to be supported by Idle No More participants' creative and extensive use of social media, as Aboriginal people and their supporters used, and continue to use, accessible technologies to spread information that previously had remained largely within Aboriginal communities and thus to share insights, ideas, and action plans among the Indigenous peoples of Canada.

Idle No More event: Elsipogtog Solidarity
rally in Vancouver on October 18, 2013.
Photograph by Lukasz Szczepanski.

SEVEN

IDLE NO MORE AND THE TECHNOLOGIES OF MASS MOBILIZATION

"There's certain ways that we can do this peacefully in trying to raise awareness. We could call upon younger people and we could do it through social media, blogs, Twitter, Facebook, writing letters to Harper, senators and the Queen. We can sign the petition, [which] is what we're doing today." —Idle No More coordinator, Prince Albert, Saskatchewan, December 10, 2012

P olitics and protest just aren't what they used to be, or so the story goes. The narrative is very simple. The advent of personal digital devices—smartphones, pagers, tablets, and the like—combined with software tools, like Facebook, Twitter, YouTube, and Spreecast, have changed the fundamentals of political organizing, mass mobilization, protest, and dissent. Being wary of technological determinism or of attributing social change to the introduction of new technologies seems to make sense here. Technology is not a simple driving force; technology produces tools that social groups, mobilized to act for a complex set of reasons, utilize to expand their reach and impact. By itself, technology is a damp squib, something without soul, purpose, or real effect. Technology mobilized to serve social forces, values, community passions, and historical grievances, however, can ignite and deliver exponential impact.

Social factors, the collective memory of historical experiences, and the interplay of politics and technology create social change. Some may think that putting smartphones in the hands of young people is far more likely to produce tweets about the Kardashians than a broad-based social movement. Technology does not change people; people change people. And yet, social media allows individuals and groups to go around government, avoid the mass media, hide from censors, make instant contact, reach out to supporters, share ideas with millions of people in seconds, and manage connections between followers and founders. The speed, affordability, and reach of social media trump all previously available means of political mobilization and public protest.

The latter part of the twentieth century was defined by the technological transformation of politics and social mobilization. Over the past two decades, however, the trend has run in the opposite direction: corporate concentration of the media, the decline of independent outlets, sophisticated use of polling and other systems that transformed organized politics into new-age, political machines, and the homogenization of Western society that is best captured in Robert Putnam's *Bowling Alone: The Collapse and Revival of American Community* (2000). Putnam's book, an impressive work of social science, documents the collapse of community, the rise of the individual, and the atomization of modern society. From the advent of the Internet, and the emergence of The Well (the first major online community, launched in 1985), the digital world has offered an alternative to a collapsing traditional world.

Digitally enabled politics changed things quickly: connecting people with shared interests and concerns; allowing groups to mobilize around, behind, and between political parties, governments, and social interests; and giving political power to the poor and dispossessed. The new technologies, which capitalize on Moore's Law (the exponential growth of computing power), improved steadily. Launched to mass effect in the industrial world in the 1990s, social media quickly spread, principally through BlackBerry and the iPhone, to the developing world. By the 2010s, smartphones had become ubiquitous, present in the profoundly poor villages of sub-Saharan Africa as well as every Aboriginal community in Canada, in authoritarian states in the Middle East and small towns in Canada's North.

Aboriginal people in Canada have embraced the Internet, social media, and smartphones. Facebook is commonplace in First Nations, Métis, and Inuit communities and is particularly well-suited for maintaining contact between families and friends stretched between home communities, kids away at college and university, and relations who have relocated to distant towns and cities. Aboriginal people have been like other Canadians: all ages—youth, adults, and the elderly alike—are enthusiastic about smartphone and social media technologies. These new tools have facilitated social relationships, connected bands with members, provided dissenters with a tool for organizing against official leaders, and otherwise transformed communications between and among community members. It is too early for researchers to say with confidence if Aboriginal use of the Internet and social media differs significantly from that of other Canadians or other cultural groups in this country or abroad, but it is safe to observe that Indigenous peoples have embraced the new technologies as a means of staying connected. Of course, any adult who has spent a few minutes on his or her teenager's Twitter account, Facebook page, Instagram, or WhatsApp sites will quickly realize there is an endless stream of aimless chatter, frivolousness, and youth angst on digital display. Social media is a platform more than it is a source of inspiration. It is, for Aboriginal people as for others, a modern version of pen and paper, and not a creator of content or an instigator of conversations. That crucial work requires human creativity and action.

Human beings are drawn to organization, and we search for ways to share ideas with each other. The powerful, in turn, have historically sought to profit from the distribution of knowledge while ensuring that systems do not undercut their privilege. So it has been with pamphlets and books, the telephone and the radio, television and the mobile phone. From this perspective, the smartphone is an evolution, a technological innovation, rather than a startling, new invention. From the early days of the telephone, organizations as prosaic as churches and high schools, political parties and protest groups, have used phone trees—the organized calling systems that connected groups of people, allowing the rapid transmission of information to large numbers of peoples. The smartphone, which digitally replicates the concept of the phone tree, capitalizing now on one's list of addresses and connections rather than the phone book, speeds up extant processes; in other words, the smartphone did not usher in the process of mass mobilization, it just makes it easier.

The advent of Idle No More brought to the forefront endless commentaries about the transformative impact of social media and smartphones. The flash mobs were mobilized by tweets and Facebook postings. Events were organized using the same social networks. People joined national conversations by placing #idlenomore in a tweet, reaching thousands of followers, and followers of followers, instantly. The impact of social media in the Idle No More movement cannot be dismissed. The new systems were fast and, even more important, virtually free. For fractions of a penny, hundreds of messages could be dispatched to potential followers. Idle No More organizers understood the potential of the new technologies and exploited them fully. When social media technologies were overlaid with the personal, professional, and family contacts of Indigenous peoples, particularly those of college and university students, formidable regional and national networks emerged.

The prototype for Idle No More, although stunningly different in intent, tactics, and outcomes, was the Arab Spring movement of 2010–2013. Protest meetings staged primarily by young Arab students popped up in a progression of authoritarian or tightly controlled Arab states, starting in Tunisia before spreading to Algeria, Lebanon, Jordan, Oman, Mauritania, Yemen, and Saudi Arabia. Egypt was next. The Egyptian movement drew crowds in the tens of thousands and threatened to topple the government of Hosni Mubarak. Twice the crowds forced Egyptian governments to step down, including the Islamist regime of Mohamed Morsi that replaced Mubarak. Rallies and protests contributed to the downfall of several Arab governments following bitter and bloody clashes between protestors and the police and armed forces. By the time the Arab uprisings ended, the protests had included Bahrain, Algeria, Jordan, and Syria, among others, with smaller rallies in other Arab nations and territories.

In the West, people understood the Arab uprisings as a region's desire for democracy and the people's collective revulsion with authoritarian or theocratic rule. In this construction, the BlackBerry and the iPhone became an instrument of democratic reform, a Western tool that had unleashed the human need for control over governments and for the chance to participate in political processes. It was a fine narrative, with more than a little substance to it. Subsequent analysis demonstrates that the Arab Spring arose primarily amongst middle-class youth, frustrated by the mismatch between their educations and career opportunities; the anger was as much socio-economic as political. The Arab Spring brought technology and protest together in a unique and powerful way, demonstrating the capacity of people to work around governments, policy forces, and the mainstream media in a manner that activists the world over found to be empowering and exciting. If nothing else, and even if the motivation and goals were misunderstood globally, the Arab Spring set a new standard for the spread, sweep, scale, and impact of youth mobilization.[1]

On the heels of the Arab Spring, and somewhat inspired by it, the global Occupy movement emerged in the fall of 2011, officially commencing with the September occupation of Zuccotti Park in New York City. Occupy had different targets: the super-rich and powerful who had rocked the global economy with the mismanagement and exploitation of world financial markets; as well as the growing economic inequality in a world dominated by the super-rich, who seemed safeguarded from the ravages of the recession. The movement spread, with rallies, occupations, and other activities happening in over eighty countries and over nine hundred cities, with the United States dominating both the activity and the publicity. The Occupy movement collapsed under its own weight, with its odd combination of social activists, anarchists, and protest followers unable to articulate a clear vision or strategy for political or economic action. The self-declared 99 per cent, it turns out, did not share a common sense of the problems and certainly had no shared vision for responding to the economic realities, even though the core of the critique of global capitalism was on the mark.

Where the Occupy movement connected with the Arab Spring and, in 2012, with Idle No More, was in the effective use of social media. In all three cases, these youth-dominated movements transformed the use of Facebook, Twitter, BlackBerry Messenger, Instagram, and other mobile media technologies into tools for social action and political engagement. Word of the actions and rallies spread rapidly among and across social groups, drawing hundreds of thousands of people into online conversations and, on occasion, direct political action. Governments learned to move warily against the protestors, knowing that they could call on many unseen followers and that they could use the highly disruptive technologies to get their word out across the nation and the world. When the Syrian protests turned deadly in the wake of the decision of President Bashar al-Assad to turn his armies loose on dissenters, the first accounts, photographs, and videos of the destructive state violence came via social media. While smartphones and attending social media technologies were not invented by or for socio-political protestors, activists discovered that they had new tools to use in sharing their stories, calling people to action, and reaching a wide and engaged audience.

In time, analysts will be able to provide a sophisticated analysis of the role of social media in the Idle No More movement. In fact, the analytical tools currently available allow for almost real-time investigation of social media activity. As an active user of social media and a student of the impact of digital technologies on society, I was intrigued from the outset about the ways in which the new systems were influencing Indigenous mobilization. It is clear that social media was, throughout the movement, a useful tool but not really a determinative factor. It is, of course, impossible to prove the counter-factual position, namely that Idle No More would have occurred without ready access to social media. It is also important, however, that one not assume too much about the role of technology in sharing the message and mobilizing the people; social media facilitates movements but does not invent them.

Idle No More tapped into existing anxieties, frustrations, and anger among Indigenous peoples and their supporters; it did not create these sentiments. Social media facilitated contact between family, friends, and political networks; it did not create these webs of connectivity. Social media was quite important in generating flash mobs in the major cities and drawing hundreds to shopping malls and street gatherings. In smaller centres, where most of the Idle No More activity took place, social media seems to have been somewhat incidental to launching the rallies but very helpful in recording and sharing the results of the meetings. On a national scale, social media certainly proved valuable in keeping the movement alive and in providing the country with a mélange of stories, speeches, ideas, and concepts shared at the level of the individual rallies.[2]

In sum, social media mattered a great deal to Idle No More, primarily because it freed the movement from reliance on traditional media sources. Digital sharing helped to solidify and express the Aboriginal voice in a way that a few mentions in the newspaper and occasional ten-second sound bites on news programs never would have done. More importantly, social media allowed First Nations to express themselves directly and not through media intermediaries. If one wants to find out what Aboriginal people had to say through Idle No More, one need only put this book aside for an hour, and enter "Idle No More" on YouTube's website. Select from among the hundreds of videos posted and listen to the words of Aboriginal peoples and their supporters, the words of protest, cultural confidence, celebration, and determination. Never in the history of Canada have so many Indigenous words, voices, and images been so readily available to so many people. Never before have Indigenous peoples across the country been able to speak to each other so easily and without non-Aboriginal intermediaries. The power of social media, in my estimation, rests far more with the sharing of stories, images, and enthusiasm than with the actual mobilization of people and generation of support for individual events.

Before reviewing the actual social media engagement associated with Idle No More, I think a bit of a primer on the new communications systems might be in order. Unless you are an adept user of Twitter, Facebook, and YouTube, or have a fourteen-year-old in the house, some of these terms and concepts might be a bit obscure. In the world of social media, however, they define participation and engagement.

1. A "tweet" refers to a short, 140-character message that may include links to websites, photos, or videos.

2. When the "@" symbol comes before a name, one knows one is reading a username or a "Twitter handle." A Twitter handle represents a person who has a Twitter account.

3. The # symbol, called a hashtag, is used to mark keywords or topics in a tweet. It was created by Twitter users as a way to categorize messages.

4.   A "Twitter follower" is a Twitter user who is following another Twitter user. By following other users, one is able to watch what others talk about in their Twitter feeds, in real time.

5.   "Likes" on Facebook refer to the act of a user clicking a "like" button on another user/group's Facebook page, which indicates interest and following of content posted by that user/group.

6.   A Facebook "post" refers to a status update post that "friends" or "public" can view, depending on the privacy restrictions the user chooses.

7.   A Facebook "comment" is a reply or response to a user's Facebook status update/post and appears after the original post.

8.   "People Talking About This" represents the number of unique users who have created a "story" about a page in a seven-day period. "Stories" are items that display in "News Feed" sections of users' Facebook accounts. Users create stories when they: like a page, post on the page wall, like a post, comment on a post, share a post, answer a question, RSVP to a page's event, mention the page in a post, tag the page in a photo, check in at a place, share a check-in deal, like a check-in deal, write a recommendation, or claim an offer.

EXAMPLE: If a user writes a status post about a certain Facebook page by using the @ function tag, this status post will add to the "People Talking About This" statistic while plain text referring to the page will not be included.

As one can see, there are many ways to engage through social media, from creating a Facebook page or entry to writing a tweet or responding to one, or simply noting one's presence in the digital conversation. Participating is inexpensive and easy and does not necessary hold much meaning. Social media participation, therefore, does not automatically indicate a person's passion about a subject or even if he or she agrees with the sentiments being expressed. "Liking" a Facebook post or page indicates a certain degree of interest or concurrence, but re-tweeting a tweet could mean anything from complete support to abject opposition. Both, however, do indicate engagement with the subject material. Yet the potential shallowness of digital participation needs to be noted. The Liberal Party recently discovered this occurrence when they celebrated the tens of thousands of "instant" party members who signed up during the Liberal leadership campaign, only to have a much smaller number carry through in voting online for the party leader. It is vital, therefore, not to overestimate the significance of social media participation.

At the same time, the digital footprints of the people tracking Idle No More provide fascinating insights into the spread of the movement, its followers, and the reach of the Aboriginal actions. The ebbs and flows of digital traffic show public interest—support or otherwise—in the activities and allow us to note the location of those participating in online debates and conversations. Many of the tweets and Facebook entries include the geo-location (map coordinates) of the device used to connect to the Internet. This permits an almost real-time exploration of the location—across Canada and around the world—of the participants in the Idle No More digital dialogue.

It is exciting to find digital tracks of conversations drawing in people from South Africa to Japan, New Zealand to Arizona, and to see engagement from followers in places as diverse as the Mackenzie River valley, Northwest Territories, and Paris, France. My favourite, still unverified, is a Facebook post that was apparently sent from the middle of the Atlantic Ocean. The mind boggles: perhaps this person was a crew member on an oceangoing cargo ship, someone using the Internet while flying and picking up an unexpected signal, a traveller on a luxury cruise ship heading to the Caribbean, or even a solo sailor making a trans-Atlantic crossing. Or, perhaps this post's recorded location, much more prosaically, represents a malfunction or inaccurate entry on a smartphone.

Still, mapping social media provides unusual insights into the shape and nature of a movement that spread like a prairie storm across the country and around the world. The following graphs and maps provide a snapshot of the social media activity on Twitter and Facebook for the Idle No More movement between December 2012 and December 2013. The Twitter data was gathered primarily from the official IdleNoMore user @idlenomore4 (https://twitter.com/IdleNoMore4). The Facebook page

"IdleNoMoreCommunity"(www.facebook.com/IdleNoMoreCommunity) had the highest number of likes and users on Facebook in relation to the Idle No More movement and is used here as being representative of the broader movement.

First, a quick comment on the scale of activity is in order. As the following data sets show, Idle No More attracted a great deal of attention, with more than 20,000 followers on Twitter and over 120,000 page likes on Facebook. By most signs of political engagement, and considering that this covers the period from November 2012 to December 2013, the numbers are truly impressive. (Occupy Wall Street's online community, in comparison, has 639,488 likes for the movement.[3]) As a study by Mark Bevis, president and digital public affairs strategist at FullDuplex.ca, demonstrates, Idle No More attracted over 1.3 million mentions in this time period. Twitter mentions (1.2 million) by Twitter participants (143,000) and Facebook mentions (100,000) were the top three most prominent social media contributors.[4] For a largely uncontrolled social movement, with a minimal budget, no paid staff, and little concerted effort to deliberately build audience size, the level of engagement is quite remarkable.

DATA SET 1: GENERAL ENGAGEMENT BY ACTIVITY LEVELS ON TWITTER[5]
@idlenomore4 Twitter Feed
Number of Tweets: 4,700
Number of Followers: 20,800

DATA SET 2: GENERAL ENGAGEMENT BY ACTIVITY LEVEL ON FACEBOOK
"IdleNoMoreCommunity" Facebook Page
Number of Page Likes: 125,686
Number of People Talking About This: 8,233
Number of Posts and Comments: 68,070

DATA SET 3: OVERALL SOCIAL MEDIA ACTIVITY
Overall Mentions: 1,366,156
Blog Mentions: 11,296
Facebook Mentions: 100,011
Forum Mentions: 13,669
News Mentions: 19,189
Twitter Mentions: 1,215,569

Twitter Participants: 143,173
YouTube Mentions: 6,422

These numbers demonstrate the reach of the movement and the scale of awareness about the movement. Idle No More had harnessed the power of the "participatory web" and "open source" ideology to a large degree, the latter referring to the fact that the system was open to all, without control from any central force.

But before we get too excited, what does this level of engagement mean in comparative terms? Idle No More was not alone in the digital space, and in fact it competed with hundreds of thousands of political, social, and economic movements for digital attention. The movement is even more impressive—with a caveat or two thrown in—when the comparative data is included. When compared to the data that I collected on Twitter and Facebook in March 2014, it becomes obvious that Idle No More's audience, even at the height of the movement in the winter of 2013, pales in comparison to a variety of competing celebrities. On Twitter in March 2014, Justin Trudeau had 339,000 followers, but he trailed that digital sensation, Prime Minister Stephen Harper, by over 100,000 followers. But even with Opposition Leader Thomas Mulcair's small numbers added in, the country's three political leaders trailed embarrassingly far behind those icons of American reality television, the Kardashians, who had almost 41 million followers.

TWITTER ACTIVITY (MARCH 2014)

Justin Bieber: 50.4M
Stephen Harper: 446K
The Kardashians: 40.98M (combined accounts)
    Khloe Kardashian: 9.58M
    Kim Kardashian: 20.3M
    Kourtney Kardashian: 11.1M
Thomas Mulcair: 63.5K
Taylor Swift: 39.9M
Justin Trudeau: 339K

The March 2014 story was much the same on Facebook. What is more, Justin Bieber and Taylor Swift attracted millions of likes and many followers. Over 1.1 million people were talking about Taylor Swift's Facebook entries, compared to the 2,300 paying close attention to NDP Leader Mulcair's postings. To put the activity of Idle No More in a different context, as of March 22, 2014, a few days into the search for the missing Malaysian air flight, the main website associated with the tragedy had over 400,000 likes and 78,000 people taking about it, both much higher than Idle No More attracted at the height of events in early 2013.

FACEBOOK ACTIVITY (MARCH 2014)[6]

Justin Bieber: 64,190,573 likes; 1,803,363 talking about this
https://www.facebook.com/JustinBieber

Stephen Harper: 105,993 likes; 15,403 talking about this
https://www.facebook.com/pmharper

The Kardashians: 16,570 likes; 619 talking about this
https://www.facebook.com/pages/Kardashians/1200517280 66503
15,987 likes; 611 talking about this
https://www.facebook.com/kardashiansrw

The Missing Malaysian Air Flight: 401,697 likes; 78,854 talking about this
https://www.facebook.com/MissingMalaysiaAirlines

Thomas Mulcair: 26,992 likes; 2,303 talking about this
https://www.facebook.com/ThomasMulcair

Justin Trudeau: 146,895 likes; 6,676 talking about this
https://www.facebook.com/Justinpjtrudeau

Taylor Swift: 57,177,228 likes; 1,140,814 talking about this
https://www.facebook.com/TaylorSwift

We see from this list that social media is, indeed, a youth environment, dominated by pop idols and movie stars, and given to the fads of the moment. It is an environment that lends itself to analytics and allows for regular and easy monitoring of "trending" topics. Indeed, rapidly evolving statistics- and data-collecting techniques allow analysts to follow, in real time, changes in digital conversations worldwide. Unfortunately, the publicly accessible analytical techniques that researchers can now utilize were not available in 2012–2013, making it more difficult to place the Facebook and Twitter traffic associated with Idle No More in comparative context. What can be said is this: Idle No More generated a truly impressive amount of digital activity for an Aboriginal topic.

While there is ample room in the social media space for serious conversation—listen to almost any news talk show or check out the major journalists in the Canadian newspapers and you will see Twitter handles and learn about their Facebook pages—social media, nevertheless, in Canada and other countries too, is overwhelmingly dominated by the not-so-serious. How else does one explain the appeal of Justin Bieber, Stratford, Ontario's own current sensation? And try to find a dozen adults who know about Carly Rae Jepsen (ever heard the song, "Call Me Maybe"?), Pattie Mallette (a trick question, the mother of Justin Bieber), or DjKingAssassin (check it out for yourself). Data taken from 2014, when newer statistical techniques became available for public use, demonstrates the degree to which popular culture personalities, themes, and events dominate the social media environment:

TOP TEN CANADIAN TWITTER PROFILES (MARCH 2014)[7]

#	Profile	Followers
1	Justin Bieber (@justinbieber)	50,427,066
2	Avril Lavigne (@AvrilLavigne)	15,265,820
3	Drizzy (@Drake)	14,530,154
4	Carly Rae Jepsen (@carlyraejepsen)	9,930,845
5	HootSuite (@hootsuite)	5,765,993
6	Nina Dobrev (@NinaDobrev)	4,517,979
7	Nelly Furtado (@NellyFurtado)	3,245,131
8	Pattie Mallette (@PattieMallette)	3,093,610
9	WORLDS⊂ DANGEROUZ DJ (@DjKingAssassin)	2,848,849
10	deadmau5 (@deadmau5)	2,694,702

Canadians' travels on Facebook are equally uninteresting. It might be heartwarming for some to see the iconic Tim Hortons creeping up on Eminem, but knowing that *Family Guy* and *The Simpsons* rank high on the list, or that Adam Sandler is catching up with Subway Canada, hardly seems reason to celebrate.

TOP TEN CANADIAN PROFILES ON FACEBOOK (MARCH 2014)[8]

#	Page	Local Canadian Fans	Fans Worldwide
1	Eminem	1,987,684	82,967,248
2	Tim Hortons	1,903,280	2, 404, 614
3	Facebook	1,791,516	142,229,356
4	Facebook	1,790,484	1,790,723
5	*Family Guy*	1,696,574	55,463,971
6	YouTube	1,609,705	78,617,827
7	*The Simpsons*	1,562,486	70,849,499
8	Subway Canada	1,344,521	1,418,873
9	Adam Sandler	1,340,378	49,831,878
10	Rhianna	1,336,624	85,716,578

And so it continues. Data on "trending" topics on Twitter give a pretty good sense of social media traffic. When hot items hit—say the latest Senate scandal revelation or news of Liberal Party transgressions in Ontario—the number of tweets and retweeted materials shoots up dramatically. Theoretically, then, the review of trending topics on Twitter gives a snapshot of the most crucial topics of the day. In the midst of the Idle No More movement, to be fair, #IdleNoMore reached into the upper brackets and clearly had the country's attention. But check out the following list from mid-March 2014. The top trending item was American college basketball, albeit with the participation of the greatest crop of Canadian elite athletes in national history. The next two related directly to the Toronto Maple Leafs, and the rest of the top ten list was also dominated by sports figures. Twitter was, in this month, hardly a national forum for sophisticated analysis of Canadian political and social issues.

TOP TEN TRENDS ON TWITTER (MARCH 2014)

#MarchMadness	#TMLtalk	#Leafs	#lupul
Reimer	Rodney	#Kindle	Xavier Thames
Bolland	Rene Bourque		

Do not read too much into this cynical reading of the digital tea leaves. Complaining about the high-ranking position accorded to pop-culture and sports fan favourites is akin to rejecting a library because it carries Harlequin romances. Beneath the mindless chatter, one *can* find some useful insights, complicated conversations, and significant analyses. The sharing of serious ideas, while happening lower on the digital radar than the love lives and misbehaviour of the pop stars and hockey players, is extensive and increasingly important, particularly as the world becomes accustomed to instantaneous updates and in-the-moment analyses of unfolding events and processes.

Recognize, too, that assessing the statistics of social media barely scratches the surface. Data points are superficial on their own and fail, in the case of Idle No More, to capture the nuances of the debate: the foundational anger and frustration that drove the movement, and the words, tone, and passion of the individuals who set out to remake both their communities and the country. What the numbers do show is how fast and how far the movement spread. Thus, following or analyzing social media is rather like taking the pulse of a social movement or social concept. Charting the spread of references to Idle No More is an excellent surrogate for understanding the sharing of the concepts, enthusiasm, and hopes for the Indigenous movement. Consider Figure 7.1, again drawn from the comprehensive work of Mark Blevis, which illustrates the spike—and rapid decline—in the activity during the first six months of the Idle No More movement.

There are many ways of presenting and reviewing the data. Consider, for example, the scale of tweeting traffic at the height of Idle No More, from November 2012 to January 2013. Blevis's research documents that over 113,000 unique tweeters issued over 850,000 tweets in this time period.

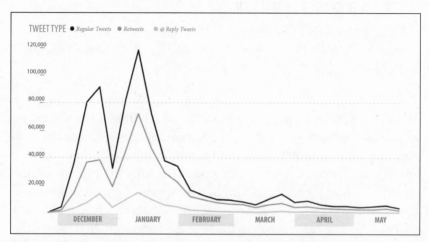

Figure 7.1. Number of regular tweets, retweets, and @ reply tweets for Idle No More for the first six months (December 2012 to May 2013).[9]

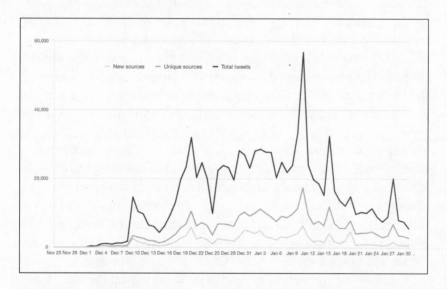

Figure 7.2. Twitter activity for Idle No More for the first two months (November 25, 2012 to January 30, 2013).[10]

As is clear in Figure 7.2, a single day—January 11, 2013—produced almost 58,000 tweets. This was a high point in Idle No More activity, brought on by Chief Theresa Spence's fast, with rallies across the country and a set of key meetings between National Chief Shawn

Atleo, some First Nations chiefs, Prime Minister Harper, and Governor General David Johnston.

Blevis and others have also documented the spread of the movement around the globe. The following map (Figure 7.3) shows the number of tweets for #IdleNoMore geographically around the world, and illustrates the movement's spread through Twitter, with the greater number of tweets coming from Canada, the United States, parts of Western Europe, the Middle East, Southern Australia, and New Zealand.

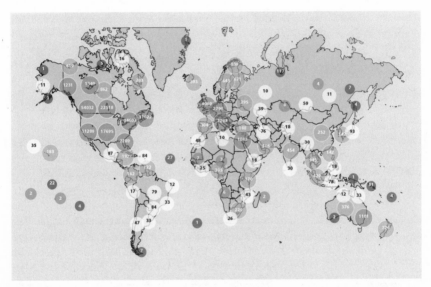

Figure 7.3. Number of tweets for #idlenomore by geographical spread.[11]

Although the majority of Idle No More events were clustered within North America, a number of events were held in various countries across Europe, the Middle East, Australia, and New Zealand. It is particularly interesting to note the rise of interest in the United States. According to Blevis, in "December 2012 through May 2013, the share of Canadian mentions decreased 22% (from 82% to 60%) while those from the U.S. increased 16% (from 14% to 30%). The United Kingdom gained a 1% share during the same period. All of this occurred while the volume of overall activity plummeted from nearly 600,000 tweets in January (equivalent of 19,000/day) to nearly 32,000 in May (equivalent of 1,000/day)." The Canadian activity appears directly connected to events and rallies; the American interest appears to be more strongly connected to the broader policy and political issues associated with Indigenous rights. In surprisingly short order, Idle No More had clearly created an internationally recognized platform for the discussion of Indigenous issues. Although far from a complete list, Figures 7.4 and 7.5 highlight some of the Idle No More teach-ins, rallies, blockades, flash mob dances, and hunger strikes that took place worldwide in 2012 and 2013.

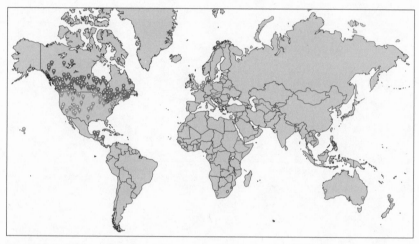

Figure 7.4. Idle No More events hosted worldwide in 2012 by geographic spread[12]

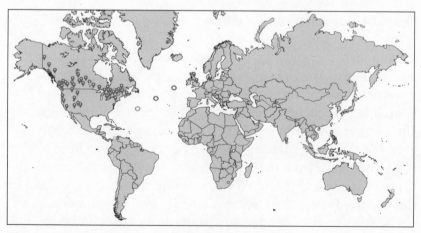

Figure 7.5. Idle No More events hosted worldwide in 2013 by geographic spread[13]

Social media analysts have an array of tools at their disposal that allow for rapid analysis of participant engagement and the spread of ideas. Blevis, for example, compiled a global "heatmap" (Figure 7.6) showing the concentration of Idle No More Twitter chatter during the first two months of the movement. The map shows where tweets originated; the more dense the concentration of issued tweets, the larger the circle. The national reach within Canada is hardly surprising. What is noteworthy is the sweeping engagement around the world, extending beyond the events themselves to produce an international conversation about the role of Aboriginal peoples within Canada and worldwide. In November 2012, four Saskatchewan women launched a conversation about an oddly comprehensive piece of Government of Canada legislation. Within two months, a truly global community of interest had emerged—fully international in scope, blisteringly fast in speed, and intense in engagement.

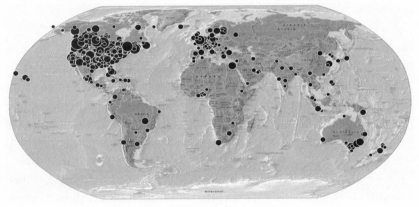

Figure 7.6. Idle No More global heatmap[14]

Twitter traffic provides a representation of the intensiveness of the global conversation. The number of tweets between December 2012 and January 2013 document the remarkable rise, quick decline, uptake over the summer of 2013, and sharp moderation by the one-year anniversary of the movement. It is also clear that the national and international conversation tracked closely specific events or touch points. The following chart (Figure 7.7) shows the number of tweets by month and the most important dates, highlighted for each month of the movement's events.

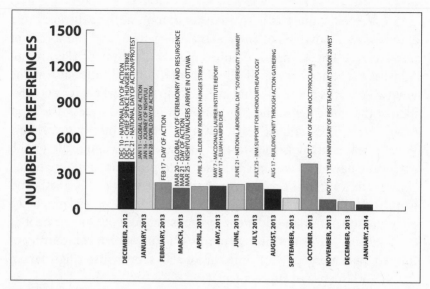

Figure 7.7. Idle No More Twitter activity, with important dates, from December 2012 to January 2014[15]

Making sense of Idle No More and social media is not an easy task. The analysis of social media as a political force is in its infancy. The election of Barack Obama as president of the United States ushered in grand enthusiasm for the new mobilization technologies, and the Arab Spring and Occupy movement solidified the reputation of social media as a political force. The organizational euphoria dissipated, however, as political parties in particular discovered that digital media was helpful mainly in speaking to the faithful and in generating quick, but typically superficial, reactions to public policy issues. As one political leader after another discovered, "likes" on Facebook pages and Twitter followers do not convert easily into financial donations, sustained interest, organizational engagement, or even votes.

This is why Idle No More's efforts to generate support extended well beyond social media. Bill C-45 opponents and Idle No More supporters produced a series of online petitions, most producing disappointing results (ranging from fewer than thirty e-signatures to over 6,500, hardly enough to generate great concern in the halls of government). Following are the statistics related to a number of Idle No More–generated online petitions.

1. British Crown: 1) Honour treaties with First Nations 2) Revoke C-45: 6,647 supporters[16]

2. Do not pass the Budget Implementation Bill C-45: 5,979 supporters[17]

3. Stephen Harper and Members of Parliament: Tell Canadians the Truth about Omnibus Bill, C-45: 3,743 supporters[18]

4. Change Omnibus Bill C-45: 1,561 supporters[19]

5. Steven [sic] Harper and the Government of Canada: Stop Bill C-45 and Honour Indigenous Rights: 812 supporters[20]

6. Stop Bill C-45, Indian Act Amendments: 236 supporters[21]

7. IdleNoMore: We Do Not Support Bill C-45 Stephen Harper. Do Not Disregard the Treaties without Consultation and Consent: 129 supporters[22]

8. Petition to Oppose Bill C-45: 27 supporters[23]

Idle No More, however, was not looking for party members, electoral votes, signatures on petitions, or even donations. The movement sought a voice, not organizational continuity. For the thousands of participants in Idle No More, sharing thoughts, beliefs, plans, and opinions was the end—there was no long-term logistical purpose. Furthermore, the core conversations—those associated with #idlenomore and a handful of key connector addresses—soon morphed into thousands of parallel or secondary discussions as individuals, community groups, and activists moved beyond the main venues into more private or specialized spaces.

Social media was, in sum, the ideal technology for a movement that aimed primarily to share ideas and commitment, rather than to focus attention on a leader or an organization. As an extended commentary on *Rabble.ca*—an activist online news resource that provided a great deal of support for the movement—opined:

Given how spread out many Indigenous folks are, living in remote or rural areas, using social media to mobilize not only made sense, but created a new space for Indigenous voices. Folks participating in #IdleNoMore streaming webinars, Twitter conversations and Facebook discussions could do so no matter where they were geographically. Much like in the Arab Spring, information and resources are shared by folks working on the grassroots for the benefit of other activists. Emphasizing the history of colonialism through an Indigenous understanding has helped link many different struggles from environmental activism, feminism and queer organizing to Idle No More. The power of the hashtag to reach out, attract attention and spark discussion was invaluable to the success of the movement.[24]

Kim Tallbear, an American social media analyst at the University of California-Berkeley, agreed: "the impact of the social media on the Idle No More movement cannot be understated," she noted. "[There are people] who have never left their home communities but have been on top of the movement through Facebook and Twitter. In this manner, Idle No More has garnered global attention."[25] Niigaanwewidam James Sinclair, Winnipeg-based observer and professor at the University of Manitoba, added that social media helped to "mobilize people very quickly and create buzz—this movement is hip, it's cool, it's cool to be resistant."[26] "Our biggest strength is that we always left it open," said Pamela Palmater. "Idle No More was to individuals whatever they wanted it to be."[27]

Idle No More made it clear that social engagement via social media broadened the reach of the movement. The empowering capacity of social media is clearly articulated in the introductory text on one of the companion Idle No More Facebook pages:

How we differ from the current Idle No More FB page: our sister site posts everything Idle No More related (and important posts can sometimes get lost in the mix), while this page is focused solely on educating and empowering organizers and worldwide supporters, as well as consolidating events and hosting a weekly radio show update.

In order to keep clear lines of communication between all organizers and supporters of the movement, this page will serve to gather all relevant information needed to empower our youth and engage the public in a unified manner. Examples include what to say to the media, and pamphlets for distribution.

Interviews with organizers, founders, and influential figures supporting the movement will be conducted and shared via Idle No More News. Contact us to promote your event.

To maintain the founders' original mission and action plan, this page will host any and all information pertaining to our situation that can be used to inform and empower our nation and the public. The founders have recommended teach-ins, and they are working to create information packages to assist you in setting up these events in your city, town, or reservation.

We will be working closely with the founders and will be able to answer all your questions—they are extremely busy and this is a way for them to not be so bombarded with messages each day.

E-mails to be sent to officials and environmental agencies worldwide will also be posted for your distribution.

Opinion polls will also be conducted on Idle No More movement developments.[28]

There is no doubt that Idle No More struck a digital cord and, equally, that social media allowed Idle No More to magnify its outreach and impact. By 2013, Idle No More had more than 1.4 million social media mentions, including over 6,400 YouTube mentions, 1.2 million Twitter mentions, and over 140,000 Twitter participants.

There is a tendency to see movements from a centre-out perspective when assessing their effectiveness in sharing core messages and coordinating activities. But Idle No More did not operate in this fashion; instead, it sought to empower all Aboriginal people to speak up and to share their experiences. Those typically viewed as being on the periphery—the urban poor, residents of isolated communities, Indigenous youth, Elders—used social media to share their words and actions with people across the country. The ease with which videos of a rally—no matter how small—could be shared globally, typically by being posted on YouTube, or Facebook, or distributed via Twitter or e-mail, allowed the Idle No More message to spread quickly and effectively, but only because this was precisely the goal and purpose of the movement. One can still view videos of events that took place along the sides of highways and in small villages from Buffalo Narrows, Saskatchewan, to Usahat, Quebec, from Manitoulin Island, Ontario, to Sagkeeng, Manitoba. These small and seemingly peripheral events were not subordinate to the movement. They *were* the movement. And social media allowed participants to both document their experiences and share their aspirations and thoughts with the broader Indigenous world.

There were key individuals associated with Idle No More, beyond the four founders and well beyond the handful of individuals who showed up regularly in the traditional media. A series of key Twitter handles stood out for their level of activity:

@chuddles11	@kal301
@teamrevoltnow	@tersestuff

As well, there were some recognizable names amongst those tweeting:

@aptnnews	@chieftheresa
@deejayndn	@ezralevant
@neiljedmondson	@pampalmater
@rabbleca	@shawnatleo
@strombo	@sunnewsnetwork
@taiaiake	@wabkinew

The presence of these well-known people—and others—connecting with Idle No More in the Twittersphere suggests their prominence in terms of sharing information about Idle No More. The official INM Twitter account, @idlenomore4, was one of the more central user accounts on Twitter. But the level of activity shown here does not necessarily correlate and connect with the core messages and values of Idle No More. For instance, Ezra Levant, a columnist, and his platform, *Sun News* (both appearing in the list above), were not supporters of the movement; they included many highly critical commentaries on the events, particularly those associated with Chief Theresa Spence. Furthermore, @teamrevoltnow, an "open Twitter stream," was not officially connected with Idle No More; "highlighting the ongoing worldwide revolution against Fascism/Oppression," this group adopted the hashtag, #idlenomore, for its own political ends—a process that often happens on Twitter wherein other groups, not officially connected with those who started the accounts, take over the hashtag for their own purposes. According to Mark Blevis, any user can retweet "any tweet which includes the hashtag #IdleNoMore, regardless of the sentiment. This is both good and bad for the movement. It can just as likely contribute to Twitter users blocking the account, or others related to [Idle No More], in an effort to prevent perceived clutter in their Twitter streams."[29] Another oddity Blevis notes is that there were "tweets about hockey which suggested players were #IdleNoMore following the end of the NHL lockout," a phenomenon that alters the significance of the movement's numbers.[30] Similarly, the hijacking of the hashtag by spambots or unrelated interest groups (i.e., @AmerikanIdle) created "noise" in the Twittersphere that could not be prevented.

As noted already, Idle No More has had an uneven relationship with traditional media. While local media typically covered smaller events appropriately, supporters believed that the radio, television, and news media responded far too slowly to the rise of the movement and missed its broad and comprehensive message. Many First Nations believed that they had to take control of the media agenda, capitalizing on social media to share their messages, bypassing the mainstream media and speaking by the people, to the people, for the people. As several participants on Twitter noted early in the process:

RIIC News @riicnews
RT @arnelltf: We can't rely on mainstream media, we have to do it ourselves. Spread the word/photos/videos on yr social networks #IdleNoMore
9:02 pm - 10 Dec 2012

MEDIA INDIGENA @mediaindigena
Big Q: What next? mt @TrevorGreyeyes: See many
disappointed w/ media coverage of #IdleNoMore but
remember: Occupy's 1st days ignored
9:08 pm - 10 Dec 2012

Waubgeshig Rice @waub
It was exciting to follow #idlenomore on twitter today,
but disappointing not to see coverage on national news
broadcasts
11:37 pm - 10 Dec 2012

Ryan McMahon Comedy @rmcomedy
No mainstream national coverage of today's
#IdleNoMore action speaks to the need for our own
independent media. #IndigenousAlJazeeraTV
11:41 pm - 10 Dec 2012

Matthew Barlow @Matthew_Barlow
I'm sorry, #Canada, but why is #ChiefTheresaSpence
not front page news? Why is this something we're not
talking about? #IdleNoMore #cdnpoli
7:22 am - 21 Dec 2012

There was a particular value gained by this silence on the traditional media's part: the movement could dominate the conversation in this way, for social media allowed Idle No More to contact thousands of people *and* also to share the right messages. As sociologist Howard Ramos from Dalhousie University observed, "The movement spread not just through social media, but when the media got it wrong."[31] For example, the media, by lumping Chief Spence's fast together with Idle No More, misrepresented what was happening across the country. In the process, however, this coverage gave more attention to Idle No More than likely would have happened otherwise. And more to the point, social media allowed Aboriginal people to ensure that their movement remained an Aboriginal story. Once the movement captured the public's attention, several key Aboriginal commentators became especially prominent, particularly Wab Kinew—who emerged as a prominent national figure through his insightful and passionate commentaries—and Palmater—who had risen to national prominence through her 2012 campaign to become national chief of the Assembly of First Nations.

Of course, not everyone was fully on board with Idle No More. While the Idle No More message dominated the digital commentary, a small number of critics used the same technologies the movement was using to speak up. In fact, a specific Twitter account was set up to highlight opposition (https://twitter.com/NoMoreIDM), and there was an anti-movement Facebook page (https://www.facebook.com/pages/Idle-No-More-Resistance-a-division-of-One-Nation-for-Equality/410479792366981) that attracted over 2,400 followers. Negative comments—on the above Twitter account and Facebook page, and elsewhere—followed key events and statements:

> **Henny Soprano** @hennysoprano 28 Jan 2013
> Ima give the panhandler natives at the red lights a new sign that reads #stillidle

> **Native Wonder** @N8ive1der 17 Jan 2013
> Dont b fooled by power movements designed to constrict the boundaries of #IndianCountry vizavi clannish cliquish delineation's. #STILLidle

> **Brennan Pitchford** @bjpitchford 1 Jan 2013
> We white people are quite content with how the government is treating us and we are gonna just sit here and take it #stillidle

Blevis's study tracked such negative tweets on Idle No More activities. Not surprisingly, major events (such as roadblocks) generated harsh comments. As he observed about January 2012:

> Criticism increased in January, driven by blockades of train and travel routes, threats to the economy and the results of a financial audit of Attawapiskat. There

was also chatter about the apparent division between chiefs and the INM movement and even differing views among Assembly of First Nations (AFN) leaders. The most dramatic drop in sentiment occurred in the low engagement category where positive sentiment dropped from 76% in December to 28% in January. This suggests diminishing public support as expressed online, combined with increased sharing of links to factual information (such as media reports) as the media directed more attention at the movement.[32]

In January 2013, the *National Post* commissioned Forum Research to conduct a poll on Idle No More (see Figure 7.8). The response was mixed. Most people knew of the movement, but most rejected the idea that government did not properly support Indigenous people. New Democratic Party members were most supportive; Conservatives most critical. Support was strongest in Quebec and lowest in Alberta.[33]

Figure 7.8. Polling on the Idle No More movement, support by key demographic. *Source: Forum Research*

Indeed, Idle No More did generate a strong, often harsh, commentary on Indigenous peoples and Aboriginal rights generally. Consider some of the negative observations made in the online commentary sections of the country's national newspapers:

BOBPOTTS: "That's because people can only read and hear lies and BS for so long, before it gets so boring and repetitive you just have to move on. Idle No More generated more total BS in a few weeks than we have witnessed in decades. The sooner they go away, the better."[34]

VALIGAL: "How Can Canada say there is Equal Rights? One group of people have to go to work everyday & they keep adding more taxes on them. The other group of people want & demand everything for nothing from the cradle to the grave & refuse to work break all the laws & nothing is [done] about it. If they don't get everything they want the[y] barricade everything like spoiled kids with temper tantrums & say the[y] want to be treated with respect. You have to earn respect which you don't no [sic] what respect is."[35]

SOMETOWN: "I'd like to see INM blockage [sic] the roads to reserves that allow Chiefs with the support of their Band Councils that have set themselves up as aristocratic landowners. This has resulted in the creation of a permanent underclass on their reserves because they don't have the right bloodlines. Why isn't INM confronting these chiefs and anti-democratic governing bodies."[36]

Not all of the negative commentary was from non-Aboriginal people. Anthony Sowan, an Alberta Cree and radio host, wrote a lengthy piece in the *National Post* that ended:

As a man who stands by his word, I pledge to never again use my native status to further myself in a way that isn't available to every other Canadian. I will leave my son unregistered, and will teach him the importance of keeping it that way. I am a proud native man, and a hard-working, forward-thinking Canadian who believes the opportunities and advantages this country has to offer should be available to everyone equally.

The first step toward healing is putting the past in its place. Only then can you work on your own personal lives, which will then naturally stem into becoming whole as a community. The healing you want and need can come from no government program, and no external source.[37]

A point that most commentators missed, however, is that popular support did not really matter. The goal of Idle No More was to empower Indigenous peoples, not bring reluctant people into the fold. It was not a public relations campaign but an assertion of Indigenous culture and determination. The movement sought community more than converts. Idle No More was more about giving First Nations a voice than answering non-Aboriginal questions or assuaging their anxieties. Social media was instrumental in giving Aboriginal people a platform and providing unprecedented access to audiences among Indigenous peoples and supporters in Canada and around the world. As one commentator observed, "In turn, Idle No More has been compared to other recent global social movements including the Arab Spring and the Occupy movement. While Idle No More primarily seeks to address Canadian issues, it bears connection with the more general global problems attacked by these other grassroots movements: social, economic, and political inequality, disregard for Indigenous rights, and exploitation of the environment and natural resources. Indeed it is these shared global problems which Idle No More is seeking to address and change, both in Canada and beyond."[38]

For many observers, the combination of the youthfulness of most Idle No More organizations, the widespread use of social media, and the global outreach drew natural comparisons to the Arab Spring. Jeff Denis of Lakehead University offered these thoughts on the movement to CBC News: "Aboriginal peoples are a very young population. . . . They are the fastest-growing population in Canada. They are increasingly well-educated and aware of injustice. They have high expectations for the future, but they still face tremendous barriers in terms of racism, lack of job opportunities, cuts to social programs and so forth. If we think about other recent social movements around the world—including the Arab Spring, for example—those are just some of the factors that might be expected to facilitate this type of movement."[39] For Denis, social media was an essential element, enabling "this new, younger generation of activists to quickly and efficiently spread the word and organize across [the country] and also increasingly internationally."[40]

In an interview with *Global News*, Greg Elmer, Bell Globemedia Research Chair at Ryerson University, concurred: "Politicians start to notice and start to worry when people show up at their constituency offices and that started to happen. . . . This particular government and governments around the world are fearful in many ways, not just of not being able to control messages, but they are fearful of the very quick, the very efficient use of social media in raising serious political concerns and activating populations."[41] Others were less positive: "So far, it's shaping up to look a lot like last year's Occupy Wall Street conniption, the thing the activist avant-garde insisted was going to be the great anti-corporate insurrection that counterculture icon Naomi Klein always wanted. Our very own Arab Spring! It ended up more like the Tanganyika Laughter Epidemic of 1962 [a case of mass hysteria that broke out in a small-town school and spread to the surrounding area], and so far, Idle No More appears headed in exactly the same direction."[42]

Social media is transitory and ephemeral. Unlike print newspapers and books, social media exists in digital formats, easily shared but seemingly temporary in reach and impact. The movement arose quickly, its message spread rapidly, and in the form of actions and activities seemed to disappear just as fast. As a means of establishing a new value system and as a confidence-building exercise, however, Idle No More was far more transformative than a mindless tweet about Justin Bieber might be.

As the rallies and online chatter peaked and slowed, the question emerged as to whether or not the movement would survive. As the Idle No More movement expanded, Canadians wondered if First Nations' determination would constitute a new normal, or if the drumming would die down, signalling another defeat.[43] The answer is not simple. The organization has lost much of its momentum, and the number and size of Idle No More–identified events has declined. Various Aboriginal activists claim to have picked up the banner of Idle

No More and push a number of different political agendas. In the end, although Idle No More events no longer happen regularly across Canada, the movement lives on as a mindset, as a set of values about how, when, and why to respond to governments, development, and the Canadian public. It remains alive as an Aboriginal tool kit, likely fixed in the collective Indigenous memory as a series of actions, processes, and mobilization techniques that can be used now and in the future for the purposes of local, regional, and national campaigns. Idle No More is still with us in the attitudes and values of the Aboriginal peoples of Canada; the real revolution created by Idle No More has taken root.

Ta'Kaiya Blaney of the Sliammon First Nation.
Photo: Christopher McLeod

EPILOGUE

More than two years have passed since the first Idle No More meeting was held in Saskatoon, and two years have passed since the Idle No More movement reached its height—when youth took up challenges to walk long distances to demonstrate their belief in their future, in their cultures, and in their ability to effect change. The movement is not as prominent now, although the movement's name and many of the more familiar faces associated with it continue to have an online presence. Among government leaders and the general public, there appears to be a certain amount of relief. Idle No More was unnerving to many, as much because it brought to the surface real reasons for anger and distress as because of the disruptions caused by the rallies and activities themselves. In many circles, from the Assembly of First Nations, where the movement worried many of the elected chiefs, to government offices, where the prospect of renewed protests still causes concern, Idle No More hangs over the country like a storm cloud on the horizon. When will it unleash its power again?

Having watched Idle No More with great interest and having thought about it a great deal since November 2012, I am still amazed by its spirit, values, and passion. Idle No More arose out of conditions of serious despair: grinding poverty, the realities of contemporary racism, the legacies of colonialism, marginalization, and seeming powerlessness. It found fuel, however, in a pattern of real and deep accomplishment, in college and university classrooms with many Aboriginal students and faculty, in a surge in Aboriginal entrepreneurship, in a series of major victories for Indigenous peoples in the courts, in the quiet assembly of hundreds of millions of dollars in investment capital that will, in short order, make Aboriginal communities real economic powers in Canada. Given all of these pieces contributing to the atmosphere that gave birth to the movement, Idle No More could have been many things: angry, aggressive, boisterous, assertive, disruptive, and even destructive. It could have, like the interminable Caledonia stand-off in southern Ontario, demonstrated the weakness of both the state and First Nations in coping with confrontation. It could have unleashed violence—Oka times ten—across the country.

Instead, drawing from the inspiration and guidance of the four founders, Idle No More was something altogether different. It was joyous—more celebratory than angry. It was cultural more than it was political. Drumming and singing, long marches and Round Dances are its legacy, not speeches and slogans. There were hundreds of events, in Canada and around the world, and they shared certain obvious characteristics: peacefulness, a desire for progress and reconciliation, openness to others, determination, and the single most sustained and inspiring affirmation in Canadian history—Aboriginal resilience and survival.

I will say it again and again: I believe that Idle No More has transformed Canadian politics and public life. It has reshaped Canada. The movement offered more than its share of harsh words directed at Prime Minister Harper and his government, but Aboriginal political leaders felt the sting of criticism as well. The marchers, dancers, and singers did not single out one person or one organization for the challenges facing Aboriginal people in Canada. Instead, they pointed at all political leaders, the political processes and structures, the values of the dominant society, the lack of interest in Aboriginal cultures, the decline of self-respect among Indigenous peoples, and the failure to look after the land that both Aboriginal and non-Aboriginal share, inhabit, and have no other choice but to nurture.

Idle No More also sent a message that peaceful assembly and positive statements of values, culture, and policy could find a real and large audience. Among First Nations, Warrior Societies have been prominent and influential in recent decades. These are most often comprised of young Aboriginal people—typically male—who are often angry and determined to stand up for their people's rights and protect their territories. They have been a formidable influence, particularly at the local and regional level. Idle No More—also young, but more female in its membership and with a message of reconciliation and cultural strength—offered Aboriginal people a different means of making their case and garnering attention. And no one can claim that the country did not sit up and take notice. But the one element that got little attention was the most important: tens of thousands of people gathered, in hundreds of events over many months, without violence, property damage, or significant disruption to the lives of others, or any harm to the Canadian economy. Idle No More, one of the largest and most powerful movements in Canadian history, attracted and required less policing or enforcement than a handful of outspoken critics who turned the 2010 G-8/G-20 Summit in Toronto into a bitter clash with police and Canadian authorities. Who applauded the Aboriginal people and their supporters for showing the country how a massive group could, with passion and dignity, make their voices heard, challenge governments and the status quo, draw thousands together time and time again, and then leave with the echoes of drummers and singers in their wake, instead of the sound of police sirens and the smell of tear gas?

While it is, in my opinion, unfortunate that more non-Aboriginal people did not see and understand what was going on with Idle No More, the movement really was not about the non-Aboriginal people and dominant groups in Canada. Instead, the movement was about Aboriginal people coming together, singing, dancing, and talking to each other. It is this affirmation of identity, a simple but powerful assertion that Indigenous peoples—First Nations, Inuit, and Métis—are a permanent feature in Canada's political, social, cultural, economic, and environmental life and future, that is the lasting legacy of Idle No More. This message, I believe, resonated deeply with Indigenous peoples, particularly the youth. This was their time, and they made the most of it, finding voice, friendly common cause, and a sense of destiny. Forget that Idle No More did not stop Bill C-45; it was never going to accomplish that narrow and difficult task. Remember, instead, that it sowed the seeds of empowerment, collective responsibility, and Indigenous determination. Now, watch these seeds grow. Watch the young people of Idle No More: the twenty-somethings who found themselves in front of a microphone, addressing hundreds of people and drawing on the power of their Elders and cultures to share their thoughts; the four-, five-, and six-year-olds brought to the events by their parents who will have, as one of their earliest memories, the sound of the drum, the chants of the singers, and the shuffling feet of the Round Dance; the youth who participated in long winter marches, enduring difficult weather conditions while covering significant distances, journeying across the provinces, inspiring others to join. This is where the future of Canada has been rerouted.

Revolutionary change happens when opponents of the current regime rise up and overthrow it. Idle No More did not effect that kind of change, and the organizers never intended it to. Although few of the commentators have said it, the reality is that Aboriginal people have found their feet—in education, in business, in politics, and in law. They know, only too well, that a great deal remains to be done. A friend and student at the University of Saskatchewan, down from the North to pursue her formal studies and take a respite from the cut and thrust of Aboriginal politics, exemplifies this reality. Smart and engaged, she struggles to balance her education with the demands of a distant family and commitments to her home region. Three times in six months, she has had to leave her studies to head home for funerals for family members who died far too young. This is still the tragic reality of many Aboriginal lives in Canada; my friend is one of the most promising, determined, and forceful women one could hope to meet—and she is exhausted by it all.

I do not know if Idle No More will be resurrected in its former form and whether or not it will come back on the same scale as we saw it at. I rather think not. The founders have a much lower profile, many people are claiming to be the inheritors of the Idle No More movement, tensions within the Assembly of First Nations have distracted attention from grassroots activity, and empowered Aboriginal people are turning their attention to local Aboriginal politics, regional issues, or specific national policy debates. But Idle No More has done its work and, in its way, it continues to affect the actions and thoughts of Aboriginal peoples across Canada. At the community level, in electoral politics, on college and university campuses, in meetings about environment and development, in countless Aboriginal gatherings across the country, the message of Idle No More lives on. It is strong, confident, and assertive. It worries old-style Aboriginal politicians, government officials, and non-Indigenous political leaders, for in Idle No More they could not find the one simple protest or problem, the quick fix that they prefer to focus on. Idle No More, it seems to me, has changed the way Aboriginal people think about their place in Canada and has shown Indigenous communities that they can and should expect far more out of life and their country than they have received to date.

In the end, I found Idle No More to be unrelentingly positive and hopeful. There were nasty bits—although the harsh words directed at Aboriginal participants greatly outnumbered any angry words spoken by the participants in Idle No More—but the positive feelings and outcomes were much stronger. Aboriginal people stood up, found others standing with them, discovered significant non-Aboriginal support at times, and realized that they had common cause with Indigenous communities across the country. The small meeting at Station 20 West launched a national evolution, not a revolution. The exciting part is realizing that, as the participants in Idle No More and their children continue to work their way through the education system, into the workforce, and into the political realm, the peaceful, hopeful, confident, and resilient spirit of Aboriginal peoples in Canada will become the defining characteristic of the Indigenous presence in this country.

And Canada, well, this evolution will help remake the country for the better—for Aboriginals and non-Aboriginals alike. Thank you, #idlenomore, for this prairie storm, for providing us with the opportunity to see Canada in this new light.

ACKNOWLEDGEMENTS

I t is a challenge to write a book on a topic as immediate and complex as Idle No More. My researcher, Joelena Leader, has been well beyond extraordinary. Her dedication to the task and the effort and skill she brought to the task have been outstanding. She was helped enormously by Rhiannon Klein, whose sharp eye for detail and nuance was invaluable as we worked through hundreds of hours of YouTube video and web-based materials. Ryan Deschamps brought his knowledge and comfort with social media to our analysis and helped us greatly. I appreciate the willingness of Mark Blevis to allow me to use his social media analyses in the book.

That this book happened at all is due in substantial measure to major contributions by others. Bruce Walsh, Director of the University of Regina Press, has made a huge splash since he arrived in Saskatchewan. His encouragement, prodding, and support have been invaluable. Karen Clark, Acquisitions Editor for the Press, saw potential in the first rough draft and devoted time she probably did not have to transforming the initial work into a decent manuscript. Meaghan Craven did a remarkable job as the editor of the work, providing insight and ideas that went well beyond the norm one expects from a professional editor. Donna Grant, the Managing Editor, guided the manuscript through its production and Duncan Campbell, the Art Director, reshaped words on a page into an attractive book. My executive assistant, Sherilee Diebold-Cooze, has been her usual remarkable and helpful self throughout this project. My wonderful staff and faculty colleagues at my shared home bases—the Johnson-Shoyama Graduate School of Public Policy and the International Centre for Northern Governance and Development—provided me with a supportive and encouraging home for my scholarly and outreach activities. I thank, in particular, Executive Director Michael Atkinson and Regina campus Director Kathy McNutt who have been greatly helpful and encouraging. Throughout all of this work, my wife, Carin Holroyd, and my at-home daughter, Hana Coates, have been tolerant and supportive in equal measure. None of these fine people have any responsibility for any shortcomings in this book.

I am most grateful to the photographers whose work is included here: Alyssa Bird, Nadya Kwandibens, Christopher McLeod, Marcel Petit, Ben Powless, Lukasz Szczepanski, and Adrian Wyld of The Canadian Press. And thank you to Ta'Kaiya Blaney and her family for permission to reprint her image here, as well.

Proceeds of the sale of this book will go to the General Scholarship Fund at First Nations University of Canada.

NOTES

PREFACE: QUIET NO MORE

1   The Kino-nda-niimi Collective, *The Winter We Danced: Voices from the Past, the Future, and the Idle No More Movement* (Winnipeg: ARP Books, 2014).

2   The Sparrow decision (R. v. Sparrow [1990]) made by the Supreme Court of Canada was a precedent-setting case that set out the official criteria for determining whether or not Aboriginal rights infringed upon by the government were justifiable based on their existence at the time of the Constitution Act, 1982. This is also known as "the Sparrow Test." The Calder Case (Calder v. Attorney-General of British Columbia [1973]) was the infamous Supreme Court ruling that legally acknowledged Aboriginal title to land that existed at the time of the Royal Proclamation of 1763. Although the court ruled against the specific claims by the Nisga'a people, the court case paved the way for the federal government's comprehensive land claims process, whereby Aboriginal groups could claim title to their territory. The Marshall court decision (R. v. Marshall [1999]) affirmed the treaty right to hunt, fish, and gather in order to pursue a "moderate livelihood," which was arising out of the 1760 and 1761 Peace and Friendship Treaties. In the recent and historic William judgment (Tsilhqot'in Nation v. British Columbia [2014]), the Supreme Court of Canada granted declaration of Aboriginal title to the Tsilhqot'in First Nation for over 1,700 square kilometres of land in British Columbia.

CHAPTER 1: MOBILIZING AN AWAKENING

1   The MPs and civil servants, through all-party agreement, had this section removed from the bill and dealt with separately.

2   "Bill C-45? What's in Omnibus Bill 2," *Huffington Post*, October 18, 2012, www.huffingtonpost.ca/2012/10/18/bill-c-45-omnibus-budget-bill_n_1981967.html#slide=1658234.

3   Jessica Gordon, "'Idle No More' Rally to Oppose Budget Implementation Bill C 45," Idle No More Facebook events page, November 2, 2012, www.facebook.com/events/299767020134614/.

4   Jessica Gordon, "#idlenomore," October 30, 2012, www.twitter.com.

5   Jessica Gordon, "#idlenomore," November 4, 2012, www.twitter.com.

6   Tanya Kappo, "#idlenomore," November 4, 2012, www.twitter.com.

7   "Idle No More Rally" poster, Idle No More Facebook album, November 5, 2012, www.facebook.com/photo.php?fbid=491567804207410&set=0a.359931934100239&type=1&theater.

8   Jessica Gordon, "'Idle No More' Rally to Oppose Budget Implementation Bill C 45," Idle No More Facebook events page, November 7, 2012, www. facebook.com/events/299767020134614/.

9   "Idle No More Interview with Nina Wilson," YouTube video, 4:56, posted by "TrevorGreyeyesNews," November 19, 2012, www.youtube.com/watch?v=L-PaAzUZ5mAE.

10   Ashley Wills, "Indian Act Amendments Need Proper Consultation: Groups Hold Protest in Saskatoon Today," News Talk 650 CKOM, last modified November 10, 2012, www.ckom.com/story/indian-act-amendments-need-proper-consultation/83104.

11   "Idle No More Is Founded by 4 Women," *Idle No More*, accessed September 1, 2014, www.idlenomore.ca/idle_no_more_is_founded_by_4_women.

12   "The Leading Global Thinkers of 2013," *Foreign Policy*, December 2013, www. foreignpolicy.com/2013_global_thinkers/public/.

13   "Biography of Founders," *Idle No More*, January 21, 2013, www.idlenomore. ca/about-us/item/121-biography-of-founders?reset-settings.

14   Jessica Gordon's LinkedIn Profile, accessed September 1, 2014, www.linkedin. com/pub/jessica-gordon/37/a02/529.

15   Febna Caven, "Being Idle No More," *Cultural Survival*, January 8, 2013, www. culturalsurvival.org/news/being-idle-no-more.

16   "9 Questions about Idle No More," *CBC News*, January 5, 2013, www.cbc.ca/ news/canada/9-questions-about-idle-no-more-1.1301843.

17   Ibid.

18   Sylvia McAdam, "Conference Presenter Profile," *Spirit of the Land,* accessed September 1, 2014, spiritoftheland.ca/conference/presenters/sylvia-mcadam/. See also, Peter Wilson, "First Nations' Culture Shared by Sask. Author," *The Star Phoenix,* March 8, 2010, www2.canada.com/saskatoonstarphoenix/ news/local/story.html?id=52a6546e-abe7-4ca0-b3a3-02486377bbeb.

19   Tom Eremondi, "A Call to Action," *Arts & Science Magazine* (Spring 2013): 8–9, quoted in "Sheelah McLean: A Call to Action," College of Arts & Science, University of Saskatchewan, April 10, 2013, artsandscience.usask.ca/ news/news.php?newsid=3522.

20   Ibid.

21   "Idle No More is Founded by 4 Women."

22   Ian Oakes, "Interview with Nina Wilson, A Founder of the Idle No More Movement," www.indiantime.net/story/2013/01/31/news interview-with-nina-wilson-a-founder-of-the-idle-no-more-movement/7359.html.

23   "The Genocide Will Not Be Televised," YouTube video, 7:45, posted by "Jessica Gordon," November 10, 2012, www.youtube.com/watch?v=nVlS3JrLNAY&-feature=youtube_gdata_player.

24   "We Are ALL at Risk," YouTube video, November 10, 2012, www.youtube. com/watch?v=wmQQtSusV8I. (As of October 2014, this video is no longer available on YouTube.)

25   Kelly Block MP, "Harper Cons Should Respect Democracy," petition, Idle No More Facebook album, accessed September 1, 2014, www.facebook.com/photo.php?fbid=10151272659375862&set=0a.359931934100239&type=1&theater.

26   Mark Bigland-Pritchard, Idle No More Facebook events page, November 10, 2012, www.facebook.com/events/299767020134614/.

27   Miki Mappin, Idle No More Facebook events page, November 10, 2012, www.facebook.com/events/299767020134614/.

28   Jessica Gordon, Idle No More Facebook events page, November 3, 2012, www.facebook.com/events/299767020134614/.

29   "Conservative Proposed Omnibus Indian Act Changes would Allow Bands to Lease out Reserve Lands Without Majority Community Support," *APTN National News*, November 21, 2012, aptn.ca/news/2012/11/21/conservative-proposed-omnibus-indian-act-changes-would-allow-bands-to-lease-out-reserve-lands-without-majority-community-support/.

30   Emma Graney, "Indigenous Unease with Bill C-45," *Leader-Post* (Regina), November 19, 2012.

31   Meagan Wohlberg, "Budget Bill Proposes Changes to Waterway Protection: New Act Will Protect Only Busiest Rivers, Lakes and Oceans," *Slave River Journal*, October 23, 2012.

32   Nina Wilson, Idle No More Facebook events page, November 10, 2012, www.facebook.com/events/299767020134614/.

33   Parliament of Canada, "Senate Committee Holds Public Hearings in Western Canada on Rights of First Nations People Living Off-reserve," Media Advisory: The Standing Senate Committee on Human Rights, November 14, 2012, www.parl.gc.ca/Content/SEN/Committee/411/ridr/press/14NOV12-e.htm.

34   "'Idle No More' Regina Rally to oppose budget implementation Bill C-45," Idle No More Facebook events page, November 17, 2012, www.facebook.com/events/130038743813408/permalink/133954686755147/.

35   "Idle No More Interview with Nina Wilson," www.youtube.com/watch?v=L-PaAzUZ5mAE.

36   "Idle No More Prince Albert," Margo Fournier Center, Facebook events page, www.facebook.com/events/379547885462660/.

37   Jessica Gordon, Idle No More Facebook events page, November 25, 2012, www.facebook.com/events/299767020134614/.

38   Originating in traditional stories, especially in the stories of First Nations located in the eastern parts of the continent, Turtle Island is the earlier name given to the land that is called North America.

39   "Press Release Idle No More," *Idle No More* (blog), accessed September 2, 2014, idlenomore1.blogspot.ca/p/blog-page_17.html.

40   Idle No More Saskatoon Facebook page, accessed September 3, 2014, www.facebook.com/IdleNoMoreSaskatoon/info.

41   D. Chidley, "Idle No More Movement Sets Social Media Ablaze," *TheStar.com*, December 20, 2012, www.thestar.com/news/canada/2012/12/20/idle_no_more_movement_sets_social_media_ablaze.html.

42   R. Lindell, "#IdleNoMore Tweets Followed Closely by Aboriginal Affairs," *Global News*, April 10, 2013, globalnews.ca/news/470073/idlenomore-tweets-followed-closely-by-aboriginal-affairs/.

43   Mark Blevis, "Idle No More at Two Months: Traffic Analysis (Part 1/6)," Mark Blevis: Digital Public Affairs, markblevis.com/idle-no-more-at-two-months-traffic-analysis/.

CHAPTER 2: THE ROOTS OF ABORIGINAL ANGER AND HOPE

1   The Marshall decision is one of the best-known Supreme Court case rulings of the 1990s, where Maritime First Nations people have a treaty right to fish and sell their catch to earn what the court claimed as "a moderate livelihood" (R. v. Marshall [1999]). See Ken Coates, *The Marshall Decision and Aboriginal Rights in the Maritimes* (Montreal: McGill-Queen's University Press, 1999).

2   Ken Coates and Brian Lee Crowley, "New Beginnings: How Canada's Natural Resource Wealth Could Re-shape Relations with Aboriginal People" (Ottawa: Macdonald-Laurier Institute, May 2013). See also Ken Coates and Brian Lee Crowley, "The Way Out: New Thinking Aboriginal Engagement and Energy Infrastructure to the West Coast" (Ottawa: Macdonald-Laurier Institute, May 2013); and Ken Coates and Dwight Newman, "The End is Not Nigh: Reason over Alarmism in Analyzing the Tsilhqot'in Decision" (Ottawa: Macdonald-Laurier Institute, September 2014).

CHAPTER 3: THE ROUND DANCE REVOLUTION

1   "Idle No More Alberta – Tanya Kappo – Introduction," YouTube video, 9:16, posted by "Karri-Lynn Paul," December 3, 2012, www.youtube.com/watch?v=YZAQBypqKyw.

2   "Idle No More Alberta – Sylvia McAdam," YouTube video, 12:05, posted by "Karri-Lynn Paul," December 3, 2012, www.youtube.com/watch?v=pKJ4m-W5urgU.

3   Ibid.

4   Ibid.

5   Jessica Gordon, Sheelah McLean, Sylvia McAdam, and Nina Wilson, "Idle No More National Solidarity & Resurgence," Idle No More Facebook events page, December 10, 2012, www.facebook.com/events/460560813989463/.

6   Ibid.

7   Ibid.

8   Jessica Gordon, "#idlenomore," twitter.com.

9   Ibid.

10   "'IDLE' No More Rally Protest @ Saskatoon, SK December 10, 2012," YouTube video, 53.02, posted by "Jamie Martell," December 10, 2012, www.youtube.com/watch?v=NLyKbTlWyuY.

11   Ibid.

12   Ibid.

13   "Solidarity Rally – Friends of Grand River ~ Idle No More ~ Save Muskrat Falls, Labrador," YouTube video, 1:30, posted by "Denise Cole," December 10, 2012, www.youtube.com/watch?v=x1wS9nrWmhM.

14   Ibid.

15   "Whitehorse Rallies at Conservative MP's Office," APTN *National News*, December 11, 2012, aptn.ca/news/2012/12/11/whitehorse-rallies-at-conservative-mps-office/.

16   Ibid.

17   "Idle No More Movement Comes to the Yukon," interview with MP Ryan Leef by Leonard Linklater, CBC North, *Airplay*, December 21, 2012, www.cbc.ca/airplay/2012/12/.

18   Kira Wilson, "Idle No More Rally Draws 300 to Manitoba Legislature," CBC *News*, Manitoba, December 10, 2012, www.cbc.ca/news/canada/manitoba/idle-no-more-rally-draws-300-to-manitoba-legislature-1.1185033.

19   Ibid.

20   Ibid.

21   Ibid.

22   "Idle No More," CBC *News*, Thunder Bay, December 10, 2012, www.cbc.ca/voyagenorth/2012/12/10/idle-no-more/.

23   Ibid.

24   Ibid.

25   Ibid.

26   Derrick O'Keefe, "On the Mainstream Media's Shameful Failure to Cover #IdleNoMore," *Rabble.ca*, December 12, 2012, rabble.ca/blogs/bloggers/derrick/2012/12/media-silence-around-idlenomore.

27   Waub, "#idlenomore," twitter.com/waub.

28   RIIC News, "#idlenomore," twitter.com/riicnews.

29   Ryan McMahon, "#idlenomore," twitter.com/RMComedy.

30   Anonymous, "#idlenomore," Anonymous @YourAnonNews.

31   Dakota J Lightning, "#idlenomore," twitter.com/dakotalightning.

32   Lauren Strapagiel, "Idle No More Day of Action Draws Aboriginal Protestors across Canada," *Huffington Post*, December 10, 2012, www.huffingtonpost.ca/2012/12/10/idle-no-more_n_2273244.html.

33   "Idle No More Halifax, NS Dec 14,2012 H 264," YouTube video, 9:55, posted by "Catherine Martin," December 14, 2012, www.youtube.com/watch?v=Ym-bqwPRlyzU.

34   Ibid.

35   Ibid.

36   Ibid.

37   "Bill C-45, Jobs and Growth Act Not to be Recognized or Enforced by First Nations in Ontario," *Chiefs of Ontario*, accessed September 5, 2014, www.chiefs-of-ontario.org/node/453.

38   "The Road Block – Idle No More," YouTube video, 30:00, posted by "douglasrthomas," December 15, 2012, www.youtube.com/watch?v=Vlyxvy6HYvA.

39   "Sandy Bay First Nation Blockade on Trans-Canada Highway," YouTube video, 04:50, posted by "cfrynews," December 15, 2012, www.youtube.com/watch?v=y67Niokf_zY.

40   Ibid.

41   Svjetlana Mlinarevic, "Aboriginal Protesters Block Highway of Heroes," *Winnipeg Sun*, December 15, 2012, www.winnipegsun.com/2012/12/15/idle-no-more-protesters-take-over-highway-1.

42   See, for example, the review of media and business commentaries in "Media Ridicules Occupy Wall Street," www.huffingtonpost.com/peter-s-goodman/media-occupy-wall-street_b_1033267.html, and "A Guide to the Smear Campaign Against Occupy Wall Street," mediamatters.org/research/2011/10/18/a-guide-to-the-smear-campaign-against-occupy-wa/181591.

43   "Idlenomore – Regina Round Dance Flash Mob," YouTube video, 8:12, posted by "Smokey01Smoke," December, 17, 2012, www.youtube.com/watch?v=QA_Hn84SrcM.

44   "Round Dance flash mob style west Edmonton mall," YouTube video, 5:47, posted by "Jamie John-kehewin," December 18, 2012, www.youtube.com/watch?v=_qz-qmApho4.

45   Neeshy, "#idlenomore," twitter.com/neeeshy.

46   "Part 1 – Flash Mob Round Dance SASKATOON Midtown Plaza IDLE NO MORE," YouTube Video, 8:09, posted by "Brown Can Shine," December 20, 2012, www.youtube.com/watch?v=IEtBobjOwJ8.

47   Melissa Martin, "Round Dance: Why It's the Symbol of Idle No More," CBC *Manitoba Scene*, January 28, 2013, www.cbc.ca/manitoba/scene/homepage-promo/2013/01/28/round-dance-revolution-drums-up-support-for-idle-no-more/.

48   "12.21.12 Idle No More Edmonton Rally Speech," YouTube video, 1:11, posted by "Brad Crowfoot," December 21, 2012, www.youtube.com/watch?v=s-0J1K-sl1EU.

49   "#IdleNoMore Denendeh Yellowknife #YZF #NWT," YouTube video, 1:36:43, posted by "George Lessard," December 21, 2012, www.youtube.com/watch?v=hVh6YWCDWZ0.

50   "Idle No More Protests Hit Calgary and Southern Alberta," CBC *News*, December 21, 2012, www.cbc.ca/news/canada/calgary/idle-no-more-protests-hit-calgary-and-southern-alberta-1.1212063.

51   David P. Ball, "Idle No More Sweeps Canada and Beyond: Aboriginals Say Enough is Enough," *Indian Country Today Media Network*, December 22, 2012, indiancountrytodaymedianetwork.com/2012/12/22/idle-no-more-sweeps-canada-and-beyond-aboriginals-say-enough-enough-146516.

52   "First Nations Idle No More Protests Push for Reckoning," *The Globe and Mail*, December 19, 2012, www.theglobeandmail.com/news/politics/first-nations-idlenomore-protests-push-for-reckoning/article6589418/.

53   "12.21.12 Idle No More Edmonton Rally Speech."

54 Nocokwis Greyeyes, Idle No More Facebook events page, December 21, 2012, www.facebook.com/events/492285850793858/.

55 "#IdleNoMore Denendeh Yellowknife."

56 "Dease Lake – Idle No More," YouTube video, 3:00, posted by "Sonia Dennis," December 21, 2012, www.youtube.com/watch?v=b2hV-Gr26j8.

57 "Idle No More - This is the face of the future, Harper! *The Indignants*," YouTube video, 1:26, posted by "Mike Roy," December 24, 2012, www.youtube.com/watch?v=y9pBux_ZYXM.

58 "Idle No More Courtenay BC," YouTube video, posted by "billiemargaret harlow," December 29, 2012, www.youtube.com/watch?v=tH5Er9y4A4U.

59 "Idle No More Protests Hit Winnipeg," CBC News, December 21, 2012, www.cbc.ca/news/canada/manitoba/idle-no-more-protests-hit-winnipeg-1.1130334.

60 "IdleNoMore Toronto FlashMob Shuts Down Dundas Square," YouTube video, 1:18, posted by "WorldTruthNow," December 21, 2012, www.youtube.com/watch?v=mG4bBu234ko&list=PLLZZvb6O8OauRptoeDJlI1foKPokNw-P3A&index=9.

61 "Idle No More – This is the face of the future, Harper!" See also "Idle No More – Aamjiwnaang Nation, Sarnia, Ontario," The Indignants Facebook page, December 24, 2012, www.facebook.com/media/set/?set=a.476734465701725.104764.257145594327281&type=3.

62 On January 2, 2013, protestors left the blockade site at around midnight. "Sarnia Railway Clear after Judge Orders End to Native Blockade," The Globe and Mail, January 2, 2013, www.theglobeandmail.com/news/national/sarnia-railway-clear-after-judge-orders-end-to-native-blockade/article6889622.

63 Norlaine Thomas, "#cdnpoli," www.twitter.com.

64 Diana Day, "#idlenomore," www.twitter.com.

65 Scott McF, "#idlenomore," www.twitter.com.

66 Arün Smith, "#idlenomore," and "#solidarity," www.twitter.com.

67 Luke Bradley, "#idlenomore," www.twitter.com.

68 "New Brunswick Natives continues [sic] to protest C Bill-45 at Regent Mall in Fredericton," YouTube video, 4:17, posted by "Charles LeBlanc," December 24, 2012, www.youtube.com/watch?v=R_fYvRN1CMM#t=159.

69 "Moncton: In Solidarity with Idle No More Part 1 – 2013," YouTube video, 0:46, posted by "wc nativenews," December 27, 2013, www.youtube.com/watch?v=3-FcGqFtLk4.

70 "Idle No More Gains Momentum," Sylvia McAdam interview with David Gray, The Calgary Eyeopener, CBC Radio, December 21, 2012, www.cbc.ca/player/Radio/Local+Shows/Alberta/ID/2319964933/.

71 For some examples of this common reference, see Facebook: www.facebook.com/pages/Idle-No-More-Get-a-damn-job/429641760440455. See also Harsha Walia, "Debunking Blatchford and Other Anti-Native Ideologues on Idle No More," Rabble.ca, December 30, 2012, rabble.ca/news/2012/12/debunking-blatchford-and-other-anti-native-ideologues-idle-no-more; Alexis Van Bemmel, "Racist Responses to Idle No More Tied to Misinformation about Canada's Past," The Straight, April 1, 2013, www.straight.com/

news/367451/alexis-van-bemmel-racist-responses-idle-no-more-tied-misin-formation-about-canadas-past; and "'Idle No More,' Protesters Confront Ezra Levant Over Alleged Racism," *Huffington Post*, January 20, 2013, www. huffingtonpost.ca/2013/01/20/idle-no-more-toronto-sun-protest_n_2516125. html.

72   Jessica Gordon's Facebook page, December 22, 2012, www.facebook.com/ jessicapearl78. See also Âpihtawikosisân, "Renewal: What Idle No More Means to Me," *Decolonization, Indigeneity, Education & Society* (blog), December 21, 2012, decolonization.wordpress.com/2012/12/21/renewal/.

73   "Idle No More Gains Momentum across Canada," Sylvia McAdam interview with Anna Maria Tremonti, *The Current*, CBC Radio, December 19, 2012, www.cbc.ca/thecurrent/episode/2012/12/19/idle-no-more-gains-momentum-across-canada/.

74   Ibid.

75   Ibid.

76   Shannon Houle, "Face and Leaders of Idle No More is the Grassroots People," *Idle No More* (blog), December 31, 2012, idlenomore1.blogspot.ca/ search?updated-max=2013-01-01T02:51:00-07:00&max-results=10.

77   Ray McCallum, Idle No More Facebook timeline photo post, December 21, 2012, www.facebook.com/photo.php?fbid=10151591904969377&set =a.10151377860889377.570480.727844376&type=1&theater.

78   "Idle No More: Indigenous-led Protests Sweep Canada for Native Sovereignty and Environmental Justice," Pamela Palmater interview with Amy Goodman and Nermeen Shaikh, *DemocracyNow.org*, December 26, 2012, www. democracynow.org/2012/12/26/idle_no_more_indigenous_led_protests.

79   JoyArc, "#idlenomore," December 1, 2012, www.twitter.com.

CHAPTER 4: THE OTTAWA DISTRACTION AND THE COMPLICATED EVOLUTION OF IDLE NO MORE

1   "Idle No More, Ladysmith, BC," YouTube video, 9:09, posted by "Phil Ives," January 2, 2013, www.youtube.com/watch?v=kpMidXplHRI.

2   "Attawapiskat Chief Theresa Spence Speaks on Parliament Hill, Dec.10 2012 Part 1 of 2," YouTube video, 9:41, posted by "Kevin Gagnon," December 10, 2012, www.youtube.com/watch?v=qzDQjvsMYMg.

3   "Chief Spence Exclusive Interview with CBC," Theresa Spence interview with Chris Rands, *CBC News*, December 18, 2012, www.cbc.ca/player/Shows/ ID/2318285061/.

4   "Attawapiskat Chief Theresa Spence Speaks on Parliament Hill."

5   Ibid.

6   Ibid.

7   "Chief Spence Exclusive Interview."

8   Krystalline Kraus, "#idlenomore," www.twitter.com.

9   Andrea Landry, #idlenomore," www.twitter.com.

10   Jorge Barrera, "As AFN Pushes for Harper Meeting, Attawapiskat Chief Spence Says Crown Needs to be Involved," APTN *National News,* December 14, 2012, aptn.ca/news/2012/12/14/as-afn-pmo-discuss-possible-harper-meeting-attawapiskat-chief-spence-says-crown-needs-to-be-involved/.

11   "Idle No More Rallies Held across Canada as Movement Grows," CTV *News,* December 21, 2012. See CTV News Channel, "Call To End Hunger Strike." www.ctvnews.ca/canada/idle-no-more-rallies-held-across-canada-as-movement-grows-1.1088765.

12   "Idle No More Rallies Held across Canada as Movement Grows," CTV *News,* December 21, 2012. See CTV News Channel, "NDP Weighs in on Hunger Strike." www.ctvnews.ca/canada/idle-no-more-rallies-held-across-canada-as-movement-grows-1.1088765.

13   Ibid.

14   Ibid.

15   Krystalline Kraus, "Toronto Solidarity Fast in Support of Attawapiskat Chief Theresa Spence," Krystalline Kraus Facebook events page, www.facebook.com/events/422975924437823/?notif_t=plan_user_joined.

16   Heather Scoffield, "Theresa Spence Says Hunger Strike's Effect on Her Health Means Meeting with Harper Must Come Soon," *Huffington Post,* January 3, 2013, www.huffingtonpost.ca/2013/01/03/theresa-spence-hunger-strike_n_2402658.html.

17   "IdleNoMore Six Nations Territory," YouTube video, 5:13, posted by "fightpollution," December 19, 2012, www.youtube.com/watch?v=hmdUJL_ro2Y.

18   "Idle No More Protests Block New Brunswick Roadways," CBC *News,* December 21, 2012, www.cbc.ca/news/canada/new-brunswick/idle-no-more-protests-block-new-brunswick-roadways-1.1257740.

19   "Idle No More at Cree Nation of Eastmain, QC, Canada," YouTube video, 3:26, posted by "Richard Cheezo," December 21, 2012, www.youtube.com/watch?v=e8Xfi98RP_4.

20   "'Idle No More' FLASH MOB Round Dance Regent Mall Fredericton NB," YouTube video, 10:59, posted by "piggylittlefish," December 24, 2012, www.youtube.com/watch?v=lIvkOom1MEO.

21   "Idle No More 7 KM March In Support of Chief Spence, Spruce Grove to Stony Plain, AB.," YouTube video, December 31, 2012, accessed March 21, 2014, www.youtube.com/watch?v=nq-YioBFWPw. (Currently unavailable on YouTube.)

22   "Idle No More Ottawa – Dec 21, 2012," YouTube video, 2:47, posted by "Tina," December 21, 2012, www.youtube.com/watch?v=wZEIdjukhYY.

23   "Clayton Thomas-Muller speech at Ottawa IdleNoMore 21 December 2012," YouTube video, 12:01, posted by "Isabeau Doucet," December 21, 2012, www.youtube.com/watch?v=49Am6sgjksA.

24   Annette Francis, "Sympathy Hunger Strikes Begin in Support of Attawapiskat Chief Theresa Spence," APTN *National News,* December 14, 2012, aptn.ca/news/2012/12/14/sympathy-hunger-strikes-begin-in-support-of-attawapiskat-chief-theresa-spence/.

25   Shawn McCarthy and James Bradshaw, "Idle No More Protestors Block Main Toronto-Montreal Rail Line in Support of Chief Spence," *The Globe and Mail*, December 30, 2012, www.theglobeandmail.com/news/national/idle-no-more-protestors-block-main-toronto-montreal-rail-line-in-support-of-chief-spence/article6802286/.

26   "Academics in Solidarity with Chief Theresa Spence: Open Letter," Academics in Solidarity with Chief Theresa Spence and Idle No More, December 21, 2012, academicsinsolidarity.wordpress.com/.

27   William Watson, "The Politics of Hunger Strikes: First Nations Chief has Clout Whether We like It or Not," *Edmonton Journal*, January 3, 2013, www2.canada.com/edmontonjournal/news/ideas/story.html?id=7a63cb28-d3b3-4fd8-8432-2b29b399be90.

28   "Chief Theresa Spence - Hunger Strike Day 20 - #idlenomore," YouTube video, 6:43, posted by "IPSMO," December 31, 2013, www.youtube.com/watch?v=McUaxs53lmo#t=76.

29   "Theresa Spence Pulls out of Meeting with Harper," CBC News, January 9, 2013, www.cbc.ca/news/politics/theresa-spence-pulls-out-of-meeting-with-harper-1.1337648.

30   Teresa Smith, "Ottawa Businesses Support Chief Theresa Spence's Hunger Strike," *Ottawa Citizen*, January 5, 2013, www.canadianprogressiveworld.com/2013/01/05/ottawa-businesses-support-chief-theresa-spences-hunger-strike/#.UwzTN_ldwso.

31   Suzanne Benally, "In Support of Chief Spence and the Rights of Indigenous Peoples," *Cultural Survival*, January 10, 2013, www.culturalsurvival.org/news/support-chief-spence-and-rights-indigenous-peoples.

32   "Joint Statement Supporting Chief Spence and 'Idle No More,'" *Amnesty International Canada*, January 2, 2013, www.amnesty.ca/news/public-statements/joint-statement-supporting-chief-spence-and-idle-no-more.

33   See full transcript of comments made regarding Theresa Spence on *The Source with Ezra Levant*, "Appendix A: CBSC Decision 12/13-0985, Sun News Network re. *The Source* (Idle No More)," CBCS document, CBCS, www.cbsc.ca/english/decisions/2013/131023appa.pdf.

34   "Prime Minister Stephen Harper Announces Meeting with First Nations Leadership," *Prime Minister of Canada*, January 4, 2013, www.pm.gc.ca/eng/news/2013/01/04/prime-minister-stephen-harper-announces-meeting-first-nations-leadership.

35   Teresa Smith, "Chief Theresa Spence Steadfast on Refusing to Eat in Idle No More Protest," *Ottawa Citizen*, January 14, 2013, www.ottawacitizen.com/news/Chief+Theresa+Spence+steadfast+refusing+Idle+More+protest/7818844/story.html.

36   Jorge Barrera, "AFN's Fault Lines Magnified by Idle No More Movement, Attawapiskat Chief Spence's Protest," APTN *National News*, January 15, 2013, aptn.ca/news/2013/01/15/afns-fault-lines-magnified-by-idle-no-more-movement-attawapiskat-chief-spences-protest/.

37   "Chief Theresa Spence to End Hunger Strike Today," CBC *News*, January 23, 2013, www.cbc.ca/news/politics/chief-theresa-spence-to-end-hunger-strike-today-1.1341571.

38   "Theresa Spence Pulls out of Meeting."

39   "Spence to Join Harper Meeting with Chiefs Jan. 11," CBC *News*, January 4, 2013, www.cbc.ca/news/politics/spence-to-join-harper-meeting-with-chiefs-jan-11-1.1346505.

40   Jason Fekete, "Stephen Harper Meets with First Nations Leaders as Sprawling Protest Unfolds in Ottawa," *National Post*, January 11, 2013, news.national-post.com/2013/01/11/harper-meeting-with-chiefs-begins-as-mass-protest-unfolds-in-ottawa/.

41   "#J11 Global Day of Action," J11action, www.j11action.com/.

42   Ibid.

43   "Idle No More Protests Held across Canada," CBC *News*, January 11, 2013, www.cbc.ca/news/canada/idle-no-more-protests-held-across-canada-1.1311721.

44   Angelique Rodrigues, "Alberta Aboriginal Leader Vows to 'Shut Down' Oil-sands During Edmonton Idle No More Protest," *Edmonton Sun*, January 11, 2013, www.edmontonsun.com/2013/01/11/alberta-aboriginal-leader-vows-to-shut-down-oilsands-during-edmonton-idle-no-more-protest. See also "Idle No More Protests Held across Canada, First Nations Chiefs, Demonstrators Threaten to Escalate Protest Movement on Wednesday," CBC *News*, January 11, 2013, www.cbc.ca/news/canada/idle-no-more-protests-held-across-canada-1.1311721.

45   "Idle No More Protests Held Across Canada."

46   "10,000 Voices Can't be Ignored," Facebook events page, January 11, 2013, www.facebook.com/events/406023956144410.

47   "Theresa Spence Speaks out, Ottawa Press Conference CBC NEWS January 11 2013 #idlenomore," YouTube video, 7:05, posted by "douglasrthomas," January 11, 2013, www.youtube.com/watch?v=h_O1WRIVDYA.

48   "Idle No More's Thunder Heard through Walls of Prime Minister's Office," APTN *National News*, January 11, 2013, aptn.ca/news/2013/01/11/protest-dying-down-as-harper-says-hell-stay-for-entire-meeting-with-fn-leaders/.

49   "10,000 Voices."

50   "Raymond Robinson at Parliament Hill – January 11," YouTube video, 5:28, posted by "Selena Flood," January 11, 2013, www.youtube.com/watch?v=G-99JzsO6mxs.

51   "INM J11 Algonquian Grandmothers, Chief Spence, Raymond Robinson, Ellen Gabriel, the Youth . . . Ottawa," YouTube video, 32:06, posted by "sky-earthstories," January 11, 2013, www.youtube.com/watch?v=ySyC5MLgEU4.

52   "Idle No More's Thunder."

53   Kaniethonkie, "Idle No More Protest on January 11, 2013," *Indian Time*, January 17, 2013, www.indiantime.net/story/2013/01/17/news/idle-no-more-protest-on-january-11-2013/6902.html.

54   Ibid.

55   Fekete, "Stephen Harper Meets with First Nations Leaders."

56   Kaniethonkie, "Idle No More Protest on January 11, 2013."

57   Introduced in March 2012, Bill C-38 sought to implement the budget mea-sures included in the 2012 federal budget. Almost half of the bill, which ran to over 450 pages, focused on amendments to environmental laws. Bill C-38 revised major portions of the Canadian Environmental Assessment Act, ostensibly to speed up the oversight and approval processes.

58   Fekete, "Stephen Harper Meets with First Nations Leaders."

59   "Theresa Spence Pulls out of Meeting."

60   Andy Radia, "Public Opinion Stands Against Chief Theresa Spence, Idle No More Protestors," *Yahoo News,* January 16, 2013, ca.news.yahoo.com/blogs/canada-politics/public-opinion-stands-against-chief-theresa-spence-idle-181852988.html. For the background survey, see "Fast Fallout: Chief Spence and Idle No More Movement Galvanizes Canadians Around Money Management and Accountability: Majority Says Most of the Problems of Native Peoples are Brought on by Themselves." January 15, 2013, IPSOS (ipsos-na.com/news-polls/pressrelease.aspx?id=5961).

61   Gloria Galloway, "With Hunger Strike Over, Chief Spence's Polarizing Legacy," *The Globe and Mail,* January 24, 2013, www.theglobeandmail.com/news/politics/with-hunger-strike-over-chief-spences-polarizing-legacy/article7760372/.

62   Roger Smith, "CTV National News: Chief Spence Ends Hunger Strike," CTV *News* video, January 23, 2013, www.ctvnews.ca/canada/attawapiskat-chief-to-end-hunger-strike-1.1125718.

63   Andy Radia, "Was Chief Theresa Spence's Hunger Strike Worth It?" *Yahoo News,* January 24, 2013, ca.news.yahoo.com/blogs/canada-politics/chief-theresa-spence-hunger-strike-worth-160446365.html.

64   Barrera, "AFN's Fault Lines."

65   Matt Sheedy, "Idle No More is about More than Chief Spence," *Waging Nonviolence,* January 27, 2013, wagingnonviolence.org/feature/idle-no-more-is-about-more-than-chief-spence/.

66   Ibid.

67   "Idle No More presentation at This is not a Gateway," YouTube video, 14:26, posted by "Pete Deane," January 27, 2013, www.youtube.com/watch?v=xN-quYwNsHm4.

68   Ibid.

69   Brian Beaton, "Honouring Chief Theresa Spence as Assembly of First Nations Support Declaration," *MediaKnet,* January 24, 2013, media.knet.ca/node/22269. See also, "Attawapiskat Chief to End Hunger Strike," CTV *News,* January 23, 2013, www.ctvnews.ca/canada/attawapiskat-chief-to-end-hunger-strike-1.1125718.

70   "Chief Theresa Spence Can End Hunger Strike with Head High: Editorial," *The Star.com,* January 24, 2013, www.thestar.com/opinion/editorials/2013/01/24/chief_theresa_spence_can_end_hunger_strike_with_head_high_editorial.html.

71   Keith Beardsley, "Theresa Spence Has Little to Show for 44 days of Protest," *National Post*, January 25, 2013, fullcomment.nationalpost.com/2013/01/25/keith-beardsley-theresa-spence-has-little-to-show-for-44-days-of-protest/.

72   "Fast Fallout: Chief Spence and Idle No More Movement Galvanizes Canadians around Money Management and Accountability," IPSOS, January 15, 2013, ipsos-na.com/news-polls/pressrelease.aspx?id=5961.

73   Andy Radia, "Public Opinion Stands against Chief Theresa Spence, Idle No More Protestors," *Yahoo News*, January 16, 2013, ca.news.yahoo.com/blogs/canada-politics/public-opinion-stands-against-chief-theresa-spence-idle-181852988.html.

74   Clinton Bishop, "#idlenomore," www.twitter.com.

75   wišqii, "#idlenomore," www.twitter.com.

76   Kateri Sa'n, "#idlenomore," www.twitter.com.

CHAPTER 5: THE WINTER OF THE DISCONTENTED

1   Tensions between Indigenous peoples and Greenpeace are well known across Canada. See Bruce Braun, *The Intemperate Rainforest: Nature, Culture, and Power on Canada's West Coast* (Minneapolis: University of Minnesota Press, 2002).

2   "InnuWebTV, Innu idle No More Uashat," YouTube video, 52:15, posted by "Moïse Jourdain," January 16, 2013, www.youtube.com/watch?v=s-rloQubT86Q.

3   "Idle No More Hits Iqaluit," Courtenay White interview with Kent Driscoll, APTN *National News*, January 17, 2013, aptn.ca/news/2013/01/17/idle-no-more-hits-iqaluit/.

4   "Idle No More – Prince Rupert BC, February 11, 2013 During All Native Basketball Tournament," Vimeo video, 27:34, posted by "terracedailyonline," vimeo.com/59783107.

5   "Amazing Grace by Ta'Kaiya Blaney at the Prince Rupert Idle No More Gathering, Feb 11, 2013," YouTube video, 5:45, posted by "TerraceDailyNews," February 11, 2013, www.youtube.com/watch?v=nC8Yk3voxhw.

6   Daniel Migneault, "« Idle no more » manifeste à Roberval pour la Journée mondiale de l'eau," *letoiledulac.com*, March 22, 2013, www.letoiledulac.com/Actualites/2013-03-22/article-3205949/%26laquo-Idle-no-more-%26raquo-manifeste-a-Roberval-po..r-la-Journee-mondiale-de-leau/1.

7   "Over 800 Attend Idle No More Rally at Manitoba Legislature," CBC *News*, January 28, 2013, www.cbc.ca/news/canada/manitoba/over-800-attend-idle-no-more-rally-at-manitoba-legislature-1.1402199. See also "Idle No More: Youth March From Reserves to Winnipeg," YouTube video, 1:03, posted by "WinnipegFreePress," January 28, 2013, www.youtube.com/watch?v=G5py-w5twN1U.

8   Ibid.

9   "First Nation Youth Walk to Protest Environment Law Changes," CBC *News*, February 11, 2013, www.cbc.ca/news/canada/manitoba/first-nation-youth-walk-to-protest-environment-law-changes-1.1362189.

10   "Indigenous Youth Gather in Winnipeg in Support of Idle No More," CBC *News*, February 10, 2013, www.cbc.ca/news/canada/manitoba/indigenous-youth-gather-in-winnipeg-in-support-of-idle-no-more-1.1363882.

11   Gloria Galloway, "Nishiyuu: A Movement of Cree Youth Who Voted with Their Feet," *The Globe and Mail*, March 25, 2013, www.theglobeandmail.com/news/politics/nishiyuu-a-movement-of-cree-youth-who-voted-with-their-feet/article10327993/.

12   Jorge Barrera, "Journey of Nishiyuu Walkers' Names Now 'Etched' into 'History of this Country,'" APTN *National News*, March 26, 2013, aptn.ca/news/2013/03/26/journey-of-nishiyuu-walkers-names-now-etched-into-history-of-this-country/.

13   Galloway, "Nishiyuu."

14   "'Nishiyuu Walkers' Complete 1,600 km Trek to Ottawa," CTV *News*, March 25, 2013, www.ctvnews.ca/canada/nishiyuu-walkers-complete-1-600-km-trek-to-ottawa-1.1209929.

15   Barrera, "Journey of Nishiyuu."

16   "'Nishiyuu Walkers' Complete."

17   Barrera, "Journey of Nishiyuu."

18   Elizabeth Curry, "A Sacred Journey for Future Generations: Stanley Mission Walkers Trek from Northern Saskatchewan to Parliament Hill to Defend Lands and Waterways," *BriarPatch Magazine*, May 21, 2013, briarpatchmagazine.com/articles/view/a-sacred-journey-for-future-generations.

19   Ibid.

20   "Featured Video of the Day: A Sacred Journey Walk in Winnipeg," *NationTalk.ca* video, posted by "douglasrthomas," April 24, 2013, nationtalk.ca/story/featured-video-of-the-day-a-sacred-journey-walk-in-winnipeg/.

21   Ibid.

22   The Haida Nation and Taku River Tlingit cases focused on First Nations' demands that they be consulted before governments authorized major resource development projects on their traditional territories. The Government of British Columbia argued that its regulatory and decision-making process met their legal requirements. First Nations argued that their Aboriginal rights necessitated more extensive consultation. The Supreme Court of Canada agreed with the First Nations. In addition to these cases, the historic William court case (Tsilhqot'in Nation v. British Columbia [2014]) saw the Supreme Court of Canada granting declaration of Aboriginal title to the Tsilhqot'in First Nation for over 1700 square kilometres of land in British Columbia.

23   "IdleNoMore II," YouTube video, 4:04, posted by "Kenjgewin Teg Educational Institute," February 15, 2013, www.youtube.com/watch?v=TaUJs00C3RA.

24   There are many stories of prophecies in the traditions and spiritual teachings of the First Nations, and here is a reference arising most likely out of what

is called the Seven Fires Prophecy. This prophecy includes the vision of the Eighth Fire, described as a time when people of all traditions, faiths, and communities conjoin, creating a Rainbow Race. This Eighth Fire will bring about peace, wisdom, and understanding throughout the world.

25   "What Does Idle No More Mean To You?" YouTube video, 3:24, posted by "SocialCoast," February 28, 2013, www.youtube.com/watch?v=F930W3qbo5I.

26   "Idle No More founders Jessica Gordon and Sheelah McLean Speak at People's Social Forum," *Rabble.ca* video, 42:33, posted by "Rabble Staff," January 28, 2013, rabble.ca/rabbletv/program-guide/2013/01/best-net/idle-no-more-founders-jessica-gordon-and-sheelah-mclean-spea.

27   Ibid.

28   Ibid.

CHAPTER 6: WHAT HAPPENED TO SOVEREIGNTY SUMMER?

1   "Sovereignty Summer Overview," Idle No More, June 27, 2013, www.idle-nomore.ca/sovereignty_summer_overview.

2   "Sagkeeng Idle No More," YouTube video, 5:15, posted by "les grosman," April 1, 2013, www.youtube.com/watch?v=v_1k2cdjxe4.

3   "Sovereignty Summer Overview."

4   Ibid.

5   "SFU Students Mount Idle No More Event," Simon Fraser University, Public Affairs and Media Relations, April 5, 2013, www.sfu.ca/pamr/media-releases/2013/sfu-students-mount-idle-no-more-event.html.

6   Ibid.

7   "Idle No More, April 8th, 2013. SFU, Burnaby, BC, Canada," YouTube video, 9:24, posted by "Resurrecting the Goddess," April 8, 2013, www.youtube.com/watch?v=9F1AbzupuzU.

8   Ibid.

9   "Youth and Politics Series – Idle No More," YouTube video, 3:09, posted by "Arooj Hussain," April 19, 2013, www.youtube.com/watch?v=JW4TQS_YYXW.

10   "May Day 2013 – Shannon Houle – Idle No More," YouTube video, 10:49, posted by "Paula E. Kirman," May 1, 2013, www.youtube.com/watch?v=8p-dVorT8xE8.

11   "Another Long Journey for Justice: Indigenous Youth Begin Walk from Winnipeg to Ottawa," *Rabble.ca*, March 28, 2013, rabble.ca/news/2013/03/another-long-journey-justice-indigenous-youth-begin-walk-winnipeg-ottawa.

12   Caelah Hardisty, Youth for Lakes Facebook community page, March 29, 2013, www.facebook.com/permalink.php?story_fbid=496162763764784&id=485867638127630.

13   Gloria Galloway, "Nishiyuu: A Movement of Cree Youth Who Voted with Their Feet," *The Globe and Mail*, March 25, 2013, www.theglobeandmail.

com/news/politics/nishiyuu-a-movement-of-cree-youth-who-voted-with-their-feet/article10327993/.

14   "Youth 4 Lakes," Youth for Lakes Facebook community post – five-hour live feed, May 13, 2013, www.facebook.com/Youth4Lakes.

15   Ibid.

16   Ibid.

17   "Youth4Lakes – Ottawa Arrival," Youth for Lakes Facebook live stream, statistics, accessed May 26, 2014, www.facebook.com/events/468021569936833/468059773266346/?notif_t=like.

18   Kevin Gosztola, "Live Blog of #OccupyWallStreet: Day Ten, Building the Hope for Reform," *The Dissenter*, September 26, 2011, dissenter.firedoglake.com/2011/09/26/live-blog-of-occupywallstreet-day-ten-building-the-hope-for-reform/.

19   "Idle No More Youth Activists Speak during National Aboriginal Day March," YouTube video, 2:35, posted by "Robin Edgar," June 21, 2013, www.youtube.com/watch?v=-ogWuQNyvZo.

20   Wab Kinew, "Canadians Call on Feds to #HonourTheApology," *Wab Kinew* (blog), July 22, 2013, wabkinew.ca/canadians-call-on-feds-to-honour-the-apology/.

21   "#IdleNoMore Yukon #HonourTheApology Prayer and Drum Rally," Idle No More Facebook events page, July 25, 2013, www.facebook.com/events/187883404713771/.

22   "#IdleNoMore Hay River #NWT greets @PMHarper," YouTube video, 8:48, posted by "George Lessard," August 19, 2013, www.youtube.com/watch?v=0P9y-2j6K0ak.

23   "Idle No More #Saskatoon," YouTube video, 5:38, posted by "bryan Myndz," September 5, 2013, www.youtube.com/watch?v=KнHCK2m1IiM.

24   Steve Rennie, "Idle No More Groups Protest on 250th Anniversary of British Royal Proclamation," *Huffington Post*, October, 7, 2013, www.huffingtonpost.ca/2013/10/07/idle-no-more-british-royal-proclamation_n_4058325.html.

25   "Idle No More Oct. 7 Global Day of Action – Travis Dugas Bellerose," YouTube video, 12:02, posted by "Paula E. Kirman," October 7, 2013, www.youtube.com/watch?v=Y3V_r2zp2OY.

26   "Idle No More Flash Mob – Saskatoon, Oct. 7," YouTube video, 1:19, posted by "MetroCanadaOnline," October 7, 2013, www.youtube.com/watch?v=AqyM-L5LSDEM.

27   "Powerful First Nation Youth @ Idle No More Oct. 7 2013," YouTube video, 3:08, posted by "thawVictoria," October 7, 2013, www.youtube.com/watch?v=9orwVsVMTUE.

28   "Idle No More Oct 7 Lkwungen WSANEC territory's," YouTube video, 2:04, posted by "thawVictoria," October 7, 2013, www.youtube.com/watch?v=4M_hTy6G_fw.

29   Ibid.

30 "Idle No More Elsipogtog Solidarity Protest In Front of Westmount RCMP HQ In Montreal 5," YouTube video, 17:15, posted by "Robin Edgar," October 18, 2013, www.youtube.com/watch?v=10c6LXmX-jU.

31 Andrew Brennan, "Montreal Shows Solidarity with Elsipogtog: Protests Arise after Violent Arrest at N.B. Blockade Site," *The Link*, October 21, 2013, thelinknewspaper.ca/article/4818.

32 "Idle No More Marks One Year Anniversary," CTV *Winnipeg*, November 11, 2013, winnipeg.ctvnews.ca/idle-no-more-marks-one-year-anniversary-1.1536900.

33 Ibid.

34 "#INM1YR WEBINAR WINONA LADUKE 'RESTORING STABLE INDIGENOUS ECONOMIES,'" *Idle No More*, November 5, 2013, www.idlenomore.ca/n10webinar?utm_campaign=n10email1&utm_medium=email&utm_source=idlenomore.

35 "Treaty 6-8 & Idle No More Solidarity Rally – Chanting," YouTube video, 1:33, posted by "Paula E. Kirman," November 28, 2013, www.youtube.com/watch?v=-wfI9vHvYmw&list=PLTeCaxT-rF4kchJskZn2EvhSxR510H_90.

36 "IdleNoMore Dec 10th 2013 #FNEA Rally," YouTube video, 4:05, posted by "Clayton Tootoosis," December 10, 2013, www.youtube.com/watch?v=luRFd_Lob6A.

37 "Idle No More | Polo Park | Winnipeg," YouTube video, 2:11, posted by "David McLeod," December 20, 2013, www.youtube.com/watch?v=5Yk4VacJuew.

38 Ibid.

39 "Idle No More Flash Mobs in 9 Cities this Weekend," CBC *News*, December 21, 2013, www.cbc.ca/news/aboriginal/idle-no-more-flash-mobs-in-9-cities-this-weekend-1.2473095. See also "Treaty Information Check Stop: 'In Memory of All the Land Defenders Who Have Lost Their Lives Defending Their Lands,'" Idle No More, December 17, 2013, www.idlenomore.ca/treaty_information_check_stop.

40 "Idle No More Flash Mob Round Dance in Toronto," YouTube video, 3:48, posted by "Civilian Media," December 21, 2013, www.youtube.com/watch?v=gPc8uYnLw8g.

41 "Thunder erupts at Metrotown center - Idle No More Anniversary 2013 Part 5," YouTube video, 6:36, posted by "wc nativenews," December 21, 2013, www.youtube.com/watch?v=QBibCuobkgM#t=314.

42 "Thunder Erupts at Metrotown Center – Idle No More Anniversary 2013 Part 10," YouTube video, 1:25:24, posted by "wc nativenews," December 21, 2013, www.youtube.com/watch?v=qCd6kv5Jeog#t=3595.

43 "The Vision," *Idle No More*, www.idlenomore.ca/vision.

44 Jason Warick, "Flash Mob Celebrates Idle No More Anniversary," *The StarPhoenix*, December 23, 2013, www2.canada.com/saskatoonstarphoenix/news/local/story.html?id=cb2fd51e-1677-4aba-9e03-c9b1456f4966.

45 Ibid.

46 Ibid.

CHAPTER 7: IDLE NO MORE AND THE TECHNOLOGIES OF MASS MOBILIZATION

1   One of the many ironies relative to the Arab Spring is that software firms whose work underpinned the social media revolution found well-paid work with the authoritarian governments, figuring out ways to use social media technologies to track dissidents.

2   Social media certainly proved useful in gathering the photographs for this book. In a few cases, for instance, tweets were sent out in an effort to make contact with photographers. Some of those tweets were answered in minutes.

3   Occupy Wall Street's Facebook page, October 27, 2014, www.facebook.com/OccupyWallSt.

4   FullDuplex.ca specializes in integrated digital communication and online reputation management. Mark Blevis's focus is on public affairs and politics with the goal of informing decisions and strategies through monitoring and analysis aimed at online engagement and community building.

5   These three data sets come from Mark Blevis, "Idle No More at Six Months: Analysis of the First Six Months of the Idle No More Movement," *MarkBlevis.com*, June 2013, markblevis.com/new-report-looks-at-idle-no-mores-first-six-months.

6   The "likes" and "talking about" data change substantially over time; the numbers are provided here for illustrative purposes only.

7   "Twitter Statistics," *SocialBakers.com*, www.socialbakers.com/twitter/country/canada/.

8   "Canada Facebook Statistics," *SocialBakers.com*, www.socialbakers.com/facebook-statistics/canada.

9   Mark Blevis, "Idle No More at Six Months: Analysis of the first six months of the Idle No More movement," fullduplex.ca/download-our-report-on-the-first-six-months-of-idle-no-more/.

10   From part one of a six-part "Idle No More at two months" analysis series of blog posts by Mark Belvis, markblevis.com/idle-no-more-at-two-months-traffic-analysis/.

11   Data from idlenomore.makook.ca/.

12   Data from Google Maps, maps.google.ca/maps/ms?msa=0&msid=2045344 03836525039663.0004d13bdc1d5b9ad39cf.

13   Data from Google Maps, maps.google.ca/maps/ms?msid=213203553366548 991650.0004d246357eadb06f9ab&msa=0.

14   Blevis, "Idle No More at Six Months."

15   Data analyzed in NVivo 10 and collected from @idlenomore4 on Twitter.

16   Trenton Oldfield, "British Crown: 1) Honour Treaties with First Nations 2) Revoke C-45," *Change.org*, accessed October 31, 2014, www.change.org/en-GB/petitions/british-crown-1-honour-treaties-with-first-nations-2-revoke-c-45.

17   Idle No More, "Do Not Pass the Budget Implementation Bill C-45," *Change.org*, accessed October 31, 2014, www.change.org/petitions/the-house-of-commons-in-parliament-assembled-do-not-pass-the-budget-implementation-bill-c-45-3.

18   Andrea Thompson, "Stephen Harper and Members of Parliament: Tell Canadians the Truth about Omnibus Bill, C-45," *Change.org*, accessed October 31, 2014, www.change.org/en-CA/petitions/stephen-harper-and-members-of-parliament-tell-canadians-the-truth-about-omnibus-bill-c-45.

19   AnonymousCanada, "Change Omnibus Bill C-45," *GoPetition*, January 9, 2013, www.gopetition.com/petitions/op-c-45.html.

20   Claudia Rubio, "Steven [sic] Harper and the Government of Canada: Stop Bill C-45 and Honour Indigenous Rights," *Change.org*, accessed October 31, 2014, www.change.org/en-CA/petitions/steven-harper-and-the-government-of-canada-stop-bill-c-45-and-honour-indigenous-rights.

21   Kainai "idle no more" nii tsi ta pi koaiks, "Stop Bill C-45, Indian Act Amendments," *Change.org*, accessed October 31, 2014, www.change.org/en-CA/petitions/canada-s-senators-and-m-p-s-stop-bill-c-45-indian-act-amendments.

22   Samantha Hebert, "IdleNoMore: We Do Not Support Bill C-45 Stephen Harper. Do Not Disregard the Treaties without Consultation and Consent," *Change.org*, accessed October 31, 2014, www.change.org/en-CA/petitions/idlenomore-we-do-not-support-bill-c-45-stephen-harper-do-not-disregard-the-treaties-without-consultation-and-consent.

23   Toby Hunter, "Petition to Oppose Bill C45," *The Petition Site*, accessed October 31, 2014, www.thepetitionsite.com/112/079/466/petition-to-oppose-bill-c45/.

24   "Tools for Success on the One-year Anniversary of Idle No More Day of Action #INM1yr," *Rabble.ca*, December 10, 2013, rabble.ca/blogs/bloggers/activist-toolkit/2013/12/tools-success-on-one-year-anniversary-idle-no-more-day-action.

25   Shari Narine, "Social Media Major Driver in Idle No More Movement," *Aboriginal Multi-Media Society* (AMMSA) 30, no. 11 (2013), ca.ammsa.com/publications/windspeaker/social-media-major-driver-idle-no-more-movement.

26   Niigaanwewidam James Sinclair, "Social Media Gives Traction to Idle No More," *CBC News*, December 20, 2012, www.cbc.ca/news/canada/manitoba/social-media-gives-traction-to-idle-no-more-1.1136443.

27   "Idle No More Anniversary Sees Divisions Emerging," *Huffington Post*, November 10, 2013, www.huffingtonpost.ca/2013/11/10/idle-no-more-anniversary_n_4250345.html.

28   Idle No More News Group Facebook page, December 23, 2012, www.facebook.com/IdleNoMoreNewsGroup/info.

29   Blevis, "Idle No More at Six Months," 14.

30   Ibid.

31   Misha Noble-Hearle, "Idle No More: A Movement for Change," *Dal News*, Dalhousie University, January 18, 2013, www.dal.ca/news/2013/01/18/idle-no-more--a-movement-for-change.html.

32   Blevis, "Idle No More at Six Months," 19.

33   Armina Ligaya, "Less than Half of Canadians Support the Idle No More Movement: Poll," *National Post*, January 21, 2013, news.nationalpost.com/2013/01/21/almost-half-of-canadians-do-not-support-idle-no-more-movement-poll/.

34   From online comments on Natalie Stechyson, "Idle No More Movement No More? Online Interest Fizzles Out, New Analysis Finds," *National Post*, February 11, 2013, news.nationalpost.com/2013/02/11/idle-no-more-movement-no-more-online-interest-fizzles-out-new-analysis-finds/.

35   From online comments on Gloria Galloway and Oliver Moore, "Idle No More Protests, Blockades Spread across Country," *The Globe and Mail*, January 16, 2013, www.theglobeandmail.com/news/politics/idle-no-more-protests-blockades-spread-across-country/article7406990/comments/.

36   From the online comments left on "Anthony Sowan: Why Idle No More Holds Back the Dream of Canadian Equality," *National Post*, fullcomment.nationalpost.com/2013/01/23/anthony-sowan-why-idle-no-more-holds-back-the-dream-of-canadian-equality/.

37   Sowan, "Anthony Sowan: Why Idle No More Holds Back."

38   Kylie Schultz, "Idle No More: Canada's Growing Indigenous Rights Movement, Fast Going Global," *The International*, January 5, 2013, www.theinternational.org/articles/292-idle-no-more-canadas-growing-indigeno.

39   "McMaster Prof Likens Idle No More to Arab Spring," CBC *News*, December 28, 2012, www.cbc.ca/news/canada/hamilton/news/mcmaster-prof-likens-idle-no-more-to-arab-spring-1.1252546.

40   Ibid.

41   Rebecca Lindell, "#IdleNoMore Tweets Followed Closely by Aboriginal Affairs," *Global News,* April 10, 2013, globalnews.ca/news/470073/idlenomore-tweets-followed-closely-by-aboriginal-affairs/.

42   Terry Glavin, "Idle No More? Let's Get Serious," *Ottawa Citizen*, January 1, 2013, www.ottawacitizen.com/opinion/columnists/Idle+More+serious/7767408/story.html.

43   Rachel Décoste, "Native Canadians Must be Idle No More on Election Day," *Huffington Post*, December 21, 2012, www.huffingtonpost.ca/rachel-decoste/idle-no-more-voting_b_2346903.html.

INDEX

A

Aboriginal development corporations, 40, 128

Aboriginal land claims, xv, xix, 30, 31, 99, 140, 218n22

Aboriginal protests in Canada, xi-xii, xxi, 40-41, 84-85, 138-43, 198
  see also Burnt Church; Caledonia; Elsipogtog; Gustafsen Lake; Ipperwash; Oka; Oldman River; Rexton; Sun Peaks

Aboriginal Peoples Television Network (APTN), 15, 49, 93, 117, 186

Aboriginal resource development, xxi, 15, 40, 42, 92, 105, 128, 140-42, 194

Aboriginal women, call for inquiry into missing and murdered, 5, 57, 99, 141, 152-54

Academics in Solidarity, 87-88

Adam, Allan, 16, 95

Alfred, Taiaiake, 49, 100

Amnesty International, 16, 64, 91, 149

Angus, Charlie, 81-82, 87

Anonymous, 55

Arab Spring, 47, 63, 112, 148, 166-68, 182, 184, 192-93, 222n1

Assembly of First Nations (AFN), xviii, 4, 49, 71-73, 78, 79, 81, 82, 91-94, 98-101, 106, 107, 190, 197, 200

Atleo, Shawn, 4, 72, 91-93, 96, 98-100, 106, 107, 113, 117, 137, 178-79, 186

Attawapiskat, Ontario, 34, 78-79, 81-82, 91, 99, 106, 108, 111, 189

B

Beardy, Stan, 57

Bellegarde, Perry, 22, 72, 98

Bennett, Carolyn, 5

Bigland-Pritchard, Mark, 13

Bill C-38, 99, 105, 216n57

Bill C-45 (omnibus bill), xiii, xxi, 1-17, 19, 20, 24, 45, 47, 51-53, 55-58, 60, 63, 66-67, 69-70, 95, 99, 105, 112, 125, 127, 129, 133, 138, 140-41, 145, 154, 182-83, 200

Bird, Simon, 50

Black power movement, xix

Blaney, Ta'Kaiya, 66-67, 114, 196, 204

Blevis, Mark, 20, 177-181, 187, 189, 203, 222n4

Bowling Alone: The Collapse and Revival of American Community, 164

Burnt Church, xi, 40, 84

C

Calder decision, *see* Supreme Court victories

Caledonia, xi, xii, xxi, 40, 83-85, 139, 142-43, 198

Cardinal, Tantoo, 67

civil rights movement, 120-21

Clark, Joe, 87

Conservative Party of Canada, 14, 190

Council for Yukon First Nations, xvi

Crowder, Jean, 5

Cultural Survival (organization), 91